Popular Music and the New Auteur

Popular Music and the
New Auteur

Visionary Filmmakers after MTV

Edited by Arved Ashby

OXFORD
UNIVERSITY PRESS

OXFORD

UNIVERSITY PRESS

Oxford University Press is a department of the University of Oxford.
It furthers the University's objective of excellence in research, scholarship,
and education by publishing worldwide.

Oxford   New York
Auckland   Cape Town   Dar es Salaam   Hong Kong   Karachi
Kuala Lumpur   Madrid   Melbourne   Mexico City   Nairobi
New Delhi   Shanghai   Taipei   Toronto

With offices in
Argentina   Austria   Brazil   Chile   Czech Republic   France   Greece
Guatemala   Hungary   Italy   Japan   Poland   Portugal   Singapore
South Korea   Switzerland   Thailand   Turkey   Ukraine   Vietnam

Oxford is a registered trademark of Oxford University Press
in the UK and certain other countries.

Published in the United States of America by
Oxford University Press
198 Madison Avenue, New York, NY 10016

Library of Congress Cataloging-in-Publication Data
Popular music and the new auteur : visionary filmmakers after MTV / edited by Arved Ashby.
pages cm
Includes bibliographical references and index.
ISBN 978–0–19–982733–6 (hardcover : alk. paper)—ISBN 978–0–19–982735–0 (pbk. : alk. paper)
1. Motion picture music—History and criticism.   2. Popular music in motion pictures.
I. Ashby, Arved Mark.
ML2075.P65 2013
781.5´42—dc23
2013007164

9 8 7 6 5 4 3 2 1
Printed in the United States of America
on acid-free paper

CONTENTS

ACKNOWLEDGMENTS

This book originated with a session on auteurs' use of popular music that I proposed in 2005 for the Chicago meeting of the Society for American Music. Julie Hubbert and Jeff Smith gave early versions of their Scorsese and Coen brothers essays, and it was their provocative ideas on those music-cinematic stylists that inspired a larger project. Because of Julie and Jeff's knowledge and eager advice, not to mention the extraordinary patience they showed while the volume slowly came together, this project is as much theirs as anyone's.

Others urged the project to fruition by suggesting additional topics and contributors. Wonderful counsel was given by such authorities—among them Anahid Kassabian, David Butler, Graham Lock, and Krin Gabbard—that the final authors have not only managed to survey a wealth of recent cinematic creativity, they've brought a remarkable variety of perspectives to their task.

All of us are very much indebted to our acquisitions editor Norm Hirschy, who was ever attentive with his wise and enthusiastic guidance, and ever encouraging from the first moment I mentioned the book's topic to him. I still have no idea how Norm can answer e-mails so fast, so wittily, and in such urbane prose. Assistant Editor Lisbeth Redfield and Kate Nunn, our project manager, were both helpful and firm in ushering the volume through production. We also owe a great deal to the anonymous reviewers commissioned by Oxford University Press, particularly the two initial readers who did so much to help focus the book.

The book also owes a debt to the students in a film music seminar that I led at Ohio State University in autumn 2008, the enrollees including Joe Nebistinsky, Andrew Martin, Alison Furlong, and Zhichun Lin. They were astute critics, and my own contributions to this volume would have been poorer without their input.

CONTRIBUTORS

Julie Hubbert, School of Music, University of South Carolina

Tim Anderson, Department of Communication and Theatre Arts, Old Dominion University

Gene Willet, Conservatory of Music, Baldwin Wallace University

Giorgio Biancorosso, Department of Music, University of Hong Kong

Jeff Smith, Department of Communication Arts, University of Wisconsin

Ken Garner, Glasgow School for Business and Society, Glasgow Caledonian University

Arved Ashby, School of Music, Ohio State University

Popular Music and the New Auteur

Introduction

ARVED ASHBY

By the late 20th century, authorship was largely defunct as cultural institution and as intellectual construct—the mindful creator of texts "killed
in Paris, embalmed at Yale, [and] mourned in Cambridge," as James Wood
put it some years ago in the *Guardian*.[1] Roland Barthes took the French
Symbolist writers' subversion—their substituting linguistic play for authorial design—as evidence of the immateriality of the latter-day author construct. Film scholars were likewise questioning the auteur idea—the notion
that a film could be defined stylistically by a single cinematic "author," usually the director—almost as soon as Andrew Sarris introduced it to the
United States in the 1960s. But more recent writers, among them Timothy
Corrigan and Gilberto Perez, have talked about a new, commercial form of
auteurism, a latter-day film authorship conditioned by the marketplace.[2] In
their view, film's commercial basis—its high production costs and financial
politics of distribution—have made it the auteurist medium par excellence.
Directors and even some producers have become brand names by which
American films, those shown in the giant cineplexes and art-house cinemas,
are sold. Moviegoers rush to a new film by Steven Spielberg, Ron Howard,
or Quentin Tarantino expecting thematic or stylistic consistency with their
earlier offerings. For such audiences, directors' names are measures of quality, uniqueness, and ultimately relevance and consequence—an equation
that began as early as D. W. Griffith with his insistence that his name be
displayed prominently on-screen, even in his early Biograph films.

So the auteur idea, once démodé in cinema studies, is again in the ascendant. The present collection of essays follows this trend by extending the
auteurism idea beyond the historical context of the politique des auteurs,
and advancing a conception different from that of Corrigan, Perez, et al.
Much recent auteurism is musically oriented, and the seven contributors to this book see important recent cinematic stylizations as specifically

music-inspired, music-based, and musically conditioned: Our book looks at cinematic visionaries who have given pop songs the kind of centrality once reserved for the script. In presenting seven influential cinematic authors in such a way, our book counters those critics of the auteur idea who stressed the scriptwriter's paper-and-ink authorship over any loosely defined notion of directorial auteurism, and thereby emphasized narrative in the narrowest sense. Two such critics were Pauline Kael and Gore Vidal, the latter of course a novelist and author in his own right. The filmmakers discussed in our own volume—among them David Lynch, Wong Kar-wai, and Quentin Tarantino—upended a basic duality. What they subverted was the long-term cinematic practice whereby popular music, if it appeared at all, served to articulate the narrative while orchestral, symphonic sounds mediated between narrative and moviegoer. The contributors to this book really follow two projects, then: They make a case for renewed understanding of auteurism, but also discuss popular music as an integral element in mise en scène.

Proponents of the auteur idea usually concern themselves with a filmmaker's consistency over time. As the second of his three premises of auteur theory, Sarris listed "the distinguishable personality of the director as a criterion of value.... Over a group of films, a director must exhibit certain recurring characteristics of style, which serve as his signature."[3] At the same time, skeptics point out the necessary creative inconsistencies in film. Opponents of auteur theory also point to the collaborative aspect of a movie; they describe multiple creativities, among them the author of the original story, the scriptwriter, the cinematographer, the production designer, and the editor. Neither of these arguments, the diachronic auteurist representation or the counter-auteurist synchronic, pluralist perspective, allows for a cinematic visionary who *changes* stylistically over time, as a cinematic original must by definition. More generally, neither of the two theories is really able to account for today's cinematic experience and its renegotiated relationship with the musical experience.[4]

The music video (MV) has changed the musical experience and the cinematic experience in fundamental ways. It widened the creative vocabulary of filmmakers, starting with MTV in 1981 and continuing through EMI's and PolyGram's founding of their own music video departments, the 1984 debut of *Nick Rocks* on Nickelodeon, the 1985 launch of VH1, the expansion of cable TV, and the proliferation of the PC and digital video. It is hard to say whether the MV was the driving force behind music's new foundational role in feature-length films, or whether the MV "sold" music only to the degree that the new audiovisual techniques were no longer conditioned *by* music, but had instead become inextricable *from* music.[5] Writers have attributed to MV influence both an increase and a decrease in speeds of events, as well as a deflection away from Aristotelian patterns of narrative, characterization, and storytelling toward a concentration on situation, feeling, mood, and new approaches to time and the passage of it. "Time in the music video is any time," remarks Ken Dancyger in his book on film editing. "With time and place obliterated, the film and video makers are free to roam in the world of their imagined media mediation." Even more important, perhaps, is the MV's introduction of ideas of performance and different performative sensibilities. Dancyger tells us how MV-influenced editing can "obliterate time and space" and thereby create a "self-reflexive dream-state [that] suggests that on another level, viewers watch or reflect upon themselves dreaming, or to put it another way, to be simultaneously very involved and not involved at all." He also speaks of how "the MTV-style film" can entail "acknowledgement by the characters that they are performing as well as participating."[6]

One often reads that filmmakers began incorporating long musical spans because the continuity of those songs allowed, by way of compensation, new temporal and spatial *discontinuities* in the visual "track."[7] We can certainly see hit songs anchoring new editing speeds in such iconic MVs as Steve Barron's rotoscope production of A-Ha's "Take on Me" (1985), Stephen R. Johnson's stop-motion rendering of Peter Gabriel's "Sledgehammer" (1986), and Mary Lambert's rendition of Madonna's "Like a Prayer" (1989). At the same time, some reflective MVs, with their cooler and statuesque performativity and their more continuous "self-reflexive dream states," have had just as strong and lasting an influence on feature films as those more active videos. One of the very first MVs is celebrated for its static, gothic portraiture, and it was produced when such productions were called "promotional clips" and people hadn't yet started using the word "video": I am referring to Bruce Gowers's audiovisual production of Queen's "Bohemian Rhapsody" (1975).[8] Fifteen years later, John Maybury presented an even quieter though no less famous example of a "slow" MV in his 1990 film of Sinead O'Connor's "Nothing Compares 2U." This video is simplicity exemplified, basically one long and unedited take of O'Connor lip-synching the song—interspersed with a few contrasting outdoor shots and some tears in the last verse. Maybury forces our gaze deep into the singer's facial texture, psyche, and barely hidden emotions. Though he eschewed the editing that many people think integral to the MV experience, Maybury truly succeeds in "obliterating time and place" and allowing a special kind of "acknowledgement by the characters that they are performing." (As one sign of her performative self-awareness, O'Connor focuses her gaze in only two directions, downward right and directly at the camera (see figure I.1); such a restricted visual composition and performative sensitivity would obviously not have worked with a faster shoot.) But then Prince's ballad of lost love makes all this possible: It serves as starting

Figure I.1: Talking head meets long take: John Maybury directs simply and continuously for Sinead O'Connor ("Nothing Compares 2U").

point and endpoint for the self-consciousness, makeup, vocal vibrato, and composition within the frame.

What is the most basic way that MVs have changed feature films? The question is not of the MV influence helping pop styles gain new inroads into film. Rather, the MV has encouraged two contrasting styles of auteurism. First among these is a synergistic approach, closer perhaps to the elusive music-filmic *Gesamtkunstwerk* presaged by the Eisenstein-Prokofiev collaborations and those 1940s Hollywood musicals where music was given an integral rather than incidental role in the narrative. Here some viewers might speak of a more "musical" cinematic experience, in the way a George Balanchine or a Mark Morris might be deemed more musical than other choreographers. Second, at the same time that it has allowed a newly synergistic approach, filmmakers' use of preexisting pop songs has facilitated Brechtian layerings of character, narrative, and music—a new dissimulation, a splitting of the cinematic seams. With this approach, relations have been renegotiated between musical style and narration, characterization, and individual subjectivity on the screen. Non-diegetic songs tend to distance the viewer from what is happening on-screen; Robb Wright recently included "their tendency to put distance between the viewer and the action" among their "subtle effects."[9] While the classic symphonic film score promised insight directly into a character's mind, the expanded role of popular music has complicated the question of when, if ever, we are allowed to see or share a character's emotions. As a result, irony and ambiguity have multiplied exponentially, narrative capacities have fragmented, and listeners have renegotiated some of their most basic instinctual connections with the human voice.

Our book describes a new, post-MTV auteurism, differentiating it from the older author-heavy stylizations of Jean-Luc Godard, Alfred Hitchcock, François Truffaut, and Stanley Kubrick. We focus, in brief, on directors of the past two decades who have reconceived cinematic stylization—or even the film experience more generally—by giving popular music a new originative function and displaying a musical influence that is deep-seated but often enigmatic. The music's new primacy is clear not only to the moviegoer, but is obvious even at the most basic levels of film production. Several popular and influential directors have confessed to giving music the kind of primary role once accorded to the narrative and script. At least two auteurs discussed in this volume, Quentin Tarantino and Wong Kar-wai, have pointed to specific songs as original inspiration for some of their movies; Wong has said that he plays music for his cinematographer in lieu of visual discussions, and that he plays particular songs on set for his actors and crew. "To me, music creates the rhythms," he has said in response to the interviewer's question: "What's the role of the music in the process of shooting and editing?"[10] This is a quite different kind of role than music had in film musicals, whether we're speaking of *An American in Paris* or the rock operas that have been reconfigured for the screen—of which The Who and Ken Russell's *Tommy* (1975) marks some kind of auteurist climax.

POPULAR SONG AND CINEMA

Filmmakers have become more and more attracted to the distinctive power of popular song, namely its seamless joining of the telling with the thing told, the how intertwined inseparably with the what. As a reflection of this, songs tend to function differently within the narrative in recent cinematic stylizations than they did in the classical Hollywood musical, following different rules of what we might call musical causation. In *The Wizard of Oz*, for instance, the causational forces that push Judy Garland over the threshold from speech into song are, by the rules of the 1930s Hollywood musical, contained within incidental aspects of the written script. We begin to sense a song's approach when Dorothy tells Aunt Em, not for the first time, that old Miss Gulch wishes to harm Toto. Too busy with work to be concerned, Aunt Em responds, "Now, Dorothy, dear, stop imagining things. You always get yourself into a fret over nothing.... Now, you just help us out today, and find yourself a place where you won't get into any trouble." Aunt Em only wants Dorothy out of the way. But her word "place" suggests the idea of transcendence, and the musical impetus begins—for Dorothy, for the moviegoer, and for the film itself. "Place" is the incitation, the incantational logos, and it gives Dorothy pause. The forces of musical causation become too strong to resist, and with mundane separations between music and everyday speech falling away, she slips into her recitative ("Do you suppose there is such a place, Toto?") and then directly into Harold Arlen's chorus-cum-aria ("Somewhere, over the rainbow way up high").

This is standard practice in the classic Hollywood musical. The song is precipitated by the word, its musical causation rooted in the logos. The specific script-based forces would attribute Arlen and E. Y. Harburg's songwriting genius to Dorothy from Kansas, and we find the forces of musical causation falling into place gradually, spontaneously, and—or so it would seem—unavoidably. "Over the Rainbow" thereby acts like an operatic musical number in that it recalls the logocentric irrationality of opera and—as Brecht described the music of *Die Dreigroschenoper*—"interrupts the plot when the action has arrived at a situation that permits music and song to appear."[11]

If the song in classic Hollywood movies is usually triggered by the word—in other words, by the script—its vocal and sonic aspect, its manner of performance, sends it to a particular place in the moviegoer's affections. Character and singer become one and the same, courtesy of the singing voice and its tone of empathy. Sean Cubitt speaks of the singing voice as an enhanced "us." "The amplified voice is an ideal form," Cubitt writes, and "...the ideal image of ourselves that it offers is the site of a complex organization of our relations with the world, the connection between our inner being and the exterior world."[12] Judy and Dorothy's rendition of "Over the Rainbow" allows such idealization because it is something of a musical-interpretive blank slate—vocally pure and without much vibrato, both boyish and girlish, and redolent less of music-hall immediacy than of idealized memory. Because the song didn't exist before the movie and is sung in the movie without obvious mannerisms and essentially without gender, the script and the vocal style come together and serve both the character on-screen and the audience's need to idealize.[13]

Some critics describe auteurism as a counteraction to genre films, and just such a contrast to script-borne musical incitation can be found in Wong Kar-wai's *Fallen Angels* (1995). Typically for Wong, this film went into production without a script (in any usual sense), the specifics of narrative and text left to develop alongside the film itself.[14] In one scene from the movie, Michelle Reis—acting as partner to the hit man played by Leon Lai—lingers erotically over a jukebox as it plays Laurie Anderson's "Speak My Language" (figure I.2).[15] Anderson's words invoke Judgment Day and bloodshed through the King James version of the Book of Peter: "Daddy Daddy, it was just like you said / Now that the living outnumber the dead."

The Reis character, drawn to music that speaks of bloodshed rather than paradise or nostalgia, becomes a kind of anti-Dorothy. As it appears in *The*

Figure I.2: *Fallen Angels:* The hit man's assistant cues up the jukebox ("Speak My Language").

Wizard of Oz, "Over the Rainbow" involves itself in a quid pro quo with Dorothy's character. Dorothy finds herself transported by the song, and in return she gives a specific human face and voice to the song's timeless innocence, its transcendence. But we're not allowed to know what "Speak My Language" means to the hit man's assistant in Wong's film: She cues it up after saying she knows "how to make myself happy," but then fails to sing, move her lips, or even empathize visibly with it. Her fellow sociopaths in Wong's movie—people glamorous and inscrutable, but at the same time strangely pragmatic—would find Laurie Anderson's parlance foreign to the same degree they would find themselves insensible to her weighty issues—here, the fate of "the quick and the dead" on Judgment Day. The Reis character and the songwriter share a certain sang-froid, but otherwise Anderson's punning, black comedy and nervy intelligence seem alien to the hit man's partner. The only real connection we have between movie and song is a cold, hard causality: a coin dropped into a jukebox followed by the sight of a CD falling into place. But these ambiguous tokens could just as easily have elicited "Over the Rainbow," "Embraceable You," or "*O Mio Babbino Caro.*"

Laurie Anderson, subjective and synthetic and immediately recognizable as a voice, cultivates a specific sense of singing "I"—mostly a matter of her distinctive, throaty, and barely song-like way of speaking—and Wong uses that sense to further mute and de-center the hit man's assistant, to relieve her of her own mental and spiritual presence. As it appears in *Fallen Angels,* "Speak My Language" personalizes and idealizes no images and suggests no particular emotional outlay—partly because its performance is so mannered, but also because it has no clear connection with what we see happening on-screen—and so we are left not quite knowing what "to do with" this not-sung song.[16] And the hit man's assistant seems no more adept at this than we are. In the end, Anderson seems to inhabit Reis's character less than the singer occupies the jukebox itself: The machine becomes more an erotic device than a mouthpiece for this love-struck woman, and stands as a kind of ventriloquist's dummy for the songwriter.

Laurie Anderson's song, then, is rooted neither in the characters nor the logos of *Fallen Angels*, and neither her performance nor Brian Eno's production helps us assimilate the song or become emotionally involved with it. The songs in Wong's film, like those in *The Wizard of Oz*, contrast with orchestral non-diegetic music in that they do nothing to advance the action. But *The Wizard of Oz* songs are still functions of the script, whereas in *Fallen Angels*, the songs become instruments of mise en scène—tools for the auteur and not for the scriptwriter, studio functionaries, and advocates of genre film, in short those "competing" with the auteur for control over the movie. In a context like *The Wizard of Oz*, music cannot function as an organ of auteurism insofar as it remains a function of the written screenplay and insofar as the music's performance doesn't encourage us to question that functioning. According to classical Hollywood studio practice, music gives voice to the sentiments and insinuations that the script cannot, though it is the script that explicitly prompts it to do so. But in the auteurist film, as is worth re-emphasizing, the music often takes on extraordinary powers because it is rooted in the ever-widening interstice between script and cinematic experience.

As described above, the contrasts between "Over the Rainbow" and "Speak My Language" speak to the differences between the filmic roles of the new song and the preexisting song. The pop song doesn't mediate in the manner of the non-diegetic orchestral score, but "sides with" the character, or sometimes with the viewer, more impartially than non-diegetic music can. If the non-diegetic orchestral score hints empathetically at what is on a character's mind, popular music—as a more obviously mediated, singular, and indeed text-based expression—gives the impression of something the character herself cues up and plays as self-expression and self-description. A preexisting pop song, however, opens a new space within the film, between the narrative situation and the music itself. Within that space, the subjectivities of the movie become allocated in a complex and sometimes conflicting way. At the most basic level, the music steps away from non-diegetic function and withholds any commentary—empathetic commentary, at least—on the narrative.

Most contributors to this book choose to describe pop songs' appearances in film as materialist: as some manner of musical "cueing up," whether they are tracks called up on a character's psychology or on an actual jukebox. The cueing-up reference shows a character's musical agency acting as metaphor for his or her subjectivity, or just as a literal reference to what's happening on screen—in *Pulp Fiction*, we actually see Mia push a button to start Dusty Springfield's rendition of "Son of a Preacher Man." In either case, the cueing-up notion brings about new issues of just what kind of agency this implies, and where it resides. Who "owns" the song? And exactly where does it "play"? And for whose sake? These are all fairly new questions and, as asked by an innovator like Tarantino, they substantiate a new brand of auteurism—a new cinematic relationship between music and narrative. At the same time, the agency interjected by a preexisting pop song can undermine any coherent sense of film authorship, suggesting the kind of decentered, postmodern subject that critics have identified as the antithesis to, and indeed the undoing of, auteurism.[18] For one thing, the musical performer's persona takes on a major role over the duration of the song. Whether performative or authoring, the agency implied by a preexisting popular song does often make a film more stylized and thereby more obviously "written," though questions of film genre—heavily involved in music as they are—are in themselves important in sensing and constructing authorship and auteurism. Wong Kar-wai, for example, sees the MTV aspect of his film *As Tears Go By* as an enhancement of its generic gangster-flick artificiality.[19] In this kind of thinking, stylization paradoxically helps emphasize authorship by removing its traces.

MUSIC AND AUTEURISM: A QUICK HISTORY

Who are the MV-influenced auteurs assayed in our book, and what are their origins and precursors? This volume can encompass only a small sample of musical-cinematic visionaries, so I should perhaps begin here by presenting a few more names and by stepping back to take a broader view of the provenance and importance of these filmmakers. Our book admittedly concentrates on recent American auteurs, to the misleading and imbalanced exclusion of filmmakers from other countries; the only figure we discuss from another continent is Wong Kar-wai. But then the Americans Tarantino and David Lynch, discussed in detail in these pages by Ken Garner and Gene Willet, have been pioneers in reassessing film through the prism of popular music. Their eccentric MV-influenced realignments of sound and vision were already in force in the later 1980s, but they have also proved to be influential on recent filmmakers whom we again do not get around to discussing: directors and scriptwriters like Baz Luhrmann, Paul Thomas Anderson, and Christopher Nolan. Starting with *Blue Velvet* (1986) and *Reservoir Dogs* (1992), Lynch and Tarantino complicated basic relations between musical style and narration, characterization, and individual subjectivity on-screen. To find precedents for their developments in musical-auteurist style, we could turn to stylistic change in opera, a genre that has approached similar issues from a different direction. To go from *Breakfast at Tiffany's* or even *The Big Chill* to *Blue Velvet* is like exiting Pietro Mascagni's *Cavalleria rusticana* for a performance of Richard Strauss's *Elektra* or Alban Berg's *Lulu*, two operas that use style not as a means of disingenuous musico-dramatic expression so much as something changeable and strategic—as rhetorical device. In short, *Elektra* and *Lulu* are like auteurist soundtracks in that they can seem to portray rather than purvey musical styles: Their dramaturgical mechanisms don't involve style as a natural and unconscious vehicle for expression, but depend on the interplay of contrasting styles.[20]

More important than opera precedents, no doubt, are several filmmakers who as early as the 1960s started to renegotiate the kinds of cinematic relations that Tarantino and Lynch came to rethink in the 1980s and 90s. By the early 1960s, Stanley Kubrick, a filmmaker of astonishing musicality, was editing to preexisting pieces of music—in some scenes, even to iconic compositions—and using them more or less at full length in order to explore new possibilities of cinematic tempo and proportion. Though he usually used classical compositions for such scenes rather than popular songs—building episodes around pieces by György Ligeti, Aram Khachaturian, Richard Strauss, Franz Schubert, Béla Bartók, and Krzysztof Penderecki—those scenes can still seem MV-like in the way the uninterrupted and unedited stretches of concert music allowed him new conceptions of cinematic time, even a new sense of timelessness.

In *2001: A Space Odyssey* (1968), Kubrick extends one montage to the full ten minutes of Johann Strauss Jr.'s "The Blue Danube." This scene becomes a performative ballet as we watch vehicles and characters negotiate zero gravity—the slow trajectories of spacecraft and the studied motions of people, individuals moving leisurely and gracefully as if they were no longer actors, persons trained to obscure any signs of enactment per se, but were instead dancers hired for their physical agency, for their *obvious consciousness*—mental and physical—of performing. "The Blue Danube" is about as far as one can imagine from classic Hollywood underscoring and its ideals of flexibility and "inaudibility," and the most famous waltz ever written does allow Kubrick to direct as if he were a choreographer.[21] The time-span and lucid structure of the piece let Kubrick juxtapose shots of the earth and spacecraft with, in one scene, the tentative footfalls of a Pan Am flight attendant during a flight to the moon (figure I.3). Strauss's leisurely pace and consistent waltz meter let us take the time to feel as if we are walking with the attendant, as if we too are learning how to put one weightless foot before the other.

Figure I.3: *2001: A Space Odyssey:* An interplanetary flight attendant walks in zero gravity ("The Blue Danube").

Because montages have been set to music since early sound films, why is Kubrick's "Blue Danube" scene so special? The answer again pertains to time and performance: While a montage represents a telescoping of time and place, an abridgement, an attempt to summarize a time-span with contrasting shots held together by a single composition in the underscoring, Kubrick's scene seems a temporal expansion, a stretching-out. He gives that impression in part with his wide variety of angles, shots, and people in the scene; if this montage represents an abridgement, it would have to be an abridgement of an entire movie. The choreographic aspect, which Kubrick might have been the first to coordinate to preexisting non-diegetic music in such a way, is entwined with that special time sensibility—but also represents, within the frame, a kind of visual precision for its own sake, a playful joy in composition and exactitude. This scene is less a narrative or character study than an abstract, spatiotemporal study of objects in gentle trajectories. And these objectifications are made possible, in a sense, by Kubrick's objectification of the Strauss waltz as a single and unbroken stretch of music.[22]

Kubrick made us realize with the "Blue Danube" sequence that a "classical music video" and a "popular music video" aren't as different as one might suppose in terms of the cinematic functions and opportunities offered by the different styles. Here musical style doesn't much matter qua style, as long as it helps the filmmaker find an alternative timeframe and an alternative rhythm—as long as it provides a situation where film can be edited to music, and a sense of broader musical-time proportion can dominate over common-practice cinematic-time proportions. Johann Strauss's "Blue Danube" doesn't have words, of course, which means it is even less directly engaged in the script than a preexisting pop song could be—and the same goes for the Adagio of Bartók's *Music for Strings, Percussion, and Celesta,* which Kubrick uses for Danny's corridor scene in *The Shining*

(1980); as well as the slow movement of Schubert's Piano Trio in E-Flat Major, Op. 100, heard in *Barry Lyndon* (1975) when Lyndon first meets the Countess. In general, Kubrick—as film aristocrat and as Wagnerian—gravitated to orchestral sounds. Ensemble works by Johann Strauss and Bartók are more likely to suggest classical Hollywood underscoring than solo instruments, and for that reason do more than popular music to clarify a film's genre aspect, whether it is horror, science fiction, or comedy.

A very different kind of musical-cinematic play, with the music inviting the viewer to a time and place even further removed from the film itself, can be found in Mike Nichols's highly original film *The Graduate* (1967). Nichols used recent recordings by Simon and Garfunkel—even adopting and retitling one song the pair had not yet released on record, "Mrs. Robinson"—and used them in their entirety, employing them as entr'actes rather than as empathetic vehicles or as emotional signifiers. The style and emotional outlook of the songs seem quite unrelated to the scenes they follow, beyond a general match between Simon and Garfunkel's acoustic sound and the movie's vein of domestic comedy, and between the duo's wistful melancholy and Benjamin Braddock's on-screen ennui. It must have been a real surprise at the time to hear songs that are neither presented by the characters—none of them desired, cued, or empathized by the characters, let alone sung by them—nor related to them specifically, causally, or thematically. Nichols thereby foretold a musical-cinematic practice that would become common at the end of the century. Instead of stemming from the diegesis or directly from characters' emotions, his chosen songs connect with the script abstractly, at the level of individual words. When Mrs. Robinson first tries to seduce Ben only to find him nervous and hesitant, she wonders if this is his "first time" and asks, "Benjamin, would this be easier for you in the dark?" We then hear the first lines of "The Sound of Silence" ("Hello darkness, my old friend / I've come to talk with you again") just as he closes their motel room door, creating a black screen.

It is important to recognize the innovations of Kubrick and Nichols; at the same time, we shouldn't neglect several 1970s filmmakers who, though not visionary in the way these other directors were, proved influential for using music compilations. Peter Bogdanovich's *The Last Picture Show* (1971), George Lucas's *American Graffiti* (1973), and Robert Altman's *Nashville* (1975) were innovative in the way they compiled disparate songs from different artists and different styles. Bogdanovich, Lucas, and Altman asked the question: How do you use songs that were already popular, even iconic and decades old, and employ them not only as period artifacts—as musical scenery—but also as narrative articulations? In addition to providing new marketing opportunities, the compilation soundtrack allowed a filmmaker more control over individual scenes than underscoring or newly commissioned songs did, and perhaps a broader range of feelings than any one musically creative presence could supply. But of course it could work against coherence in a film. The compilation soundtrack, in short, sharpened the cinematic duality between details and the whole, and thereby raised the stakes for musical auteurism by intensifying the forest-or-trees problem that has always occupied auteurs. With the wide stylistic range of their compilation soundtracks, these directors widened the musical-affective spaces in film, thereby allowing later filmmakers to pit the musical-stylistic expression of individual songs against their expected functions as set pieces within the film—a kind of tension that paved the way for Lynch's and Tarantino's own forms of musical-cinematic alienation.[23]

Finally, we must address recent questions of how auteurism relates to media and how it is a changeable phenomenon insofar as it is inextricable from those media. Though auteurism is usually described in cinematic and non-societal terms, Spike Lee demanded a change in those terms of discussion when he turned his stylizations to TV and concerned himself with issues of media and audience. Lee is important to any account of musical auteurism, not only because of his cinematic signature, but also because he is so involved in recent media issues and his work is so deeply musical. Victoria Johnson traces Lee's concomitant musicality and "media-lity" as far back as *Do the Right Thing* (1989):

> The fundamental aurality of *Do the Right Thing* combined with its hot look and camera movements conspires to create an address that is perhaps much further in its operation from cinematic suturing than it is similar to the affective, physiological response generally attributed to music as music and, perhaps most provocative for further study, to the interpellative strategies of television as an "ongoing video collage."[24]

With Radio Raheem's boombox, a tape player that sets the narrative of *Do the Right Thing* in motion and is in turn silenced at its turning point, we see that Lee is highly attuned to media and to music's materiality. Part of what Johnson is saying is that Lee likes to make visible things audible and—for the most part—audible things visible, and this creates a crowded, combative, and cinematic musical texture. The dissonant style is a vivid analogy for the ethnic tensions in the movie, as they've developed in a diverse community with local history.

What this means for the present book is that Spike Lee is a deeply musical audiovisual stylist who presages either an end to auteurism or a redefinition of it. His renegotiation of music's relationship with cinema goes quite beyond Lynch's and Tarantino's own renegotiations. Lee's productions of the new century tend to have so much going on in a hot cinematic texture that the referential aspect of individual songs breaks down, and with it the various forms of legibility, distance, empathy, and tension that I discuss above. Ellen C. Scott speaks of Lee forming his sonic-musical practices at a time when New Hollywood practices, promising musical affinities, and exploiting utopian visions were more or less standard in studio production. As Scott describes him, Lee ended up turning those musical-cinematic strategies inside-out and, in Trojan-horse manner, "uses the New Hollywood merchandized soundtrack to confront auditors with historically referential, complicated sampled sounds that operate, much like his image track as challenge, stumbling block, and site of knowledge acquisition." *He Got Game* (1998), for instance, shows Lee appropriating "classic" film scoring for narrative voices that Hollywood would have marginalized.[25]

Victoria Johnson has described Lee's recent work for TV as a form of "convergent auteurism," adapting the term from Henry Jenkins's notion of a media-induced "convergence culture."[26] She discusses Lee's paradoxical, basic redefinition of mediated aural-visual experience, an art form that we might better understand and have a specific term for in a decade or so. We can see his "convergent auteurism" in the New Orleans documentaries *When the Levees Broke: A Requiem in Four Acts* (2006) and *If God Is Willing and Da Creek Don't Rise* (2010). Here classic cinematic style mixes with video style, Hollywood with DIY and commercial styles, and televisuality with a big-studio manner. The past mingles with the present and big-budget with low-budget. These films are mostly scored by Terence Blanchard with newly created, eclectic, obviously contemporary, yet rather classically situated music. Each of Lee's post-Katrina New Orleans films is a Wagnerian four hours in length. The first one is "A Requiem in Four Acts," a subtitle that itself refers to European classical traditions, and one that forces a convergence between the sacred and the profane, the orthodox and the vernacular. At the end of *When the Levees Broke,* Shelton Alexander commemorates his city's tragedy with a spoken word poem at a cemetery in the devastated Ninth Ward (figure I.4). This is a site-specific documentary with interviews, an example of visual and audio historiography, but in this final scene, the stationary camera points up from a low POV in film-class style; the viewer is expected to focus on multiple things in an almost Wellesian depth of field, and Lee's composition within the frame is classical and studied. So in visual terms, Lee's documentary ends as a kind of 21st-century update on *Citizen Kane*, though the soundtrack here precludes auteurism in the pre-convergent sense: The director finishes not with any authorship-bolstering, Bernard Herrmannesque underscoring, but to the sounds of a quiet, improvised verbal essay in African American vernacular.

Figure I.4: *When the Levees Broke: A Requiem in Four Acts*: Shelton Alexander closes Spike Lee's televisual lament for New Orleans.

CONTRIBUTIONS TO THE LITERATURE

As a subject of scholarly interest, film music has advanced through three phases. First, there is the relatively recent institution of film music—any kind or aspect of film music—as a disciplinary category. In their joint contribution to the 2001 collection *Film Music: Critical Approaches*, David Neumeyer and James Buhler summarize some of the reasons for this neglect, among them the fact that musicologists became interested in film music only recently. And film studies itself, as K. J. Donnelly describes it, has "roundly failed to incorporate the study of film music into its schemes."[27] Second, there is the even more recent interest in popular music, as opposed to non-diegetic symphonic scoring, as a vital aspect of film. Scholars have been late in coming around to popular film music largely because they have mislabeled, or more broadly misunderstood, it as source music. According to Buhler, the relative lack of scholarly interest in source music is one remnant of "a lingering cultural elitism: orchestral music is where the art is."[28] Third and most recently, researchers have taken notice of filmmakers' use of preexisting music. It is not difficult to understand why scholars took so long to arrive at this discussion: There are aesthetic and intellectual property controversies, and musicians have painful memories of Walt Disney, Stanley Kubrick, and others using music with minimal compensation for its composers. More to the point, music scholars would seem to find something awkward about studying filmmakers' musical tastes and selections—about theorizing the musical decisions of non-musicians.

Important work has certainly been done on compilation soundtracks and on popular music in movies more generally. The essays in Pamela R. Wojcki and Arthur Knight's 2001 collection *Soundtrack Available: Essays on Film and Popular Music* address issues of cultural and gender politics raised by filmmakers' use of popular music, questions of film genre and musicianship, and the ramifications of audiovisual technology. Anahid Kassabian devotes much of the third chapter in her 2001 book *Hearing Film* to a trend in narrative films about women with "abandon[ing] the symphonic Romanticism of classical Hollywood in favor of pop—and especially compiled—soundtracks."[29] Specifically, she traces connotations of desire and agency in the popular music of several Hollywood compilations. Similarly, Ian Inglis's 2003 edited collection *Popular Music and Film* largely concentrates on cinematic uses of pop for purposes of scene-setting, helping specific audience demographics identify with a film, and detailing the work of pop musicians who have appeared in movies. Most recently, Phil Powrie and Robynn Stilwell's 2006 edited volume *Changing Tunes: The Use of Pre-existing Music in Film* describes the ways films have become involved in the social and historical meanings of the preexisting musics that they use. Ronald Rodman's chapter in that book, "The Popular Song as Leitmotif in 1990s Film," takes a largely structuralist perspective and concludes by saying that the turn to pop music means "the abstract discourses of musical style and social practice, once the realm of connotation in the musical score, now become sources of denotation in film music."[30]

In our own book, we discuss such "borrowings" of music as they have become involved in recent renewals of cinematic stylization and authorship. These contributors theorize individual film stylists' uses of preexisting popular music, focusing primarily on the textual aspects of the films in question though also bringing viewership, cultural politics, and music performance into the discussion. Following the developments in film music studies described above, our approach would seem a natural next step, indeed a necessary one. That we are now seeing renewed interest in auteurism, specifically in an influential filmmaking culture that is both highly stylized cinematically and musically oriented, makes our study all the more imperative. If Buhler is correct in attributing scholarly disinterest in source music to its dearth of art, one can only wonder if disinterest in the musical aspects of auteurism can be attributed to *too much* art being brought to bear on film music. There have been few discussions of preexisting music as it has become involved in specific filmmakers' styles and creative avenues; for examples of such, we could turn to the discussions of Stanley Kubrick in my own essay "Modernism Goes to the Movies" and Claudia Gorbman's exploration of the same director's musical choices in "Ears Wide Open: Kubrick's Music."[31] These two essays complement each other nicely, as the first concentrates on *2001: A Space Odyssey* and the second on the director's last film, *Eyes Wide Shut*. Because she surveys a wider swathe of Kubrick's career and asks larger filmmaking questions, Gorbman comes closest to the provocative issues in the present book. She tells us, for example, how this director employs the terrifying sparseness of Ligeti's *Musica Ricercata* to articulate a typically Kubrickian tale of one male character's ruin—in this case, Bill Harford's humiliation and downfall.

As I have already said, contributors to the present book are interested not only in popular music as it appears in film, but they also ask specifically how such appearances have been mediated and colored by the MV. Ours is a new topic; there has been little discussion of the MV aesthetic as an influence—both cinematic and musical—on recent film stylists. John Mundy is one writer who has theorized the MV in broader cinematic terms. In addressing the special qualities of the MV's style, storytelling, and sense of time and performance, Mundy relates it to cinematic traditions of the spectacular—specifically, to the early-20th-century "cinema of attractions" described by Tom Gunning as an exhibitionist form of filmmaking, a confrontational, carnival-like play of images that chooses to show things rather than narrate stories. "This is a cinema that displaces its visibility," Gunning writes, "willing to rupture a self enclosed fictional world for a chance to solicit the attention of the spectator."[32] As Mundy presents it, this "attractions" aesthetic of the MV erases differences between narrative and performance, with a concomitant transformation of time passage from clock time to the kind of time stoppage that attends acts of showing.[33]

An additional, fourth stage of film music scholarship has arrived with Claudia Gorbman's recent account of "Auteur Music." Brief as it is, this essay is a signal event in that it brings together auteur theory and film music studies. Note the word order in Gorbman's title: She comes close to redefining the auteur construct, re-emergent and commodified, as a form of music-making rather than an art of filmmaking. She calls music-loving, stylized filmmakers *mélomanes*, or "music fans." More and more, such *mélomanes*, she says, conceive of music as "a key thematic element and a marker of authorial style." Digital technology encourages such music-loving directors by allowing them to take more and more control of the music "as a key thematic element and a marker of authorial style."[34] Describing auteurism as "a film-historical self-consciousness that encourages individuation and even excess," Gorbman says that music has become "a platform for the idiosyncratic expression of taste, and thus it conveys not only meaning in terms of plot and theme, but meaning as authorial signature itself." As she describes it, the new *mélomane* auteurism represents an emancipation, a reprioritization, a relaxing of rules, a glorification of excess, and an opening-up of sound and sight, and ultimately a transformed understanding: New musical usages in cinema have brought us to the exciting point, she says, where "the sky's the limit with respect to the possible relations between music and image and story."[35]

THE BOOK AND ITS CHAPTERS

So Gorbman thinks of the new auteurism almost as a kind of musicianship. She discusses Godard, Tarantino, Tsai Ming-Liang, and late Kubrick, describing those *mélomane* auteurs as music fans who grab you by the collar and express their creative ideas and cultural situations by playing their latest CDs or MP3s for you. Yet Gorbman doesn't explore the fact that today's music enthusiasts are perforce video enthusiasts, and she makes no mention of the MV and the importance of its video-musical stylizations for filmmaking more broadly. Probably because of the brevity of her essay, she also takes no particular interest in the duality of popular and symphonic music, or in textual issues—specifically, in the preexistence of songs, their pre-cinematic lives as co-opted and manipulated by the filmmaker. Possibly for similar reasons, she discusses songs not as spans of musical and historical reference, but as entities that are—by virtue of auteurism's definition—edited, cut, and all-around manipulated by technology-aided cinema stylists.

Our book ventures in those directions that Gorbman chooses not to follow: We ask what auteurist "cueings up" might mean with regard to the cultural construct of popular music generally, the songs themselves as music-historical entities, and authorship in broader terms. We also take up the fascinating issues of just what kind of musical aesthetics and canons are devised and curated by these auteurist musician-cineastes. One important discovery, for instance, is that musically involved irony has become one of the major issues of cinema aesthetics, yet it is tough to define and discuss irony vis-à-vis the authorial signature. Music has become a tool of unprecedented cinematic expression and a major aspect of auteurist style; this is a basic understanding of this book's contributors. At the same time, it needs emphasizing that with music's increasing cinematic importance, it has taken on a paradoxical aspect, and many of the contributors to this book look closely at the ways music has helped redefine auteurism at a time of unbridled irony and intertextual reference. Whether Andrew Sarris would recognize auteurism in the multivalent film texts that we uncover is open to question, but we thereby acknowledge the changeability of the auteur construct, or rather the presence of a nouvelle auteurism.

Julie Hubbert presents Martin Scorsese as a *mélomane* and a Janus figure, a cinema veteran whose approach to filmmaking has changed along with his dramaturgical involvements with popular music—the question of which instigated the other becomes unanswerable and perhaps irrelevant. For Scorsese, the need for new narrative rhythms and textures, for things "to move faster" and more obliquely are tied not just to contemporary cinematic styles, like the high-concept film, but more fundamentally to the specifically musical media that inspired them. As Scorsese sees them, changes in film rhythm and texture have been inextricably tied to changes in visualizing music, to some of the challenges Richard Lester tested in the early Beatles films, but more important, to the contemporary innovations of the music video. Hubbert devotes most of her attention to *Goodfellas* (1990) as Scorsese's pivotal work. The music in this film functions on multiple levels. The oblique texts and "decadent" psychedelic style of the songs comment on protagonist Henry's mental disintegration and on the disintegration of his life as a gangster. But it is the placement of these songs and the independent interpretive structure they create that are most striking. When the narration comments on what's taking place and emphasizes Henry's actions—driving, cooking, picking up his brother—the music articulates a separate commentary. Its seams emphasize Henry's increasingly dangerous and paranoid behavior—the near crash, the drugs, the capricious and irrational changes of plans.

As Tim Anderson discusses them, Sofia Coppola's films use popular songs in the classical tried-and-true manner of the melodrama and the musical: The songs have the function of stopping narrative time to make room for gesture and the primacy of the individual cinematic moment. These functions also help Coppola carve out what could be called a gendered, "feminized" sense of time. As Anderson describes it, this filmmaker's singular sense of time has incurred considerable scorn—puzzlement at her disinterest in the Aristotelian, transformational narrative and the character development that attends it. Indeed, the songs Coppola uses often shoulder much of the narrative enactment of her characters, projecting characterization and the drama of the moment from screen to soundtrack, and back again. This singular conception of time has peaked in her third and most controversial feature film, *Marie Antoinette* (2006). Coppola's supposed anachronism here of using new music to accompany an old tale—of mixing pop-culture vernacular with, as the first-time viewer must presume, authentic historical orthodoxy—has been called incompetent and shallow. Instead, as Anderson suggests, we should understand these apparent instances of auteurism (winning out over convention and good taste) as a postmodern cinematic sensibility being brought to bear—as was inevitable—on a real historical subject. And music, this filmmaker seems to suggest, can never be "of the past," or historical in the narrower sense. In this way, we might understand Coppola's sensibility as not only auteurist, but innately musical.

David Lynch's authorial signature is unmistakable, yet his cinematic-musical meanings are famously evasive—and intrinsically ironic, some would say. Gene Willet helps us locate this director as auteur and music lover by turning the discourse surrounding Lynch not toward the subject of irony, but toward the imagined. Willet talks about popular music as a means of creating fantasy, but fantasy in the Lacanian sense—not as a means of staging wish-fulfillment, but rather as a way of creating desire itself. In examining the soundtracks of *Lost Highway* (1997), *Mulholland Drive* (2001), and *Blue Velvet* (1986), Willet reveals music's fundamental role in Lynch's construction of fantasy. This filmmaker uses popular music not simply as an old-fashioned cue for fantasy, rather music seems to function as a screen upon which fantasy itself is projected. These fantasy worlds provide protection from reality but are presented in an unmediated, stark, and pure form that often overwhelms the audience. Willet's analysis complements the book's other chapters primarily in the way it exposes cinematic appearances of irony. Critics tend to see irony in Lynch's use of Bobby Vinton's and Roy Orbison's music in *Blue Velvet*, and thereby hear those songs as the film's external critiques of some "reality." But as Willet tells us, the movie presents a more complex staging of desires and their satisfaction than ideas of irony can encompass. In this way, Lynch is seen to interpret and indeed interrogate the songs he uses to a greater degree than we have previously suspected. And we see that his use of popular music offers more intricate layers of allusion and double meanings than a symphonic non-diegetic score could.

Like Willet, Giorgio Biancorosso examines music's role in fantasy and image-making and doesn't see those pursuits as limited to cinema. Indeed, the Biancorosso and Willet chapters show us film not as an escape from reality, but as a kind of working-out of real life, a place where images and dreams prove more tangible and important than reality itself. Biancorosso discusses Wong Kar-wai's *Happy Together* (1997), *Fallen Angels* (1995), and *In the Mood for Love* (2000) in terms of remembrance and self-fashioning and desire, presenting this director as a purveyor of moving images whose sensibility is nevertheless defined by *still* images and all their attendant nostalgia. Wong is a portraitist in much the same way all of us are portraitists—of ourselves and of desired and loved ones, mostly. Here the filmmaker's signature is scattered and diffracted by popular music—music belonging to everyone and trailing a fragmented history, a history free of meta-narratives. With his implication that Wong's soundtracks cannot be accounted for in terms of auteurist personal expression, Biancorosso also seems to challenge Gorbman and her view of "auteur music." Wong seems instead to collaborate with us, his viewers, when he chooses music: He gives us songs as enabler or fellow fantasist. And so his films are all the more film-like in that they seem very much lifelike, or similar to those especially real lives that we live in our own minds. His music can also play with that divide between fantasy and reality: As Biancorosso describes Wong and his deployment of songs, it is when his films become most like real life that "music comes to our rescue as either explicit reference or allusion, helping us see Wong's characters as celluloid fantasies, a gallery of jigsaw puzzle cuts...."

In his chapter on the Coen brothers, Jeff Smith gives an idea of how this pair of *mélomanes* has deployed a wide variety of songs in films rife with cross-purposes, ironies, and multivalent meanings. As Smith describes them, the Coens have developed their own humorist "signature"—be it dark, quirky, or otherwise—and within that aesthetic, they use preexisting songs both as a kind of intertextual "wink" and as a means—joyful, not dutiful—of "period and place" authentication. Smith's discussion of "Danny Boy," as it accompanies a failed hit on mob boss Leo O'Bannon in *Miller's Crossing* (1990), helps demonstrate the different layers of significance that an older song can have in a Coens movie: The famed Irish ballad functions, alternately and simultaneously, as a musical commonplace and as a wry reference. For Smith, the song presents "perhaps the most conclusive evidence that the Coens' tendency toward intertextual allusionism is inextricable from their use of classical storytelling techniques. The cue's jokiness and its status as a musical cliché do not negate its essentially classical function." As Smith discusses it, the song's seamless progression from source music—we first hear and see it playing on a Victrola in Leo's room— to ostensibly empathetic underscoring only serves to accentuate the Coens' sardonic and slippery employment of this music. The scene becomes a kind of catalogue for the ways in which a folk ballad can be used in a movie, and the film asks us to understand and believe them all.

As already mentioned, Tarantino is the auteur who has almost single-handedly managed to make preexisting songs function differently, even *sound* differently, in the movie theater. The revolution of the earlier, pre-millennial Tarantino was in creating new manners of distance or disjunction between narrative and song—an inversion of classic Hollywood practice where it was the newly composed underscoring, and not the diegetic pop music, that told us about the characters. The characters in those earlier Tarantino films cued up relatively obscure preexisting pop records, and like real people in real life, "played" the songs not only to enhance their own pleasure, but also to lose control. The pop songs in question became tools, avenues to danger and possibility. Thus Tarantino's earlier practice, as Ken Garner described it in an earlier study of this filmmaker's music, covering the films through *Jackie Brown* (1998).[36] In his contribution to the present book, Garner focuses on Tarantino's more recent musical strategies—his use of popular music in *Kill Bill* (2003–2004), *Death Proof* (2007), and *Inglourious Basterds* (2009). With these considerably new strategems, Tarantino now uses preexisting music perhaps less to focus our attention on individual characters than to invoke authenticity and perhaps historicity: He tends to home in specifically on earlier film music cues, thereby circumscribing the whole notion of popular music rather differently than before. In doing so, he emphasizes the materiality and age of these cues, and painstakingly exaggerates their provenance in some cases—even, as in the case of the café scene in *Inglourious Basterds*, making up a provenance as it suits him. Devising new means of allusion, fictitious vinyl surface noise among them, the recent Tarantino has become newly aware of the intertextual nature of media and expression; as Garner puts it, music has become for him a way of inviting his audience "to be conscious above all else that this film is a construct formed of various media and ways of telling."

In my own chapter, I pursue the notion of musical-cinematic irony to its logical—or, better said, illogical—conclusion, as set out by incorrigible ironist Wes Anderson in *The Royal Tenenbaums* (2001), *The Life Aquatic with Steve Zissou* (2004), and *The Fantastic Mr. Fox* (2009). My broader proposal is that all auteurism is ironic, though in accordance with the less obvious connotations of that much-abused word. Anderson's importance lies with his creation or reactivation of a form of irony auteurism that is very different from the irony auteurisms of Welles and Kubrick, less like a disaffected worldview that yearns to be less estranged, and more like a fleeting complacency in a complex universe, a set of perceptual quirks. Auteurs tend by nature to be controversial filmmakers, and Anderson divides opinion more than many. As I present his work, however, he is an author whose particular foregrounding of irony, digression, and distraction is all but necessary to an understanding of auteurism more generally. In short, Anderson is to be taken seriously as an auteur, even when—especially when—he insists that we *not* watch and listen to him in earnest. Using wide ranges of songs—most of Anderson's soundtracks are too far-flung to be considered compilations—he forges unattentive, idiosyncratic, sort-of narratives from anti-narrative elements. Anderson shows an increasing general discomfort with narratives, as do so many of the auteurist chroniclers discussed in this book—Lynch's stories hollow, Sofia Coppola's wandering, Wong's fragmented, Tarantino's paper-thin. It seems in the end that this narrative disaffection is the dominant theme of our book, and that all the musical selections we describe directly reflect this sort of disillusioned manner of non-storytelling, one that recent auteurs have refined, literally, to an art form.

In discussing the ascendant future of cinematic auteurism alongside the less assured fate of orchestral underscoring, it is difficult not to conclude that the increasing role of popular songs as a kind of "music proper"—as a deeply allusive and specifically contingent, and therefore ultimately definitive, form of music—says something more generally about music's current cultural roles. As described by W. J. T. Mitchell, postmodernism represents a basic reorientation from the word to the image, from the syntactic to the iconic. In other words, living as we are after "the pictorial turn" in "a culture totally dominated by images," we don't read things anymore; we look at them.[37] Music seems both to have followed and encouraged wholesale changes in film aesthetics, jumping in to transform, expedite, and magnify the individual looked-at cinematic moment in an age when movies don't tell stories the way they used to, and human sensibilities have been transformed by digital editing. While auteurism resurges in our age of looking, it has come to rely on and redefine music as an art of listening-as-looking. Music has never been more necessary to filmmakers or, in terms of split-second visual and narrative change, more deeply cooperative in the cinematic venture. And as regards music, the emerging art of listening-as-looking is a topic of great importance, a topic that the contributors to this book are in the vanguard of theorizing.

No theory of auteurist filmmaking is really able to account for today's cinematic experience and its renegotiated relationship with the musical experience. The various arguments fail to account for auteurism as an art of the all-subsuming and poly-sensual instant within a buyer's market—a propensity toward originality of sound and vision that charges and changes the individual moment just as strongly as it does the complete film. For almost half a century, film criticism has hypothesized the auteur as a specific and historically substantiated filmmaker. But for present-day purposes, given the increasingly organic, all-enveloping, and inclusive nature of the cinematic experience, with music given an integral role, we would do well to theorize auteurism as a quasi-theistic impulse on the part of the moviegoer. For what kind of cultural arbiter beside the filmmaker remains as influential and powerful as she is enigmatic? How dare the critic declare on the moviegoer's behalf that the auteur does or does not exist, when the mysterious auteur construct—whether in the narrow sense of the politique des auteurs or in some more colloquial sense—helps the spectator either envelop herself unknowingly in a film or try to understand the experience in phenomenological rather than technical terms of control, omniscience, personality, and mastery?[38] The more powerful, all-enveloping, and even bewildering encounter a film provides, the more the viewer confronts the filmmaker as a variant of the Cartesian subject. In discussing individual directors, contributors to the present book ask the basic question: *Creat ergo est; the filmmaker creates, therefore she is—so who is she?*

In William James's conception of theism, heavily influenced by Darwin, the believer creates the one god that precisely and efficiently fulfills her needs. *Creat ergo est.* The moviegoer creates the god auteur as an essential yet virtual presence—an overseer without a face, as both a synecdoche for the experience and a (virtual) finalizer of signification. The spectator is confronted by an all-enveloping experience that can only be ascribed to someone other than herself, and thereby finds herself caught up in a secularized version of James's "ultimate duality of God and his believer." In this sense, the filmic creator's power is a function more of her intangibility and persuasiveness, and therefore a function of her musicality, than of whom she actually is. "God's personality is to be regarded," writes James, "like any other personality, as something lying outside of my own and other than me, and whose existence I simply come upon and find. A power not ourselves, then, which not only makes for righteousness, but means it...."[39] At its most basic, then, the spectator's auteurist impulse becomes a need for order bound inextricably with a sense of wonder.[40] And the "power not ourselves" of cinema, never more omniscient or more persuasive or more image-driven than in recent films, is becoming ever more a musical one.

NOTES

1. From Wood's review of Seán Burke's *The Death and Return of the Author* (Edinburgh, UK: Edinburgh University Press, 1992), as cited on the back cover of that book in its second edition.

2. See Timothy Corrigan, "The Commerce of Auteurism: Coppola, Kluge, Ruiz," in *A Cinema Without Walls: Movies and Culture after Vietnam* (New Brunswick, NJ: Rutgers University Press, 1991), 101–136; and Gilberto Perez, *The Material Ghost: Films and Their Medium* (Baltimore, MD: Johns Hopkins University Press, 1998), 3–13. According to Corrigan, "Auteurs are far from dead...they may in fact be more alive now than at any other point in film history" (135). Frederic Jameson offered his own problematization of auteurism at about this same time and proposed that pastiche has replaced auteurism in postmodernity; see Frederic Jameson, "Historicism in *The Shining*," in *Signatures of the Visible* (New York: Routledge, 1992), 82–98. Catherine Grant, in a post-Corrigan and post-Perez essay that includes some valuable summaries of late-century auteurist theory, concludes that the auteur construct is proving remarkably resilient in our age of global/ postnationalist capital. Despite the talk of "deterritorialization" under globalization, she says "auteurism still appears to be playing a rather similar role within regional frameworks, or 'territories'...as it has since the 1950s and 1960s." Grant, www.auteur.com, *Screen*, vol. 41, no. 1 (Spring 2000), 101–108.

3. From Sarris, "Notes on the Auteur Theory in 1962"; reprinted in *Theories of Authorship: A Reader*, ed. John Caughie (London and New York: Routledge, 1981), 64.

4. The Sarris theory tries to define a filmmaker by a specific set of traits, and the pluralist/ poststructuralist can't recognize the kind of creative stewardship seen in other art forms that are just as socially, technically, and financially encumbered as film. An example of the latter is orchestral performance, where the conductor has been considered the visionary and definitive idiosyncratic presence for some 150 years. If the cinematic auteur idea is

to be denied because film is a collaborative and industrial art form, then the notion of a distinctive and pervasive conducting style must be denied as well.

5. John Mundy, writing in 1999, disregarded any such convergences between visual and musical styles when he averred that "music video remains, whatever else it is, a musical event." Mundy, *Popular Music on Screen: From Hollywood Musical to Music Video* (Manchester, UK, and New York: Manchester University Press, 1999), 240.

6. Dancyger, "The MTV Influence on Editing I," in *The Technique of Film and Video Editing*, fourth edition (Amsterdam and Boston: Focal Press, 2007), 184, 190.

7. "Music videos use the continuity of a popular song to give the visuals coherence as they defy spatial and temporal logic." Timothy Corrigan and Patricia White, *The Film Experience: An Introduction* (Boston and New York: Bedford/St. Martins, 2004), 120.

8. Gowers designed the "Bohemian Rhapsody" clip largely as a replication of the *Queen II* album cover. The original photographer for that cover, Mick Rock, recalled that his inspiration for the album image was yet another still, a shot of Marlene Dietrich in *Shanghai Express*. See Rock as interviewed in "More than Meets the I: Classic Rock Art—Queen II," http://www.dangerousage.com/classiccovers/index.php?page=queen-ii, accessed April 29, 2012.

9. Wright, "Score vs. Song: Art, Commerce, and the H Factor in Film and Television Music," in *Popular Music and Film*, ed. Ian Inglis (London and New York: Wallflower, 2003), 15.

10. Quoted in Peter Brunette, *Wong Kar-Wai* (Chicago and New York: University of Illinois Press, 2005), 128.

11. Brecht quoted by Joy H. Calico, *Brecht at the Opera* (Berkeley and Los Angeles: University of California Press, 2008), 36.

12. Sean Cubitt, " 'Maybellene': Meaning and the Listening Subject," in *Reading Pop: Approaches to Textual Analysis in Popular Music*, ed. Richard Middleton (New York and Oxford, UK: Oxford University Press, 2000), 155.

13. Camille Paglia writes of Garland, "for the generation that experienced the Depression and World War II, she was a link to an innocent past, the Arcadia of pre-industrial America. In the *Wizard of Oz*, she sang 'Over the Rainbow' with an already perceptible nostalgia for the paradise lost of a childhood she never had." Paglia, "Judy Garland as a Force of Nature," *New York Times*, June 14, 1998, http://www.nytimes.com/1998/06/14/arts/judy-garland-as-a-force-of-nature.html.

14. "First of all, normally we shoot without a script, or without a real script or [even] a fake script, but we have an idea." Wong Kar-Wai quoted in Peter Brunette, *Wong Kar-Wai*, 125.

15. My description of the jukebox scene from Wong's *Fallen Angels* owes a great deal to Giorgio Biancorroso's essay "Global Music/Local Cinema: Two Wong Kar-Wai Pop Compilations," in *Hong Kong Culture: Word and Image*, ed. Kam Louie (Hong Kong: Hong Kong University Press, 2010), 229–245; see especially his discussion of the Michelle Reis character's delusion and "jukebox melancholia" at 237–239. See also Biancorosso's conclusion to his chapter in this volume.

16. Of course the style of "Speak My Language" was itself a strategic choice on Wong's part, in that Anderson's song disinvites empathy and identification. In the words of a critic for the *All Music Guide*, the Anderson album containing "Speak My Language" is "filled with images of disconnection, miscommunication, and fear . . . it's nearly impossible to make any sort of emotional connection with this music." Stewart Mason, "Laurie Anderson: *Bright Red*," *All Music Guide*, fourth ed. (San Francisco: Backbeat, 2001), 13.

17. Ian Garwood, "Pop Music as Film Music," in *Close-up 01*, eds. John Gibbs and Douglas Pye (London: Wallflower, 2006), 96–103. As Garwood says, "the relationship between song and character . . . allows the viewer to understand, in a way that the characters do not, the extent to which each character fails to project his desired self-image onto the world around him" (134). Garwood contrasts popular song with the non-diegetic orchestral

score, describing the way that the John Sayles film *Baby, It's You* explores the consequences of characterizing its music as working determinedly from the "outside-in": "being taken on by its characters in their efforts of self-display" (159).

18. Writing from this perspective of poststructuralism and the decentered subject, Roger Beebe has contrasted "the postmodern auteur" with the old "modernist aesthetic valorization of 'expression' (the exteriorization of a 'deep' interior existence)." See Beebe, "Paradoxes of Pastiche: Spike Jonze, Hype Williams, and the Race of the Postmodern Auteur," in *Medium Cool: Music Videos from Soundies to Cellphones*, eds. Beebe and Jason Middleton (Durham, NC, and London: Duke University Press, 2007), 303–327.

19. "Everybody has already said the same thing [in gangster movies], and I didn't think people would believe it anymore. So I was trying to do it with the form of MTV, which just made it more fake, you know. You don't have the feeling that I'm trying to tell you a really serious story." Peter Brunette, "Interview with Wong Kar-Wai," in *Wong Kar-Wai* (Urbana, IL, and Chicago: University of Illinois Press, 2005), 120.

20. Judith Lochhead speaks of a duality between "parodic" and "authentic" idioms in *Lulu*, proposing that Berg didn't necessarily use diatonic tonality as a natural mode of compositional-stylistic expression, but employed it as part of an allusive gender-performative strategy; see her essay "Lulu's Feminine Performance" in *The Cambridge Companion to Berg*, ed. Anthony Pople (Cambridge, UK, and New York: Cambridge University Press, 1998), 227–244.

21. Kubrick probably chose Herbert von Karajan's 1967 recording of "The Blue Danube" for its grace, smoothness, and leisureliness; a critic writing for *Gramophone* in 1967 praised the record for the conductor's way of "surrendering himself to the melting mood of the waltz."

22. As Claudia Gorbman describes Kubrick's appropriation of preexisting music, "the exactitude of his visual compositions and editing finds an aural equivalent in the music cues." Gorbman, "Auteur Music," in *Beyond the Soundtrack: Representing Music in Cinema*, eds. Daniel Goldmark, Lawrence Kramer, and Richard Leppert (Berkeley, CA, and Los Angeles: University of California Press, 2007), 152.

23. As Jeff Smith describes it, the compilation soundtrack "emerges as a curious hybrid of the musical and the traditional classical Hollywood score. Like the musical, each song of the compilation score retains a certain measure of structural unity and integrity.... At the same time, however, the individual songs of the compilation score are typically utilized in ways that are not unlike the cues of the conventional orchestral score." Smith, *The Sounds of Commerce: Marketing Popular Film Music* (New York: Columbia University Press, 1998), 155.

24. Victoria E. Johnson, "Polyphony and Cultural Expression: Interpreting Musical Traditions in *Do the Right Thing*," in *Do the Right Thing*, ed. Mark A. Reid (Cambridge, UK, and New York: Cambridge University Press, 1997), 69–70.

25. Scott, "Sounding Black: Cultural Identification, Sound, and the Films of Spike Lee," in *Fight the Power! The Spike Lee Reader*, eds. Janice D. Hamlet and Robin R. Means Coleman (New York: Peter Lang, 2009), 230. For a fascinating account of Lee's appropriation of Aaron Copland's film and stage music to represent young black sportsmen in *He Got Game*, see Krin Gabbard's 2004 essay, "Spike Lee meets Aaron Copland," as reprinted in *The Spike Lee Reader*, ed. Paula J. Massood (Philadelphia: Temple University Press, 2008), 175–195.

26. "Welcome to convergence culture, where old and new media collide, where grassroots and corporate media intersect, where the power of the media producer and the power of the media consumer interact in unpredictable ways." Jenkins, *Convergence Culture: Where Old and New Media Collide* (New York and London: New York University Press, 2006), 2.

27. K. J. Donnelly, "The Hidden Heritage of Film Music," in *Film Music: Critical Approaches,* ed. K. J. Donnelly (New York: Continuum, 2001), 4.

28. Neumeyer and Buhler, "Analytical and Interpretive Approaches to Film Music (I): Analysing the Music," in *Film Music: Critical Approaches,* 43.

29. Kassabian, "A Woman Scored," in *Hearing Film: Tracking Identifications in Contemporary Hollywood Film Music* (New York and London: Routledge, 2001), 69.

30. Rodman, "The Popular Song as Leitmotif in 1990s Film," in *Changing Tunes: The Use of Pre-existing Music in Film,* eds. Powrie and Stilwell (Aldershot, UK, and Burlington, VT: Ashgate, 2006), 135.

31. Ashby, "Modernism Goes to the Movies," in *The Pleasure of Modernist Music: Listening, Meaning, Intention, Ideology* (Rochester and New York: University of Rochester Press, 2004), 345–386; Gorbman, "Ears Wide Open: Kubrick's Music," in *Changing Tunes: The Use of Pre-existing Music in Film,* eds. Phil Powrie and Robynn Stilwell (Aldershot, UK, and Burlington, VT: Ashgate, 2006), 3–18.

32. Gunning, "The Cinema of Attractions: Early Film, Its Spectator, and the Avant-Garde," in *Early Cinema: Space, Frame, Narrative,* eds. Thomas Elsaesser and Adam Barker (London: British Film Institute, 1990), 230.

33. Mundy, *Popular Music on Screen: From Hollywood Musical to Music Video* (Manchester, UK, and New York: Manchester University Press, 1999), 226–227, 239–240.

34. Gorbman, "Auteur Music," in *Beyond the Soundtrack: Representing Music in Cinema,* eds. Daniel Goldmark, Lawrence Kramer, and Richard Leppert (Berkeley, CA, and Los Angeles: University of California Press, 2007), 149.

35. Gorbman, "Auteur Music," 151.

36. Garner, " 'Would You Like to Hear Some Music?' Music In-and-Out-of-Control in the Films of Quentin Tarantino," in *Film Music: Critical Approaches* (New York: Continuum, 2001), 188–205.

37. William J. Mitchell, *Picture Theory* (Chicago and London: University of Chicago Press, 1994), 15, and passim. See also Arved Ashby, "Mahler as Imagist," in *Absolute Music, Mechanical Reproduction* (Berkeley and Los Angeles: University of California Press, 2010), 221–251.

38. As Patrick Phillips has observed, auteur theory has gone some way toward helping explain "exactly how are the makers of film and the audience bound together in the activities of creation, communication, and comprehension." Phillips, "Genre, Star and Auteur: An Approach to Hollywood Cinema," in *An Introduction to Film Studies,* ed. Jill Nelmes (London and New York: Routledge, 1996), 134.

39. "Reflex Action and Theism" (1881), reprinted in James, *The Will to Believe and Other Essays in Popular Philosophy* (New York: Dover, 1956), 122, 134.

40. In his own discussion of auteurism in the new century, Adrian Martin follows a line of thought similar to my own but arrives at a drastically different scenario: In his political, as opposed to quasi-religious scenario, it is the public, not the filmmaker, that has a god-like presence. In his view, "the rise of the director as superstar, as media celebrity . . . is an increasingly irritating phenomenon." In an age tired of such pronouncements and commercialism, Martin continues, there is increasing ambivalence toward the auteur. "To the auteur-as-commodity we are effectively saying: get lost, we can get by without you." Adrian Martin, "Possessory Credit," *Framework,* vol. 45, no. 1 (Spring 2004), 95–99.

PART ONE

Music and Cinematic Time

CHAPTER 1

"Without Music, I Would Be Lost": Scorsese, *Goodfellas*, and a New Soundtrack Practice

JULIE HUBBERT

In the critical literature on the filmmaker Martin Scorsese, the discussion of music occupies an unusual position. Although scholars have acknowledged the significant presence music has in his narrative films, popular music especially, most of the analysis has focused on the filmmaker's documentary films. Over the course of his decades-long career, Scorsese has made numerous documentary films about prominent musicians or musical events, from *The Last Waltz* (1971) to the more recent television documentaries *The Blues: Feels Like Going Home* (2003), *No Direction Home: Bob Dylan* (2005), and *Shine A Light* (2008).[1] These films have repeatedly shown Scorsese to have a deep, critical interest in pop and rock music, a fascination that has overshadowed all others including his interest in his Italian heritage and the history of the cinema.[2] Although few scholars have considered it to any significant degree, music also enjoys an enormously privileged position in Scorsese's narrative films.[3] This neglect seems particularly glaring considering the emphasis Scorsese has placed on music as a formative aspect of his narrative filmmaking style. As he himself has remarked on a number of occasions, music is an essential ingredient in his fiction film work. Its centrality not only challenges the conventional privileging of imagery over sound but the conventional placement of music in the filmmaking process. For Scorsese, music is not merely a secondary or postproduction addition to the images on the screen, but rather a primary element in the conception of the film. In an interview in 1995, for instance, he observed that

[m]usic has always been for me a major source of inspiration. Stanley Kubrick said once that it is the combination of images and music that is of the greatest importance to the cinema, and one is convinced of the accuracy of this observation when one watches his films....I know that without music, I would be lost. Very often it is uniquely on hearing a piece of music that is right for one of my films that I begin to visualize it.[4]

For Scorsese, music is an essential part of the narrative filmmaking process. Its place is so privileged, in fact, that it subverts conventional film hierarchies. It is the combination of image and music (not image and dialogue), he asserts, that defines cinema as a unique art form.

This reversal, this privileging of music over dialogue, Scorsese notes, is not without precedents. Kubrick also prioritized music over dialogue.[5] For all its overlap with Kubrick's, however, Scorsese's musical aesthetic is distinct from it, especially in the way that its priority is achieved. As Scorsese sees it, in narrative filmmaking, music should be not only central but fundamentally authentic. It should function much as it does in a documentary in the sense that it should not act just as decoration but emanate from the content of the film. Scorsese roots this aspect of his musical aesthetic, as he does much of his filmmaking style, in autobiographical or personal experience:

When I was young, popular music formed the soundtrack of my life—rock 'n' roll and Neapolitan love songs would rise from the jukeboxes in the little bars of my old neighborhood, New York's Lower East Side, day and night. And so it was only natural that it would become such an important part of my work as a director, beginning with my first student films. Music has always been a key source of inspiration for me—it has the power to bring entire sequences to life.[6]

This observation explains much about the stylistic preferences Scorsese exhibits in his films. His soundtracks are full of pop and rock music, particularly from the 1960s and '70s, because these are the styles he is most familiar with, the music that accompanied formative personal experiences. But the autobiographical component of his musical aesthetic also explains the placement he gives music in his films. For Scorsese, music must authenticate time and space. It must emanate visually from on-screen sites, jukeboxes, record players, car radios, etc. Scorsese privileges music but unlike Kubrick, he additionally mandates that music authenticate narrative content. For him, the combination of music and image becomes central precisely in the moment when it becomes real, when it can be literally linked to the images on the screen.

Although Scorsese has collaborated with composers in some of his films, it is in those films with compiled soundtracks where Scorsese himself has acted as composer, selecting and placing preexisting music in his films, that this aesthetic has been most visible.[7] In *Mean Streets* (1973), *Raging Bull* (1980), *The Color of Money* (1986), *Goodfellas* (1990), *Casino* (1996), and *Bringing Out the Dead* (1999), the length of the soundtracks Scorsese constructs from preexisting music alone speaks to the general priority that music has as a narrative element in his films. In all of these soundtracks, the music is additionally chosen to be "period" and to satisfy general conditions of authenticity by being placed primarily diegetically within the film. Beginning with *Goodfellas*, however, a change in Scorsese's musical aesthetic and his soundtrack construction is evident. In *Goodfellas*, the music Scorsese uses can also be seen to satisfy a new and additional imperative for visual "movement," one rooted in contemporary music video practices. In this respect, the film articulates a turning point in Scorsese's musical aesthetic and the evolution of his soundtrack practice. All of Scorsese's narrative films with compiled soundtracks privilege music. This priority is arguably one of the conditions that define Scorsese as an auteur.[8] But in *Goodfellas*, that authorial voice is particularly clear not only in the substantial amount of music Scorsese uses, but in the way that he also uses music to experiment with narrative tempos and textures and to create more fluid and independent uses of cinematic space. In this sense, the *Goodfellas* soundtrack represents an expanded music aesthetic and a new soundtrack practice for one of cinema's most musical auteurs.

FROM VÉRITÉ TO VIDEOS: TOWARD A NEW MUSICAL AESTHETIC

The foundation for Scorsese's narrative musical aesthetic was crystallized in his first studio film, *Mean Streets* (1973), an intimate and autobiographical look at the small-time neighborhood gangsters Scorsese grew up with in New York's Little Italy in the 1950s and '60s. The film follows a close-knit circle of friends as they roam the neighborhood engaging in various petty crimes and misdemeanors. It also follows them with a kind of documentary enthusiasm. As Scorsese observes, *Mean Streets* was "an attempt to put myself and my old friends on the screen, to show how we lived, what life was like in Little Italy. It was really an anthropological or sociological tract."[9] To create this sense of anthropology, Scorsese borrowed heavily from the tradition of documentary filmmaking, especially the newly minted styles of the cinema vérité and direct cinema movements. Scorsese began his post-film-school career in the late 1960s working for direct cinema pioneers Al and David Maysles, and their influence is visible in the film. The film uses a number of documentary, or specifically vérité, techniques: shaky cameras, long uninterrupted takes, abrupt jump cuts, a disjunctive narrative structure, and natural lighting. Sonically, it revels in "found" sound. Sections of the dialogue are often improvised, muffled, or fragmented, and ambient sounds are often unusually loud or unbalanced with dialogue. The film's music soundtrack also articulates a sense of vérité. All of the music is diegetically placed and is stylistically "period" or authentic to the narrative action of the film. Set in the early 1970s, the film has a soundtrack that features songs by the Ronettes, the Chantels, the Aquatones, the Nutmegs, the Paragons, the Shirelles, the Miracles, Eric Clapton, and the Rolling Stones. The songs are additionally heard spilling out from objects seen on the screen: jukeboxes, car radios, television sets, and street bands.[10] Like the sets, costumes, and dialects, the style, placement, and often fragmented structure of the music works to authenticate or document the film's mise en scène.

These vérité elements in *Mean Streets'* compilation defined Scorsese's early soundtrack practice and articulated the foundation of his musical aesthetic by reprioritizing music as a narrative element and making it authentic, literally locating it in the film as a fundamental part of its imagery. This anthropological privileging also gave the cinematic depiction of gangsters and mob culture a new sound. It replaced the conventional orchestral, thematic score, in particular Nino Rota's majestic score for *The Godfather* (1972) that premiered the year before *Mean Streets*, with contemporary rock music. This substitution of popular for orchestral music had a permanent and dramatic effect on cinematic depictions of mob culture.[11] But it also had a significant effect on Scorsese's musical aesthetic. It codified his interest not only in prioritizing music as a central and defining element in his cinematic style, but in having music participate in the film's documentary intentions.[12] Well into the 1980s, Scorsese was still compiling his soundtracks first and foremost to satisfy a vérité aesthetic. In *The Color of Money* (1986), for instance, the music was stylistically selected and spatially placed primarily for the familiar purpose of reinforcing visual authenticity. As Scorsese observes,

> Most of the film takes place in bars and pool rooms and when you go in these places there is always music playing on a jukebox. Everywhere we went we'd hear rock 'n' roll, black music or swing. I wanted to reflect that the way I did in *Mean Streets*.[13]

Although Scorsese's aesthetic in the late 1980s was still essentially anthropological or vérité-inspired, the director also acknowledged that the studios were increasingly pressuring him to make his selections with financial incentives in mind. In *The Color of Money*, some songs were selected for their temporal and stylistic authenticity, but some were selected for their commercial appeal, for their ability to be marketed on a soundtrack album outside of the film. Because the film was financed by a major Hollywood studio, Touchstone Pictures, Scorsese admits to becoming aware of a different soundtrack formula, a practice at odds with his own. "Since *The Color of Money* was going to be a commercial movie," he observes, "in America today you have to, if at all possible, make a tie-in album.... Touchstone made a deal with MCA, so that Robbie [Robertson—the music supervisor for *The Color of Money*] could talk to their artists like Don Henley and Eric Clapton...."[14] Some selections in the soundtrack, he admits, were included not just for vérité purposes, but also because of a preexisting contractual arrangement between Touchstone and MCA records to use the record label's artists in their film soundtracks. Although *The Color of Money* soundtrack in general still adheres to vérité practice, especially in terms of the diegetic placement of the music within the film, it also shows some modifications, concessions that Scorsese made to accommodate a new, commercially motivated studio soundtrack practice.

Synergic or conceptual cooperation between record companies and film studios to maximize profits was not the only concern motivating changes in both Scorsese's and the studios' soundtrack practice. It was also changing in response to the growing popularity of a new visual vehicle made expressly for the promotion of popular music: the music video. Whereas previous visualizations of popular music, like jukebox "soundies," concert films, and television shows, featured performances of band members playing and singing, the music video distinguished itself by detaching the visual performance of the music from the musical work.[15] It replaced static concert-like performances with constructed montages of non-performance scenarios. The stylistic characteristics of this mode of visualized performance varied widely. Sometimes music video montages unfolded cinematically, forming a rudimentary narrative around the lyrics of the song with either band members or actors executing the action. Just as often, however, music videos featured non-narrative scenarios. They borrowed design techniques from abstract and experimental film—surreal imagery, hyperbolic costumes, disparate set elements, unusual locations, animation—as well as camera techniques common to abstract and experimental film—double exposures, superimpositions, flash-cuts, and juxtapositions.[16] In both approaches, the music video accomplished something previous musical performance formats had not. It created a new and uniquely dense cinematic texture, one that allowed musical style, song texts, and imagery to articulate separate but related texts and subtexts. Music videos also reveled in new and decidedly non-cinematic editing tempos. The montaged images were often cut together not according to conventional cinematic tempos, but according to a song's tempo and phrase structure.[17] In comparison with other visual media, the conventional Hollywood film in particular, the music video flowed at a uniquely fast speed and with an unusual and un-cinematically dense visual texture.

The exposure to this new medium was immediate and widespread primarily because of the rapid growth of cable television. The Music Television channel, or MTV, which began broadcasting in 1981 with the novel idea of reconceptualizing television as a "visual radio," exhibited a continuous 24-hour stream of music videos. With little serious competition, MTV quickly became one of the most subscribed networks on cable television, establishing itself in 22 million homes by 1984 and growing steadily to well over 30 million subscribers by the end of the decade.[18] Because of its visual format, MTV soon replaced radio as the most essential tool for promoting music and promoting film soundtracks. Videos were perfectly suited for cross-promoting film soundtracks, especially because those songs had already been cinematically visualized. Because videos of soundtrack songs often featured film imagery, sometimes even condensed film narratives, the film industry took particular interest in them. Studio executives especially began investing in the production of music videos of songs featured on film soundtracks, because such videos increased soundtrack sales and boosted ancillary film profits.[19]

Film executives were not the only ones interested in music videos, however. Directors also studied the medium and began importing music video techniques and structures into their narrative films. They began to infuse the montages that traditionally accompanied soundtrack selections with music video tempos and editing techniques. Although these musical interpolations created interruptions similar to song performances in classical film musicals, the visual imagery that accompanied the music did not. It moved at a different, much faster pace, and often with a more oblique visual style.[20] As music supervisor Bob Last observed, "You can always tell a song is coming, because the visual pace of the film changes. There are subtle cues in the pacing of a movie.... There's a change in the pace, it adjusts itself sometimes very subtly... [with] an MTV moment, [the film] clearly just changes gear...."[21] These "MTV moments," the dramatic shifting back and forth from cinematic to video style, created a distinctively "modular" structure, as film scholar Justin Wyatt describes it.[22] The highly stylized and fast-paced interruptions were especially well suited to the new so-called high-concept films, films that distinctly emphasized visual style over narrative complexity. Contemporary popular music was an essential element in them, but as one critic observed of two early high-concept films, *Flashdance* (1983) and *Footloose* (1984), part of what made these films so successful was not just the sonic space they gave to popular music, but the visual space they gave to music video style. In *Flashdance*, the film overtly accommodated the soundtrack by very suddenly adopting a new visual style, a music video style that interrupted the film with "quick-cut montages set to a driving beat."[23] In *Footloose*, the allusions to MTV were not only overt but intentional. The "dance-and-romp sequences," as one critic described them, "were modeled after the fare on MTV which director Herbert Ross confessed to watching religiously throughout production."[24]

The crossover between film and music videos was also accomplished physically, with a literal exchange of personnel. Film directors like John Landis, Nicolas Roeg, William Friedkin, and Brian de Palma began directing music videos, and likewise, many music video directors like David Fincher, Lasse Hallstrom, Spike Jonze, and Michel Gondry became film directors after achieving recognition directing music videos.[25] Scorsese, curiously, was also one of these crossover directors. In 1987, he directed "Bad," the high-profile music video that Michael Jackson made of his hit song (figure 1.1). Instead of experimenting with new music video techniques, however, Scorsese used the video as an opportunity to explore classical film musical conventions and to create an homage to one of the great directors of film musicals in the 1940s and '50s, Vincente Minnelli.

> I'd always been fascinated by Michael Jackson's performances and especially his dancing. For years I'd been watching the Minnelli musicals, and I had applied the same camera techniques in the musical sequences of *New York, New York*....So I was dying to do it again and I realized that Michael's rock video, or whatever you want to call it, would involve dancing and I'd be able to move the camera and have some fun with it. [26]

Figure 1.1: A classicist Scorsese pays homage to Vincente Minnelli in Michael Jackson's "Bad" video.

Although Scorsese professes an ignorance of music video techniques, his statement reveals not so much a lack of knowledge as a continued resistance to contemporary musical formats and their distinctive visual styles. By intentionally adopting classical camera techniques instead of using contemporary ones, Scorsese acknowledges an awareness of contemporary techniques and the distance between them and his own method of visualizing music. Just as he resisted commercializing the soundtrack to *The Color of Money*, he similarly resists the "video-izing" of popular music by infusing the "Bad" video with classical film musical conventions of visual style and tempo.

In his next film, *Goodfellas* (1990), however, that resistance breaks down. Scorsese adopts a new visual texture and an editing style that appears to be highly influenced by music video techniques. Unlike the high-concept approach to soundtrack construction and film structure, however, Scorsese's new style is not interruptive. It does not pursue a "modular" format of shifting back and forth from cinematic to video style and tempo. Instead of having selected moments in the film articulate a video-ized aesthetic, Scorsese instead adopts a faster tempo and denser narrative texture throughout the film as a whole. In the way that it expands vérité practice to accommodate a new mandate for visual movement and for a faster and more dense narrative texture, *Goodfellas* articulates an important turning point in the evolution of Scorsese's musical style.

GOODFELLAS AND A NEW MUSICAL AESTHETIC

Although *Goodfellas* is separated from *Mean Streets* by over 15 years, it is connected to it in several important ways. Like *Mean Streets*, *Goodfellas* also has basic documentary intentions. It is based on a true story, the experiences of mobster Henry Hill as described in Nicholas Pileggi's best-selling nonfiction book *Wise Guy*.[27] The film tells the story of Hill (Ray Liotta) and his 30-year involvement with the mafia, from his earliest days as an errand boy in the 1950s to his eventual entrance into the Witness Protection Program as a government informant in the early 1980s. During the course of the film, the action centers on Hill and his relationship with crime bosses Jimmy Conway (Robert de Niro), Tommy DiVito (Joe Pesci), and Paulie Cicero (Paul Sorvino) and explores Hill's relationship with Karen (Lorraine Bracco), a Jewish girl who becomes his wife.

Scorsese reinforces the film's documentary intentions in a number of familiar ways. Visually, the film features an array of cinema vérité techniques. Scorsese makes liberal use of jump cuts, long fluid takes, handheld shots, and freeze-frames. "I wanted a very fluid style," he notes, "as if I had been doing an Al and David Maysles cinema vérité documentary on these guys for 25 years with the ability to walk in and out of the rooms with cameras."[28] The quasi-documentary style of the film persists in other ways as well. The costumes, sets, and locations authenticate the film in visual ways, as do the intermittent title cards and texts that tell us the day and time the action is taking place. Documentary intentions also surface in the script's colloquial, seemingly improvised dialogue and in the persistent use of voiceovers. Although the perspective of the narration alternates back and forth between Henry and his wife Karen, their voices lend an air of authority and authenticity to the action in the film. As Scorsese himself points out, although not literally adhering to the same level of vérité as *Mean Streets*, *Goodfellas* is nonetheless meant to be viewed as a kind of "staged documentary," a film "in the *spirit* of a documentary."[29]

Scorsese also uses music to reinforce the film's sense of realism. All of the musical selections for the film were made first with the idea of being authentic or "in period." In constructing the soundtrack, Scorsese observes, "The only rule was to use music which could only have been heard at that time."

> If a scene took place in 1973, I could use any music that was current or older. For example, I wanted to use a Rolling Stones song at the end, "She Was Hot"—for that last day in 1979, but it came out a year later, so I had to use something else.[30]

Scorsese's "current or older" policy, when applied to the film's 30-year time span, results in a surprisingly wide variety of musical styles—from Neapolitan love songs and Tony Bennett ballads to three decades of rock music from groups like the Cadillacs, the Chantels, the Marvelettes, the Shangri-las, the Rolling Stones, Cream, Nilsson, and the Sex Pistols.

The style of the selections is not the only musical element that reinforces a sense of realism. The placement of the music, the fact that Scorsese ties it to period sound reproduction technologies, also articulates a sense of vérité. This devotion to authentic technologies also has much to do with the soundtrack's wide variety of musical styles.

> The thing is, believe me, in a lot of these places [mob hangouts] you had jukeboxes, and, when the Beatles came in, you [still] had Benny Goodman, some old Italian stuff, Jerry Vale, Tony Bennett, doo-wop, early rock 'n' roll, black and Italian.... There's a guy who comes around and puts the latest hits in. [But] when you hang out in a place, when you are part of a group, new records come in but [people] request older ones. And they stay.... Basically there are certain records that guys like and it's there.[31]

Scorsese uses music to suggest time and place, intentionally locating the source of the music visually on-screen in order to authenticate its performance. He also authenticates the music by privileging the technology used to reproduce the music, by emphasizing the performance of the music on jukeboxes, record players, and car radios.

With *Goodfellas*, however, Scorsese's longstanding "vérité-only" music policy also weathers some changes. In an interview in 1991, shortly after he made *Goodfellas*, for instance, Scorsese surprisingly reveals significant misgivings about the practice of using music only to satisfy temporal and geographic concerns. Suddenly the idea of using music simply to define when or where a scene is taking place, of using it *only* to document time and place, is simplistic and problematic, especially in the way that it deemphasizes and de-prioritizes music. "A lot of music is used in movies today just to establish time and place," he asserts, "and I think that is lazy."[32]

> I think they are using it [music] cheaply. I think they're using it unimaginatively. I think they're using it basically to say "Okay, its 1956." They're using it to tell you what period you are in.[33]

Starting with *Goodfellas*, the criticism of studio soundtrack practices becomes not only a fixed part of his discussion but a decidedly negative one. Mainstream studio filmmaking has not only overused popular music, it has made bad or hackneyed use of period music. What was once a fresh approach to film music has now become so conventional that Scorsese deems it "lazy." Because it has been co-opted by commercial studio filmmaking, the vérité soundtrack is no longer effective. It joins the purely commercial inclusion of music, the high-concept soundtrack, as being equally untenable and limited. With *The Color of Money*, the boundaries between his own practice and the studio's were visible but still permeable. The inclusion of music simply for commercial purposes to draw soundtrack sales, although not ideal, was permissible. With *Goodfellas*, however, that gap between his own filmmaking and mainstream filmmaking has become rigid and unfathomable. In the way that it rejects both the overuse of period music and the over-commercialized use of popular music ("cheap and unimaginative" uses of popular music), Scorsese shows clear signs of forging a new musical aesthetic.

With *Goodfellas*, Scorsese's discussion of music contains an increased level of rhetorical distancing from contemporary studio practices. But it also contains a prescription for a new and emerging musical mandate. Stylistic and temporal authenticity still plays a central role in his soundtrack compositional process. But increasingly, an additional element begins to assume equal importance in his discussion: movement. In *Goodfellas*, the problem of movement, of using music to help establish a new narrative rhythm and a new level of textural density, assumes an equal if not greater share of the soundtrack discussion as "anthropology" once did. By adjusting his vérité practice to include new elements, ones suggestive of but separate from video-ized or high-concept soundtrack construction, Scorsese reveals a new aesthetic mandate that uses music to reinforce both authenticity and movement.

As Kolker has noted, Scorsese has always been interested in experimenting with ways of creating movement in his films. "Of all the young, post-New Wave filmmakers," he notes, "he [Scorsese] has retained his excitement about the narrative possibilities of cinema, his curiosity about cutting and camera movements, and his delight in toying with the conventions of the classical form." In *Goodfellas*, this curiosity in playing with both camera and editing conventions is in full display. Although some of the unique visual style he develops in the film is inspired by the vast temporal expanse of Pileggi's book, it also stems from Scorsese's deep interest in experimenting with cinematic conventions in time and movement. In this film, Scorsese is fully occupied with the need to compress time and to move as quickly through the narrative as possible. As a result, the idea of movement, both physical and temporal, assumes an important part of the film's visual and sonic aesthetic. In discussing *Goodfellas*, he observes:

> The idea was to get as much movement as possible—even more than usual. And a very speeded, frenetic quality to most of it in terms of getting as much information to the audience—overwhelming them, I had hoped—with images and information. There's a lot of stuff in the frames. Because it's so rich. The lifestyle is so rich.[34]

Whereas in his previous films, Scorsese focused more exclusively on issues of authenticity, in this film, he has a new concern for establishing "as much movement as possible." Movement is now equally essential, and it guides the disposition of visual and sonic elements in the film. In identifying this new, larger consideration, however, Scorsese is also quick to dissect it into smaller component parts. Getting as much movement into the picture more specifically means experimenting with the cinematic conventions of tempo and texture. The need to establish a new and unconventional sense of tempo especially surfaces regularly in his discussion of *Goodfellas*. For Scorsese, movement is achieved most prominently through a new "speeded" or faster narrative rhythm. To get a film to move faster, the editing pace must be altered. Scorsese touches on this topic, on speed and a faster editing tempo, on a number of occasions in his discussion of the film. "I wanted *Goodfellas* to move as fast as a trailer," Scorsese said, "and to go on like that for two hours."[35] "I figure to do it as if it was one long trailer," he continues, "where you just propel the action and you get an exhilaration, a rush of [the] lifestyle."[36] In a trailer's compressed narrative structure, Scorsese finds a similar sense of speed, and in his repeated reference to it, he underscores his interest in altering conventional narrative rhythm to give the film this greater sense of movement.

Speeding up the tempo is not the only way Scorsese achieves movement. As his discussion reveals, he also challenges soundtrack conventions through the use of rhythmic inconsistency, through the quick alternation between conventional and non-conventional tempos. Just as the film should move faster, he asserts, it should also move "frenetically." It should shift unpredictably between classical narrative pace and new, faster tempos. Movement can also be created by varying editing tempos and by doing so unpredictably. Scorsese discusses his general interest in experimenting with rhythmic instability in the film on a number of occasions, but it surfaces most prominently in the additional consideration he gives to the technique of freeze-framing. [37] He achieves a frenetic tempo for the film not just by speeding up the pace of the editing, but also by literally stopping it, by intermittently freezing it on selected actions. As Scorsese describes it,

> I wanted images that would stop because a point was being reached in his [Henry's] life; like "everyone has to take a beating sometime"—freeze—then go back to the whipping.... The next thing is the explosion and the freeze-frame, with Henry frozen against it and the hellish image of a person in flames.... It's very important where the freeze-frames come in that opening sequence because I wanted to recreate the sort of things that make an imprint.... It's a dramatic and unexpected way of dealing with how these people behave.[38]

It is not just a fast tempo but an inconsistent tempo that can give a film a rushed and frenetic quality. The unpredictable alternation of fast and slow tempos can contribute an interpretive complexity not possible through the conventional articulation of a single consistent tempo.

For Scorsese, varying tempos facilitates a greater amount and range of narrative information. But in his expanded aesthetic, movement is accomplished through the use of new cinematic textures as well. *Goodfellas* moves differently than his previous films because the frames are stuffed with visual and sonic information. This new stuffed or dense texture is created primarily through the establishment of a more oblique relationship between visual and sonic material. The film's visual images are moving faster and more inconsistently but also more independently from the other narrative elements in the film. That the discussion of this new texture is often bundled with the related topic of tempo (fast, speeded editing) only underscores the importance that both elements play in the elucidation of the new aesthetic concern for movement.

It's the way things go. Things have got to move faster. [With *Goodfellas*] I was interested in breaking up all the traditional ways of shooting the picture. A guy comes in, sits down, exposition is given. So the hell with the exposition—do it in the voiceover, if need be at all. And then just jump the scene together. Not by chance. The shots are designed so that I know where the cut's going to be. The action is pulled out of the middle of the scene, but I know where I'm going to cut it so that it makes an interesting cut.... Compressed time. I get very bored shooting scenes that are traditional scenes. [39]

A new sense of movement can be achieved, he theorizes, by "breaking up" the conventional approach to rhythm and tempo, and also by weakening the conventional relationship between diegetic and non-diegetic space. Instead of using the dialogue to describe or reinforce the actions depicted on screen, Scorsese allows the two cinematic dimensions, image and soundtrack, to work independently. He uses narration obliquely and selectively to highlight or "pull out" some actions and ignore others. By engineering it so that non-diegetic elements move independently of diegetic elements, by allowing sonic elements (i.e., voiceovers or narration) to move distinctly and separately from imagery, Scorsese imagines a new, thicker and busier cinematic texture. He achieves a distinct sense of movement by overwhelming the viewer with a complex interplay of sonic and visual information.

In these verbal descriptions of *Goodfellas*, the repeated need for establishing a faster and more flexible editing pace, denser textures, and greater spatial independence show Scorsese to be auditioning a new, expanded aesthetic. Authenticity and anthropology are still central and controlling concepts, but the discussion is increasingly preoccupied with the need for creating a sense of movement, for establishing unconventional conceptions of tempo, texture, and cinematic space. Kolker has, to some degree, acknowledged this expanded musical aesthetic in *Goodfellas*, especially in his discussion of the film's unusual camera and editing work. Although he also sees the emphasis on movement as evidence of a new level of cinematic self-consciousness on Scorsese's part, his observations describe a similar change in Scorsese's filmmaking style. Starting with *Goodfellas'* famous four-minute-long shot of Henry and Karen entering the Copacabana nightclub, Kolker observes:

The long take is, of course, only one aspect of the self-conscious narration. Editing is another and very subtle element. Scorsese's editing style is carefully executed and tuned to create the appropriate dramatic rhythm of a given sequence. The angularity of the cutting, making arrhythmic joins between the movements in one shot to the movement in another, speeding things up—as in the cocaine sequences, where the cutting suggests the characters' paranoid state of mind—provide a kind of rhythm section for the shots that together compose the movement and meaning of the film.[40]

Kolker recognizes an increased level of visual movement in *Goodfellas* in the persistent use of freeze-framing, flash cutting, long takes, zooms, and pans. Apart from a general acknowledgment that the music is "tightly bound to the structure of the film," however, he says little about how individual songs or the soundtrack in general participates in this project.[41]

As Scorsese himself describes it, however, music was an integral component of this new mandate for movement. The vérité practice of rooting the selection and application of music in an aesthetic of "found" sound, he recognizes, is no longer adequate. In order for music to participate in the larger need from movement, Scorsese develops a new soundtrack aesthetic, one strangely rooted in that musical genre that he had been resisting for so long: the music video. Whereas before, music videos and the commercial application of them in high-concept studio films were anathema, in *Goodfellas*, music videos are suddenly useful, especially in their ability to help generate new cinematic tempos and textures. Although Scorsese additionally credits television and distant anticipations of the music video for having inspired aspects of his new musical aesthetic, it is the contemporary music video, he suggests, that was most influential in helping to create a sense of movement.

> I think the formula [is]—what do they call them?—high-concept pictures, probably. A high concept picture should have a basic theme....A lot of it[s influence] is, I think, the flash kind of cutting that goes on. The man who broke that into films originally was Richard Lester with *A Hard Day's Night*. You really saw the influence of television commercials on the film, and it worked. And now—this is old hat what I'm saying, really, it's really not even very good—the influence of MTV, let's say, over the past eight years on movies, maybe the audience attention space is a bit of a problem now. Things have to move faster. And you feel that.[42]

For Scorsese, the need for new narrative conventions of rhythm and texture, for things "to move faster" and more obliquely, are tied not just to contemporary cinematic styles, like the high-concept film, but more fundamentally to the quasi-cinematic and specifically musical media that inspired them. As he sees it, changes in film rhythm and texture are inextricably tied to the changes in the visualizations of music, some of which earlier filmmakers like Lester experimented with but most of which can now be routinely found in contemporary music videos.

While Scorsese now suddenly allows music videos to inform his new, expanded musical aesthetic, the soundtrack practice that results is different from contemporary studio practice. It is an approach that bears little resemblance to the high-concept practice, with its modular structure of carefully prepared "MTV moments." Instead of applying video techniques piecemeal as commercial studio films were doing, in *Goodfellas*, Scorsese experiments with generating a sustained texture from them. He experiments with using music video techniques not just at selected moments but throughout the film as a whole to create a faster and more flexible approach to rhythm and tempo and a richer and denser narrative texture. In *Goodfellas*, Scorsese outlines a new filmmaking style in general, one that revels in faster tempos and oblique editing techniques. But he also outlines a new compilation soundtrack practice, one that both corrects the misappropriation that commercial films had been making of music video concepts and expands the boundaries of his own aging vérité soundtrack formula.

GOODFELLAS AND A NEW SOUNDTRACK PRACTICE

One of the most striking features of the *Goodfellas* soundtrack is the way Scorsese uses music to alter conventional approaches to tempo and texture. Although the style of music Scorsese selects still addresses an anthropological imperative, the amount of music he uses answers to the need for a new and particularly dense cinematic texture. Part of this density comes from the fact that the film is quite literally saturated with music. The soundtrack features 46 separate pieces of music, a number nearly double that of Scorsese's previous soundtracks and double the size of conventional high-concept soundtracks.[43] In the film's nearly three-hour running time, only a few scenes, together lasting less than a half hour, do not have music. To some degree, the size of the soundtrack is made possible by the length of some selections. Although some excerpts are little more than fragments, lasting only 20 to 30 seconds long, other songs are heard in their entirety. The soundtrack has the distinction of being almost continuously heard, but like the visual tempo of the film, it also moves inconsistently and unpredictably.

Just as the quantity of music gives the film an unconventionally dense cinematic texture, Scorsese also uses song texts to generate movement and narrative density. On some occasions, they are used conventionally to comment on the action and narration. Scorsese coordinates it so that song lyrics, imagery, and narration all work to reinforce a single theme. When Henry begins courting Karen in earnest, for instance, taking her to the Copacabana nightclub and later a lover's lane for their first kiss, Scorsese connects these disparate scenes that have been jump cut together with narration from both Henry and Karen and also with a song, the Crystals' "Then He Kissed Me," which runs continuously under the scene. Likewise, when Henry, Tommy, and Jimmy take their mistresses out to the nightclub, singer Bobby Vinton serenades them with the song "Pretend You Don't See Her," which describes the men's wish to forget their wives, a wish additionally articulated in Henry's narration. When Henry later recruits the babysitter into his drug-smuggling operations, loading his own baby's diaper bag full of drugs, the Rolling Stone's song "Monkey Man" with the lyrics "I'm a flea-bit peanut monkey and all my friends are junkies" is played to reinforce Henry's drug-fueled obsessive behavior and rapid-fire narration. At times, Scorsese's use of music, song texts in particular, is conventional. "Sometimes," Scorsese admits, "[I] put the lyrics of songs between lines of dialogue so that they comment on the action."[44]

Just as often, however, Scorsese uses music to contradict or counterpoint narrative elements. Instead of using music uniformly or monolithically, he uses it selectively to comment on imagery or narration separately. Kolker describes the unusual interpretive range Scorsese achieves through the shifting gaze of the camera and the continually shifting perspective offered by multiple narrators.[45] What he doesn't consider, however, is the degree to which this fast- shifting perspective is also created with music. Some of the film's rapidly changing perspective is generated by the construction of the soundtrack. When Jimmy begins to grow weary of his partners in the Lufthansa heist who are impatient for their payoff, Maury especially, the introduction of a song complicates the scene. While we see images of Jimmy, Henry, and Maury interacting affably, Cream's 1968 hit "Sunshine of Your Love" begins to play. The song's refrain, "I've been waiting so long, to be where I'm going, in the sunshine of your love," is particularly audible and describes the seemingly mutual and genuine affection shared by the characters depicted on-screen. Henry's narration, however, suggests otherwise. In contrast to the imagery, it tells us that Jimmy will soon brutally murder Maury for his greed and impatience. For Maury, the payoff will not be warm and loving, as the song lyrics suggest, but instead a violent and brutal end. In this instance, the song has an unconventionally bifurcated role. While commenting directly on the imagery, the song text simultaneously ironizes the narration. By underscoring the quasi-familial ties we see among the characters on the screen, the lyrics make the narrated description of Maury's murder shocking and unanticipated.[46]

The film opens with a similar interpretive independence among music, imagery, and narration. We are introduced to the film's central characters Henry, Jimmy, and Tommy by watching them brutally bludgeon and shoot a man to death in the trunk of their car. When the camera freezes the action, Henry's narration only partly explains: "As far back as I can remember, I always wanted to be a gangster," his voiceover declares. As the imagery of the film flashes back and we literally see Henry's transformation from innocent youth to petty criminal, Henry's narration parallels the action on the screen with descriptive details of his adoption into the mob. Scorsese uses music to reinforce this narration, but also uses it for other purposes.

When Tony Bennett's ballad "Rags to Riches" begins playing at the end of the trunk scene and into the flashback of Henry's childhood, the music physically links the scenes together. But it also provides a different subtext for each. The song's highly audible first stanza of text—"You know I'd go from rags to riches / if you would only say you care / and though my pockets may be empty / I'd be a millionaire"—parallels Henry's economic transformation from a poor immigrant kid to an affluent young man. The insouciant style of the ballad reinforces Henry's delight in the process. But the text and style of the song also comment ironically on the brutal murder, on the opening scene it punctuates, underscoring the callousness of Henry's violent actions. The love and transformation the lyrics describe speak to Henry's naïve understanding of what it means to be a mobster, and to his idealized conception of the casual brutality and crime that come with being mafioso. Scorsese frequently credits previous filmmakers for informing his musical sensibilities, his use of textual irony in particular. He cites William Wellman's *The Public Enemy* (1931), for instance, for influencing his decision to pair popular music with brutal on-screen violence.[47] Although that sense of irony and contradiction is still available in Scorsese's soundtrack practice, it is also subsumed by a new, more complex treatment of music as an interpretive element. In *Goodfellas*, Scorsese uses music to contradict the action of the film and the narration separately, and often in quick alternation. He uses song texts to stuff the frame with an interpretive subtext that comments independently and separately on both the imagery and the narration. As a result, the interpretive alliances between imagery, music, and narration are constantly shifting. By giving musical texts a flexible interpretive range—parallel and counterpoint, and an interpretive independence—to move back and forth from image to narration, Scorsese uses the soundtrack to establish a new and uniquely dense cinematic texture.

Even more distinctive than the range and independence Scorsese gives musical texts, however, is the unique use he makes of musical style and performance practice. On several occasions, Scorsese stuffs the frame by stratifying music material, by using both a song's lyrics and its performance style to comment on the action or the narration. This stratification of music into component parts is most evident in the use Scorsese makes of song covers, of non-original performances of well-known pop songs. For Scorsese, covers are different from newly composed songs because they come loaded with additional information and layers of meaning. Because they access the associations of two performance styles, the original and the cover, one old and one new, they bring more than just textual considerations to bear. They bring questions of authorship and stylistic practice into the interpretive equation as well. When Jimmy and Henry celebrate the announcement that Tommy is to become a "made" man, Scorsese chooses "Unchained Melody" to accompany the action. By controlling the dynamics, Scorsese makes sure we hear the song's opening stanza, "Oh, my love, my darling / I've hungered for your touch." When paired with immediate action, the overlap between text and action is direct. Being promoted to a made man in the hierarchy of Paulie's crew is the "touch" or attention that Tommy has been seeking. The song's "love" speaks to Tommy's desire for professional acceptance. Because much of the song after the opening stanza plays at a volume that renders the remainder of the lyrics obscure, it is the style of the song that informs the rest of the scene. The performance is not the original version of the song, the slow instrumental theme that composer Alex North wrote for the film *Unchained* (1955), however, but instead a fast, syncopated, rock 'n' roll version of it from 1964 performed by Vito and the Salutations. This discrepancy between stylistic periods in popular music allows the song to articulate additional commentary. For Scorsese, the gap in performance practice makes the song not just different or faster but, as he puts it, "decadent."

> You have "Unchained Melody" being sung in a decadent way, like the ultimate doo-wop—but not black, it's Italian doo-wop....And I like the Vito and the Salutations version of "Unchained Melody." Alex North wrote it...for this movie made in the early fifties called *Unchained*. And it's unrecognizable. It's so crazy and I enjoy it. I guess I admire the purity of the early times...but I'm part of the decadence of what happened in the seventies and eighties.[48]

For Scorsese, choosing a song cover opens the soundtrack up to providing not just textual but stylistic interpretations. In this case, while the smooth and melodic performance practices of the 1950s he considers "pure," the faster, more disjunctive rhythmic practices of the '70s and '80s he considers corrupt and "decadent."[49] As a result, when placed within this scene, the song has an additional and contradictory subtext. If the text of the song could be said to speak for Tommy's desire to become a made man, then the style of it speaks for his corrupt and decadent behavior and the surprising, violent conclusion waiting for him.

Song covers and their doubly allusive texture play an important role in another striking moment in the film. At the end of the film, when we see Henry and hear him describe his life as a government informant, Sid Vicious's cover of the Paul Anka song "My Way" plays prominently then and into the credits. In this epilogue, we see the aftermath of Henry's decision to betray his mob family. The stark contrast of Henry's new life in the Witness Protection Program is depicted in the bland and featureless

Figure 1.2: Henry laments the suburban lifestyle ("My Way").

suburban housing development where he lives and in his disheveled appearance (figure 1.2). The anonymity and loneliness of his new existence is reinforced in his voiceover where, instead of celebrating the evasion of a lengthy prison sentence, he laments the lack of good food, friends, and family. "My Way" enters prominently at the end of Henry's narration. On a textual level, the song contradicts both the imagery and the voiceover. The text is heroic, an anthem to independence and self-determination.

> *And now, the end is near*
> *And so I face the final curtain*
> *My friend, I'll say it clear*
> *I'll state my case, of which I'm certain*
> *I've lived a life that's full*
> *I've traveled each and every highway*
> *But more, much more than this*
> *I did it my way*

Because we see nothing to suggest that Henry's betrayal has been noble or self-empowering—his life as a government informant is tedious and lonely, and as the text epilogue discloses, Karen divorces him, and Jimmy and Paulie are sent to prison for life—the song's text seems particularly ironic. For Scorsese, however, the song contributes more than just a textual overlay. The performance style of the song also adds a layer of commentary. Instead of Paul Anka's or Frank Sinatra's iconic performances of the song, we hear Sid Vicious and the Sex Pistols' distorted, half-screamed, almost atonal cover of it. When asked why he chose the Sex Pistols' version of the song, Scorsese observed:

Oh, it's pretty obvious, it may be too obvious. It's period, but also it's Paul Anka and of course Sinatra—although there's no Sinatra in the film. But "My Way" is an anthem. I like Sid Vicious's version because it twists it, and his whole life and death was a kind of slap in the face of the whole system, the whole point of existence in a way. And that's what is fascinating to me—because eventually, yeah, they all did it their way. [And] because we did it our way, you know.[50]

The selection still functions significantly on an anthropological level; it places and dates the time of Henry's demise. Sid Vicious and the Sex Pistols were a prominent part of the punk-rock scene in early 1980 when the film ends. But Scorsese also selected the cover for its "twisted" punk-rock rendering of the song. The performance is decadent because it lacks or twists Sinatra's vocal purity, but also because it references the biography of the performer, Sid Vicious. It references images of Sid Vicious's own twisted life, his well-known self-destructive and drug-fueled behavior on and off the stage. When placed under the epilogue, it asks us to see Henry's tedious and anonymous suburban life in the Witness Protection Program as decadent and subversive.

But the song offers more than just ironic commentary on Henry's final act as a mobster. In this last scene, Scorsese inserts an overt quotation from another film. For a few brief seconds, Tommy shoots a gun directly into the camera, as director Edwin Porter had his protagonist do at the end of *The Great Train Robbery* (1903), one of the first feature-length gangster pictures. Most scholars view the quotation as evidence of a kind of anxiety of influence. Kolker, for instance, reads the reference as overt proof of Scorsese's self-consciousness about not only previous films and filmmakers but the whole tradition or genre of gangster pictures.[51] What he fails to mention, however, is how the soundtrack also contributes to this overt self-consciousness. Like the visual quotation, the quotation of "My Way" also has genre implications. Because it is virtually impossible to hear "My Way" without thinking of the song's foremost interpreter—Frank Sinatra, whose voice has come to symbolize cinematically the music of the mob, a voice conspicuously absent from this and all of Scorsese's mob film soundtracks—Sid Vicious's performance is not just a criticism of '50s "purity." It can also be heard as a critique of contemporary mob soundtracks. On selected occasions, Scorsese has openly criticized the authenticity of other gangster film soundtracks. Jonathan Demme's contemporary mob satire *Married to the Mob* (1988) was undermined, he observes, by its clichéd use of 1950s pop music, Rosemary Clooney's "Mambo-Italiano" in particular.[52] A similar criticism of the cinematic misuse of popular music is also available in the "My Way" cover. In its intentional and studied avoidance of Frank Sinatra, in his use of Sid Vicious's twisted cover, Scorsese critiques the conventional Hollywood reduction of mob criminality to the clichéd sounds of Anka, Sinatra, and Clooney.

Scorsese's interest in using music to generate a greater sense of movement is also visible in the placement he gives music in the film. Although all of the music is temporally authentic, most of it is *not* given an authentic placement. Little of it appears strictly as source music, for instance, but instead plays from the background, from the same unreal, non-diegetic space that the narration occupies. Scorsese uses this conflict between real and unreal, foreground and background, for the purpose of creating a uniquely fluid sense of filmic space. He often disregards the boundaries that typically separate diegetic from non-diegetic space by ignoring the priority dialogue traditionally maintains over narration and music. Instead he equalizes all three of these elements by moving constantly and fluidly among them. Through the placement of music in particular, he allows the perspective to shift seamlessly back and forth and often quickly from narration to dialogue to music, with each element taking a turn in guiding or articulating the narrative action of the film. Song lyrics and musical performance style still provide overt and direct commentary on both the action and narration of the film. But on many occasions, the interpretive range of these elements is enhanced by the unusual spatial treatment of the music.

A good example of this fluid use of music and the role it plays in establishing a uniquely dense cinematic texture is Henry and Karen's wedding scene. At the start of the scene, we see a glimpse of the formal Jewish ceremony Henry and Karen have with Karen's family, but after a few moments, we abruptly jump to the setting that will occupy most of the scene, the reception that Henry's mob "family" hosts for them. The importance of this adopted family is suggested not just by the length of the scene, but by the song that accompanies it. The Harptones' 1955 song "Life Is But a Dream" plays prominently and seemingly diegetically in the scene. The opening text of the song is clearly audible, playing at the same volume as the dialogue and narration that follow. "Will you take part in / My Life, my love, / That is my dream," the song states. Because it is Henry's mob family that we see in this scene, the lyrics seemingly speak for Henry and his invitation to Karen not just to marry him but to become a part of this extended family. Although the song continues to play throughout the scene, its function as speech or dialogue is altered after the opening stanza when Scorsese lowers the volume to accommodate other diegetic and non-diegetic elements. As the camera fluidly surveys the room, we hear family members Paulie, Jimmy, Tommy, and others and their wives and families talking. The camera samples snippets of casual and trivial conversation from each table. Moments later, the volume of the dialogue is lowered to make room for Karen's narration. As she describes the complexity of getting to know her new family and the bewildering array of children—"where the boys are all named either Peter or Paulie and the girls Marie"—her observations are given emphasis with brief fragments of dialogue that often literally repeat or describe the content of her narration.

Behind these quick and seamless alternations of dialogue and narration, the Harptones' song continues to play and occasionally interrupts through to the foreground. When Henry and Karen begin receiving gifts as they sit at the head banquet table, and the camera pans out to show us an unending line of Henry's "family" waiting to give envelopes of cash to the newlyweds, we suddenly hear the last phrase of the third stanza: "…Come here to my open arms." The lyrics temporarily emphasize Karen's perspective and her pleasure at the excessive generosity of her new "family." It no longer comments on the action as a whole but speaks directly for the couple as they embrace their new life. One phrase later, however, the music seamlessly recedes again to make way for dialogue. As Henry and Karen take their first dance together as a married couple, we hear them talk about their future (figure 1.3). But as their conversation reaches its conclusion, the song returns again to full volume, reestablishing its priority over the dialogue and narration. The final stanza, a repeat of the opening text, is again prominently heard, but this time the "dream" the song describes speaks for the couple and their hope for a happy future. By prioritizing music and equalizing it with dialogue and narration and allowing it to move effortlessly back and forth between foreground and background, Scorsese uses music to challenge the conventionally fixed boundaries of cinematic space. He creates a dense narrative texture through a uniquely fluid sense of cinematic space.

Figure 1.3: Henry and Karen ponder their future ("Life Is But a Dream").

Narration also plays an important structural and rhythmic role in the film. Scorsese uses the voiceovers to facilitate speed and temporal compression, and to give coherence to the often abrupt and obliquely edited images within scenes.[53] But he uses music in this capacity too. He often uses the interpolation of a song, for instance, to articulate structural emphasis. On other occasions, he uses a single song to suture together a complex of individual scenes giving them shape and unity. Most of the time, this suturing and structuring are done in coordination with the narration. Typically, the music begins or changes when the narration starts or changes perspective. On several occasions, however, Scorsese intentionally designs the soundtrack so that the musical changes are not coordinated with changes in the narration. Instead of having narration and music work together, Scorsese engineers it so that they simultaneously delineate two separate and distinct substructures within the film. Just as he uses music to make the movement between diegetic and non-diegetic more fluid, he also uses music to stratify the non-diegetic space of the film. He uses the placement of music to create an interpretive space separate and independent from the narration.

This unusual stratification of space surfaces most prominently near the end of the film when Henry's and Karen's criminal activities and behavior are centered around drugs. The visual rhythm of the film picks up noticeably through the persistent use of flash cutting and through frequent visual interruption of on-screen dates and times. On "Sunday, May 11, 1980," the day before his arrest, we see Henry working assiduously and at times frenetically to accomplish a host of activities: He sells some guns to Jimmy, picks up his brother from the hospital, cooks dinner, picks up drugs for his Pittsburgh connection, all while trying to evade the real or imagined surveillance of police helicopters. A frenetic quality in these scenes is suggested not just by the fast editing pace but by the appearance of Henry himself who gets increasingly paler, sweaty, and agitated as the scene progresses. The music that plays under the scene contributes to this growing sense of mental and physical instability. As the day starts, Nilsson's 1972 hit "Jump into the Fire" plays prominently in the foreground. Both the text and style of the song comment directly on Henry's behavior and actions. "You can climb a mountain / You can swim the sea / You can jump into the fire / But you'll never be free / You can shake me up / Or I can break you down." The abstract text, the distorted electric guitar accompaniment, and the half-screamed quality of the singer's performance all project the psychedelic style of rock music Scorsese defined as "decadent." Musical style and lyrics both comment on Henry's growing mental instability, but the placement of the song in the scene also contributes to this sense of disintegration. When Henry visits Jimmy to sell him some guns, "Jump into the Fire" continues to play throughout the scene but with its volume lowered to accommodate both narration and dialogue. When Henry resumes driving after failing to unload the guns with Jimmy, the scene change is articulated by the resumption of narration and by the introduction of a new song—"Memo from Turner," the Mick Jagger song from the 1970 film *Performance*. The visual jump cut is underscored by an abrupt cut in the soundtrack. Like the unconventional visual editing, the sudden change of songs, tempos, and texture, and the change from lyric to instrumental music emphasize Henry's erratic behavior.

Midway through this scene, however, the music abruptly asserts its independence from both the narration and the image track. When Henry, in his obsessive need to check for surveillance helicopters, nearly crashes into a car in front of him, the moment is marked not visually but aurally with an abrupt change of music (figure 1.4). "Memo from Turner," which had been playing in the background is suddenly interrupted by the return of Nilson's "Jump into the Fire." Fragmentation counts for some of the sense of interruption. When "Jump into the Fire" returns, it is not the beginning of the song but a fragment from the chorus that is heard. The discontinuity of this interruption is further magnified by the singer's vocal style. The lyric "We can make each other happy" is screamed at near full volume as Henry forcefully applies the car brakes. The sharp juxtaposition of two different song fragments emphasizes Henry's increasingly irrational behavior and appearance, but so does the placement of those fragments. By introducing the interruption mid-scene, by creating a separate seam within the film's non-diegetic space, Scorsese allows the music to act independent of the narration. He gives the music an interpretive independence by allowing it to articulate a structural point separate from both the action and narration in the scene.

Figure 1.4: Henry steps on the brakes, and the score fragments ("Jump into the Fire").

Scorsese continues to use the soundtrack in this independent and stratified way throughout this section of the film. As the day progresses and Henry's physical appearance and behavior continue to disintegrate, Scorsese also speeds up the tempo of the musical interruptions.[54] When the action jumps abruptly ahead, as the on-screen text tells us, to "8:45 a.m." and to Henry's trip to the hospital to pick up his brother Michael, this visual demarcation is strikingly not reinforced by a similar change in music. No music, in fact, plays at the beginning of the scene. Halfway through the scene, however, when Michael's doctor, in response to Henry's sick and exhausted appearance, gives Henry more drugs to take, a fragment of "Jump into the Fire" suddenly returns to underscore the absurdity of the moment. The song continues to play through the remainder of the scene and into the next. It remains unchanged despite another deliberate visual seam, an abrupt change in time and location—"11 a.m.," when Henry returns home to cook dinner. When Henry and Karen suddenly suspend dinner preparations in order to finalize their drug deal in Pittsburgh, the visual disruption is smoothed over by the soundtrack. "Jump into the Fire" continues to play as they drive to the dealer's house. When they abruptly change course mid-scene to stash the guns they are trying to sell at Karen's mother's house, however, their erratic decision is underscored by another song interruption, an abrupt entrance of the Rolling Stones' "Monkey Man." The drug-related imagery of this song text comments on the characters' erratic and paranoid behavior. But it is the placement of the music, the sudden shift in musical rhythm, tempo, and texture that speaks the loudest. By stratifying non-diegetic space, the song's unanticipated and displaced entry mid-scene creates an independent interpretive layer of information separate from the narration. When Henry's narration attempts to impose an air of calm, order, and structure, the music underscores Henry's and Karen's frenetic and paranoid actions.

In the afternoon of the final day, the temporal collapse happens even faster and more erratically. Between "1:30 p.m." and "10:45 p.m.," there are five titled scene changes in less than five minutes with several scenes lasting less than 30 seconds. In addition to the rapid tempo change, Scorsese further destabilizes the texture with erratic camera movements, with an unusual number of zooms and pans. This abrupt and fragmented visual style is reinforced by an equally fast, erratic, and fragmented soundtrack. A quick succession of disparate songs is also jumped or flash-cut together. The musical cuts, however, are not always coordinated with these visual cuts. While this cinematic stretto starts out in sync—the "1:30 p.m." scene change is accompanied by the Stones' "Monkey Man"—this coordination soon disintegrates. Halfway through the "1:30 p.m." scene, as Henry and Karen frantically look for helicopters, George Harrison's "What is Life" suddenly begins to play. This interruption continues unpredictably for several minutes playing across not one but the next three scene changes, right through the "3:30 p.m." drug deal, the brief "6:30 p.m." cooking scene, and the "8:30 p.m." visit to the mistress's apartment for more drugs. It doesn't end until mid-way through this scene when, as Henry inhales a fresh round of cocaine, Muddy Water's "Mannish Boy" suddenly interrupts. "Mannish Boy," in turn, again plays over the next scene change, the "10:45 p.m." dinner at home, only to fade out half way through it. Silence takes over the soundtrack until a brief isolated drum beat is heard punctuating Henry's arrest.

Throughout this extended sequence, the music functions on multiple levels. The lyrics and decadent psychedelic style of the songs comment on Henry's mental disintegration and on the literal disintegration of his life as a gangster. But it is the placement of these songs and the independent interpretive structure they create that is most striking. When the narration comments on the action and works to emphasize the activities that Henry is attempting to accomplish—driving, cooking, picking up his brother—music articulates a separate commentary. Its seams emphasize the manifestations of Henry's increasingly dangerous and paranoid behavior—the near crashes, the drugs, the pills, the capricious and irrational changes of plans. With the unusual placement of the songs, Scorsese stratifies the film's non-diegetic space. He complicates the text and subtext of the scenes by engineering the music and the narration to act independent of one another, to articulate separate and independent commentaries on the visual action. By allowing the music to change quickly and erratically and by allowing it to be structurally independent, Scorsese uses music to create a uniquely fast-paced and dense cinematic texture.

In many ways, the soundtrack for *Goodfellas* is the musical expression of the tension that underlines the general aesthetic Scorsese envisioned for the film when he describes it as a "staged documentary." While the film depicts the real-life actions of mobster Henry Hill, it also presents those actions within the context of a new visual practice, one that emphasizes a new narrative rhythm and an increased independence of diegetic from non-diegetic material. The intentionally unprocessed production values of his earlier films like *Mean Streets*, the long takes, shaky cameras, and natural lighting and sound, have been replaced with a new visual vocabulary. The heavy use of flash cutting, zooms, and freeze-frames has expanded Scorsese's still active interest in establishing a general anthropology with a new and additional need for movement, speed, and density.

That music is a fundamental component of this aesthetic expansion is something that is also revealed in the *Goodfellas* soundtrack. Documentary intentions still motivate Scorsese's selection process. He still chooses material for the compilation based first on the recording date of each song to ensure that all of the music in the film is stylistically authentic or "period." But in the way that he expands this practice to include additional considerations, to include new manipulations of musical text and style and new placements for music, Scorsese uses it to realize the new desire for increased movement. The soundtrack is crowded nearly wall-to-wall with an expansive variety of popular songs, but the structure and placement of the music also contributes to the film's fast and rich texture. The often fragmented presentation of songs, the audible jump cuts between them, the independent layering of musical text and style, and the fluid and flexible placement all contribute to an unusually rich and dense cinematic texture. Things move faster in *Goodfellas* not just because scenes and images are more obliquely and quickly edited together, but because the soundtrack moves quickly and flexibly between and within cinematic spaces.

In this way, Scorsese's new soundtrack practice could also be considered to be video-ized. The music is still tightly integrated with the image track, but in the same way that visual imagery is independent of music or performance in a music video, Scorsese experiments with the relationship between sound, music, and image, creating an oblique and complex relationship among them. He pursues video tempos and style not just sporadically in isolated "MTV moments" but throughout the film. The whole film revels in fast, rhythmic editing tempos, oblique relationships between music and imagery, and a fluid use of visual space. Scorsese also integrates music into his new mandate for movement by video-izing it, by creating a new crowed, fragmented, and omniscient soundtrack.

In this regard, the *Goodfellas* soundtrack is essential not just to the evolution of Scorsese's musical aesthetic but also to the evolution of the pop compilation soundtrack. In *Goodfellas*, Scorsese gives the pop compilation soundtrack an interpretive range and a command of cinematic space that it did not previously have with either the vérité or the high-concept commercial filmmaking approach. Although these innovations bring attention to Scorsese as one of the most important authors or composers of the pop compilation soundtrack, they also bring emphasis to the pivotal and essential role music plays in Scorsese's filmic style. Without music, without the practice of the compilation soundtrack in particular, his films would be missing a great deal of their authorial style.

NOTES

1. One of Scorsese's first professional experiences was working as a cameraman on Mike Wadleigh's Oscar-winning 1970 documentary *Woodstock*. A few years later, he made his own highly acclaimed documentary *The Last Waltz* (1978), which chronicled the rock group The Band's final concert in 1976, as well as Scorsese's close friendship with lead

singer Robbie Robertson. Three recent efforts have emerged to reaffirm Scorsese's documentary interest in popular music. In 2003, he made "Feels like Going Home," a documentary that aired as the first episode in the seven-part PBS television documentary *The Blues*. In 2005, *No Direction Home: Bob Dylan* (2005), a documentary about the legendary pop musician, aired on PBS as part of the network's "American Masters" series. In 2008, Scorsese finished *Shine a Light*, a concert film of the Rolling Stones' performances at New York's Beacon Theater. And in 2011, he released *George Harrison: Living in the Material World*, his biopic of the Beatles member. For a discussion of his earlier documentary work, see "Robbie Robertson's Big Break: A Reevaluation of Martin Scorsese's *The Last Waltz*," *Film Quarterly*, 56/2 (Winter, 2002–2003), 25–31; Lawrence S. Friedman, "The Sound(s) of Music: From the Bands to The Band," in *The Cinema of Martin Scorsese* (New York: Continuum, 1997), 88–112; and selected chapters in Les Keyser, *Martin Scorsese* (New York: Twayne, 1992); Mary Pat Kelly, *Martin Scorsese: The First Decade* (1980) and *Martin Scorsese: A Journey* (New York: Thunder's Mouth, 2004); Marie Kathryn Connelly, *Martin Scorsese: An Analysis of His Feature Films, with a Filmography of His Entire Directorial Career* (Jefferson, NC: McFarland, 1993); Ben Nyce, *Scorsese Up Close* (Lanham, MD: Scarecrow, 2004); David Ehrenstein, *The Scorsese Picture* (New York: Carol, 1992); and Andy Dougan, *Martin Scorsese* (New York: Thunder's Mouth, 1998).

2. Scorsese has made two documentary films about film history: *A Personal Journey with Martin Scorsese Through the Movies* (1995) and *My Voyage to Italy* (1999), which is a narrated history of Italian cinema. Other topical preoccupations include his Italian-American heritage (*Italianamerican*, 1974), the Italian influence on fashion (*Made in Milan*, 1990), and New York City (*American Boy*, 1978, and *Lady By the Sea: The Statue of Liberty*, 2004). None of these fascinations has the sustained longevity in his critical imagination, however, as popular music has.

3. A few exceptions to this are Robert Kolker's discussion of Scorsese in *A Cinema of Loneliness* (Oxford, UK: Oxford University Press, 2000), 175–246; and Lawrence S. Friedman, *The Cinema of Martin Scorsese* (New York: Continuum, 1997), 88–112. Although both acknowledge the significant space music occupies in the narrative films, those with compiled soundtracks in particular, neither follows up on this observation with any sustained analysis.

4. Quoted in "*Sans la musique, je serais perdu*," translated into French by Serge Grunberg, *Hor série spécial musique, Cahiers du cinema* (Dec. 1995), 17. The retranslation back into English is mine.

5. For a good discussion on Kubrick's musical aesthetic, see Claudia Gorbman, "Ears Wide Open: Kubrick's Music," in *Changing Tunes: The Use of Pre-Existing Music in Film* (Burlington, VT: Ashgate, 2006), 3–18.

6. Martin Scorsese, "Preface," *Celluloid Jukebox: Popular Music and the Movies since the 1950s*, eds. Jonathan Romney and Adrian Wootton (London: BFI, 1995), 1.

7. On several occasions, Scorsese has worked with a composer and traditional orchestral scoring. Such is the case with *Taxi Driver* (1977) scored by Bernard Herrmann, *The Last Temptation of Christ* (1988) by Peter Gabriel, *Cape Fear* (1991) and *Age of Innocence* (1993) by Elmer Bernstein, and *Kundun* (1997) by Phillip Glass. Significantly, most of these "scored" films have non-contemporary settings or settings with a weak connection to popular music. The most obvious exception to this is *Cape Fear*. A remake of J. Lee Thompson's 1962 film, the film featured Elmer Bernstein's adaptation of Bernard Herrman's original score. *Taxi Driver*'s contemporary setting should have made it a good candidate for a compilation soundtrack, but it's an exception too because, as Scorsese puts it, one of the primary expressions of the central character Travis Bickle's mental instability was his avoidance of popular culture and music. See *Scorsese on Scorsese*, eds. David

Thompson and Ian Christie (London: Faber & Faber, 1989), 62–63. *Gangs of New York* (2002), *The Aviator* (2004), and *The Departed* (2006) have some pop music, but because they also have orchestral scoring, in all three cases by the composer Howard Shore, they are in the margins of the soundtrack category and may more comfortably belong in a separate, post-classical category. See Kevin Donnelly's discussion of the post-classical marriage of score and compilation soundtrack, "The Classical Film Score Forever? *Batman, Batman Returns* and Post-classical Film Music," in *Contemporary Hollywood Cinema*, eds. Steve Neale and Murray Smith (New York: Routledge, 1998), 142–155. *The King of Comedy* (1983), it should be noted, anticipates this kind of post-classical hybridization by also mixing a soundtrack of popular music with thematic orchestral scoring by composer Bob James, albeit to a lesser extent.

8. For those filmmakers whose cinematic style is defined in large part by their unusual employment of music, Gorbman uses the term *"mélomanes."* See her article, "Auteur Music," *Beyond the Soundtrack: Representing Music in Cinema*, eds. Daniel Goldmark, Lawrence Kramer, and Richard Leppert (Berkeley, CA: University of California Press, 2007), 149–162.

9. *Scorsese on Scorsese*, eds. David Thompson and Ian Christie (London: Faber & Faber, 1989), 43, 47.

10. "For me *Mean Streets* had the best music because it was what I enjoyed and it was part of the way we lived. Suddenly a piece would come on and we'd stay with it for two or three minutes. Life would stop, so I wanted the film to stop and go with the music. *Mean Streets* has that quality, whether it's rock and roll, opera, Neapolitan love songs. In our neighborhood you'd hear rock 'n' roll, playing in the little bars in the back of the tenement building at three in the morning, so that was 'Be My Baby,' when Harvey's [Keitel's] head hits the pillow. For me, the whole movie was 'Jumping Jack Flash' and 'Be My Baby.' " See *Scorsese on Scorsese*, 45.

11. When asked in an interview if he meant for *Mean Streets* to "serve as an antitdote for *The Godfather*," Scorsese replied: "Yes, absolutely....By the time I did *Mean Streets, The Godfather* had already come out. But I said, it doesn't matter, because this one is really to use the word loosely, anthropology—that idea of how people live, what they ate, how they dressed...." See Gavin Smith, "Martin Scorsese: Interviewed (1990)," in *Martin Scorsese: Interviews*, ed. Peter Brunette (Jackson, MS: University of Mississippi Press, 1999), 148. And although Scorsese doesn't say it, one could also add "what they listened to." The film's substitution of styles, of contemporary rock for orchestral thematic scoring, proved not only striking but enduring as witnessed most recently in the hit HBO television show about New Jersey mobsters, "The Sopranos." As David Milch, the creator of the series noted in the HBO documentary film *The Making of the Sopranos: Road to Respect* (2006), the show borrowed heavily from Scorsese in creating the cable television show's similarly rock-heavy soundtrack. See also Maurice Yacowar, *Sopranos On the Couch: Analyzing Television's Greatest Series* (New York: Continuum, 2003), 224–225.

12. Scorsese was not the only proponent of the vérité compilation soundtrack formula in the 1970s. Other directors like Lucas and Bogdanovich also made prominent use of it. See my article, "Whatever Happened to Great Movie Music: Cinema Verite and Hollywood Film Music in the Early 1970s," *American Music* 21/2 (Summer, 2003), 180–213. For a thorough discussion of the use of popular music in these 1970s films, see Jeff Smith, *The Sounds of Commerce: Marketing Popular Film Music* (New York: Columbia University Press, 1998), 196–209.

13. *Scorsese on Scorsese*, 110.

14. Ibid., 110–111.

15. Some scholars have approached the music video by placing it within a longer history of visualized musical performances. See Andrew Goodwin, *Dancing in the Distraction*

Factory: Music Television and Popular Culture (Minneapolis: University of Minnesota Press, 1992); R. Serge Denisoff and William D. Romanowski, *Risky Business: Rock on Film* (New Brunswick, NJ: Transaction, 1991), 345–398; and Charles M. Berg, "Visualizing Music: The Archaeology of the Music Video," *OneTwoThreeFour: A Rock 'n' Roll Quarterly* No. 5 (Spring 1987), 94–103.

16. For a more detailed analysis of the music video's unusually broad and disparate repertoire of visual techniques, see Andrew Goodwin, "From Anarchy to Chromakey: Music, Video and Media," *OneTwoThreeFour: A Rock 'n' Roll Quarterly* No. 5 (Spring 1987), 17–32; Marsha Kinder, "Music Video and the Spectator: Television, Ideology and Dream," *Film Quarterly*, vol. 38, no. 1 (Autumn, 1984), 2–15; Will Straw, "Music Video in its Contexts: Popular Music and Post-Modernism in the 1980s," *Popular Music*, vol. 7, no. 3 (October, 1988), 247–266; Carol Vernalis, *Experiencing Music Video: Aesthetics and Cultural Context* (New York: Columbia University Press, 2004); and essays in *Sound and Vision: The Music Video Reader*, eds. Simon Frith and Andrew Goodwin (New York: Routledge, 1993).

17. As market research proved, the resulting fast and irregular visual rhythm suited the shortened attention spans of the medium's target audience: youths aged 12–25. See R. Serge Denisoff and William D. Romanowski, *Risky Business: Rock on Film*, 350–352.

18. Initially, MTV had some competition from the NBC program "Friday Night Videos" and TBS's program "Night Tracks," but its 24-hour programming soon made it the dominant cable television station. See Maira Viera, "The Institutionalization of the Music Video," *OneTwoThreeFour: A Rock 'n' Roll Quarterly* No. 5 (Spring 1987), 80–93; and Denisoff and Romanowski, *Risky Business: Rock on Film*, 345–357. See also R. Serge Denisoff, *Inside MTV* (New York: Transaction, 1988), foreword, 2; and E. Ann Kaplan, *Rocking Around the Clock: Music Television, Postmodernism and Consumer Culture* (London: Methuen, 1987), 1–2.

19. That the music video was a valuable marketing tool for film soundtracks and films themselves was most effectively pointed out by critic Marianne Meyer, who in an article in *Rolling Stone* magazine coined the phrase: Movie + Soundtrack + Video = $$$!!! See Marianne Meyer, "The Rock Movideo," *Rolling Stone Review*, Ira Robbins, ed. (New York: Charles Scribners & Sons, 1985), 168. For discussion of the new marketing "synergies" that music videos and MTV created, see R. Serge Denisoff and George Plasketes, "Synergy in 1980's Film and Music," *Film History* 4/3, 257–276; and Alexander Doty, "Music Sells Movies: (Re)New(ed) Conservatism in Film Marketing," *Wide Angle* 10/2 (1988), 70–79. See also R. Serge Denisoff and William Romanowski, *Risky Business: Rock in Film* (New Brunswick, NJ: Transaction, 1991), 399–468; and Jeff Smith, *The Sounds of Commerce: Marketing Popular Film Music*, 186–230.

20. Rick Altman, *The American Film Musical* (Bloomington, IN: Indiana University Press, 1987), 345–346. Altman considers the similarities between classical film musicals from the 1930s, '40s, and '50s, and 1980s films with music video-like interruptions. Others have also discussed in greater detail the effect music videos had on film style and structure. See Kay Dickinson, "Pop, Speed and the 'MTV Aesthetic' in Recent Teen Films," 143–152; and John Mundy, *Popular Music on Screen: From the Hollywood Musical to Music Video* (Manchester, UK: Manchester University Press, 1999), chapter 7, "I Want My MTV...and My Movies with Music," 221–247.

21. *Celluloid Jukebox: Popular Music and the Movies Since the 1950s*, eds. Jonathan Romney and Adrian Wootton (London: BFI, 1995), 139. As Last also describes it, "MTV moments" also began conforming to certain length requirements dictated by commercial pressures. Whereas song interruptions in film musicals were typically the length of an entire song, in video-ized soundtracks, the interruptions or modules varied but on the whole were shorter. They could include whole songs, but more often than not only parts of songs were heard, frequently lasting only two times through the chorus, a length studio executives deemed sufficient to inspire viewers to purchase the soundtrack.

22. For a detailed discussion of the high-concept film, see Justin Wyatt, *High Concept: Movies and Marketing in Hollywood* (Austin, TX: University of Texas Press, 1994); also Stephen Prince, *A New Pot of Gold: Hollywood Under the Electronic Rainbow, 1980-1989* (Berkeley, CA: University of California Press, 2000), 132–141; and Mark Crispin Miller, "Hollywood: the Ad," *The Atlantic Monthly* 265/4 (April 1990), 41–54.

23. Meyers, "The Rock Movideo," 168.

24. Ibid.

25. Prince, *Pot of Gold*, 132–141; *Celluloid Closet*, 119–123.

26. Quoted in *Scorsese on Scorsese*, 113.

27. Kathlyn Murphy, "Made Men," *Film Comment* 26/5 (Sept.–Oct. 1990), 25–30, 69; see also Jim Sangster, *Scorsese* (New York: Virgin Books), 151–154.

28. *Scorsese on Scorsese*, 154. As several biographers have pointed out, one of the first jobs that Scorsese got out of film school was working with the pioneers of the direct cinema movement, the Maysles brothers, an influence readily apparent not only in his early narrative film but in his early interest in making documentary films. See Lawrence Friedman, *The Cinema of Martin Scorsese* (New York: Continuum, 1998), 7–19.

29. When asked by an interviewer what kind of film he saw *Goodfellas* as being, Scorsese answered, "I was hoping it was a documentary. [Laughs] Really, no kidding. Like a *staged* documentary, the *spirit* of a documentary. As if you had a 16mm camera with these guys for 20, 25 years; what you'd pick up. I can't say it's 'like' any other film, but in my mind it [has] the freedom of a documentary, where you can mention 25 people's names at one point and 23 of them the audience will not have heard of before and won't hear of again, but it doesn't matter. It's the familiarity of the way people speak." Quoted in Gavin Smith, "Martin Scorsese: Interviewed (1990)," 146.

30. *Scorsese on Scorsese*, 161.

31. Gavin Smith, "Martin Scorsese: Interviewed (1990)," 150.

32. *Scorsese on Scorsese*, 160.

33. Anthony DeCurtis, "What the Streets Mean (1991)," in *Martin Scorsese: Interviews*, 175.

34. Gavin Smith, "Martin Scorsese Interviewed (1990)," 153.

35. Amy Taubin, "Martin Scorsese's Cinema of Obsessions," in *Martin Scorsese: Interviews*, 141–142.

36. Anthony DeCurtis, "What the Streets Mean (1991)," 160.

37. An astute student of the cinematic past, Scorsese not surprisingly locates the elements of this new aesthetic—speed, density, and spatial independence—in the work of a previous generation of filmmakers. He credits New Wave directors Truffaut and Godard, for instance, with inspiring his interests in unconventional narrative rhythms in *Goodfellas*. "The freezeframes are basically all Truffaut," he says of the visual style of *Goodfellas*. "The[y] come from the first two or three minutes of *Jules and Jim*." Ibid., 154. "The Truffaut and Godard techniques from the early sixties that have stayed in my mind—what I loved about them was that narrative was not important." Later in the same interview, he again refers to the editing experiments introduced by New Wave directors and other influential directors from that generation. "I always loved those jump cuts in the early French films, in Bertolucci's *Before the Revolution*." Ibid, 154.

38. *Scorsese on Scorsese*, 154.

39. Gavin Smith, "Martin Scorsese Interviewed (1990)," 154.

40. Kolker, *A Cinema of Loneliness*, 197.

41. Ibid, 186–187. Speaking of the music in *Goodfellas*, Kolker observes: "The soundtrack of popular music contemporary to the time of the narrative becomes an inextricable part of that narrative. The very rhythm of the songs being played becomes integral to the movement of the camera and the editing pattern of a given sequence...this "found" music becomes so tightly bound to the structure of a film, the cutting, shot composition, and music begin to infiltrate each other so that film and music become a seamless rhythmic

construction that, despite its tight integration, always remains on a conscious level influencing viewer response to the film."

42. Anthony DeCurtis, "What the Streets Mean (1991)," 174-175.

43. The *Mean Streets* compilation, for instance, consisted of 22 pieces of music. *Flashdance* (1983) a contemporary high-concept film soundtrack, in comparison, featured only 17 selections. Size is a distinctive characteristic of the *Goodfellas* soundtrack, but it is also a characteristic that is observable only in the film itself. The commercially released soundtrack album, prepared by the studio's subsidiary record company, Atlantic records, contains only 12 of the film's 46 songs and is hardly representative of the film's soundtrack. It is instead more representative of the high-concept tie-in album phenomenon, the 1980s and '90s practice that dictated that every film produce a CD-length (around one hour) collection of music that could be marketed outside the confines of the film.

44. *Scorsese on Scorsese*, 161.

45. Kolker, *A Cinema of Loneliness*, 199–201.

46. According to Scorsese, "Some people said it was impossible that gangsters would have been listening to 'Sunshine of Your Love' by Cream in 1967, but I pointed out that the song was on American radio in the Top 40, so they heard it anyway, whether they listened to it or not! I used that song for the scene when Jimmy is at the bar looking around and deciding that he has to get rid of all these people, and the camera moves into his face slowly. We tried ten songs and the most interesting turned out to be 'Sunshine.' " *Scorsese on Scorsese*, 161.

47. See Scorsese's preface to *The Celluloid Jukebox: Popular Music and the Movies since the 50s*, 1.

48. Gavin Smith, "Martin Scorsese Interviewed (1990)," 150.

49. *Goodfellas* is not the only film in which Scorsese displays this opinion of the evolution of popular music. The soundtrack for *Casino* was also constructed with this personal judgment of historical periods in mind. In this film too, early rock 'n' roll and '50s pop music is "pure," and the psychedelic and punk rock of the late '70s and early '80s is "decadent" and "degenerate." As Scorsese puts it, "For me, every piece of music used has its own associations.... There's [a] breakdown in style in 'Satisfaction,' from the Stones to Devo." *Scorsese on Scorsese*, 207.

50. Gavin Smith, "Martin Scorsese Interviewed (1990)," 151.

51. As Kolker puts it, "Scorsese pays his cinematic debts" with the quotation, "he links his films to the gangster tradition." See *A Cinema of Loneliness*, 195.

52. *Scorsese on Scorsese*, 147. The use of clichéd 1950s faux-Italian pop songs in particular, Scorsese argues, rendered the film more of a "cartoon" of mob life than a satire. "As far as an Italian-American thing, it's really like a cartoon. When he starts with 'Mambo-Italiano,' Rosemary Clooney, I'm already cringing because I'm Italian-American, and certain songs we'd like to forget! So I told Jonathan he had some nerve using that, I said only Italians could use 'Mambo-Italiano' and get away with it." In contrast, Scorsese did admire *Married to the Mob*'s visual authenticity, enough in fact to use that film's production designer, Kristi Zea, for *Goodfellas*.

53. As Kolker describes it, "The voice-overs in *Goodfellas* are not psychotic, but seem rather to be the words of two good-natured guides—commentators, memorialists, even moralists—reflecting on the pleasures and fears of the gangster life in ways meant to ingratiate. They are, of course, fictional voices, which are mediated by another narrator, the controlling voice of the film itself." See *A Cinema of Loneliness*, 195.

54. The film's final '80s sequence," Scorsese agrees, is about all "losing control." As he puts it, "Henry disintegrates with drugs. With Jimmy Conway, the disintegration is on a more lethal level, the elimination of [everybody else]." Gavin Smith, "Martin Scorsese Interviewed (1990)," 152.

CHAPTER 2

Lost in Transition: Popular Music, Adolescence, and the Melodramatic Mode of Sofia Coppola

TIM ANDERSON

I like movies that just meander along, where it's more about the feelings.... I was just compiling all these different things that I liked and hoped that it would all add up to the feeling I wanted to give.

Sofia Coppola[1]

Ever notice how nothing actually happens in Sofia Coppola's movies?

Liz Armstrong[2]

Strolls through Versailles, Tokyo, and Grosse Pointe, Michigan, are all important parts of the stories of Sofia Coppola films, although the stories themselves don't necessarily go anywhere. Coppola's films do not have much of a beginning, middle, or end; nor do they disrupt or restore much of anything. For example, Coppola's first feature, *The Virgin Suicides* (1999), is ostensibly about the suicide of the Lisbon girls and how these events affect their family, the community, and the young adolescent men who worshipped them. However, the film offers no resolution, only speculation about why these young women would take their lives. Similarly, both *Lost in Translation* (2003) and *Marie Antoinette* (2006) provide no "life lessons" or moral clarifications. In fact, it is not clear what anyone "learns" in these films, films where black and white moments of moral crisis do not exist, protagonists are not heroic, and antagonists are hard to find. Coppola's films do get from beginning to end, but they wander quite a bit along the way.

Although this tendency to wander has generated a significant amount of critical condemnation, much of Coppola's creative energies are deposited onto specific moments rather than weighty narratives. At the same time that Coppola is often lauded for her cinematic impressions, she is consistently marked down by critics for her narratives. Writing about *The Virgin Suicides*, Mark Olsen notes that "Coppola frequently frames moments as if taking a still photograph, aiding the film's air of suffocating memory" and that *Lost in Translation* "seems driven more by its tone than by the mechanics of getting from A to B."[3] Elvis Mitchell observes that *Translation* is "about a moment of evanescence that fades before the participants' eyes."[4] In the case of Coppola's third and most controversial feature film, *Marie Antoinette*, the majority of critical opprobrium is applied to her emphasis on style over story. J. Hoberman's review notes that it is "basically a small story in a gilded frame," while Stuart Klawan in *The Nation* states that although *Marie Antoinette* "goes a little flat," "the tired businessman in me enjoyed every joke, musical number and costume change."[5] In her assessment of Coppola's oeuvre, Anna Rogers succinctly sums up her tendency to meander:

> The trajectory of Coppola's films is far from predictable and smooth; they lack narrative arcs because they detail a world where the link between things has broken down and the protagonists are no longer able to react in an effective fashion. Her protagonists are pertinent examples of people who are incapacitated or overwhelmed by the situation with which they are presented, yet this does not have to be one of explicit danger. Rather, the protagonist's crisis is often a case of trying to navigate a path for oneself in a world that is confusing and unresponsive to one's needs.[6]

It is in these moments of sophisticated drift and tread, moments of potential transition, where we witness Coppola at her best. Coppola's narratives specifically concentrate on the generation of melodramatic moments that are expositional and reveal characters' states of mind, specifically what they themselves cannot communicate. Throughout these momentous experiments, popular music is mobilized as an essential element to illustrate these moments. This is particularly true of those moments of experience that are crucial to psychic development in feminine adolescence. As Pam Cook points out, all of Coppola's four films "[borrow] elements of the teen-pic such as the rites-of-passage narrative and contemporary-music soundtrack but giving it an arthouse, European flavour."[7] This chapter examines these moments of audiovisual confluence to better understand how Coppola, working in concert with her music supervisor Brian Reitzell, has asserted an idiosyncratic, melodramatic style that underscores and emphasizes the importance of specific moments of subjectivity.

Brian Reitzell's efforts and partnership with Coppola cannot be understated. The primary music supervisor to have worked on Coppola's feature films, Reitzell has a practice that is anything but standard. He goes beyond the typical role of the music supervisor, who acts as a "liaison between director and the film's musical personnel," negotiates music licensing, and provides aesthetic consultation.[8] For example, Reitzell does not employ a "temp score," the music score typically assembled at the earliest stages of the film's edit that expresses the director's aesthetic intentions. Instead,

[f]or all his movies—regardless of the director—Reitzell creates a mix CD of existing tracks that allows the director to hear the direction he feels the music should follow. "It's so much better that way," he says, even though the process can be very time-consuming. "I have to do my private investigator work," he says. "I'm spending hours in record shops, on the Internet, and I usually go to the place" where the movie is based to get a sense of the geography.[9]

Because this contribution comes at the preproduction phase, Reitzell's mix CD goes far beyond the process of simply providing music. In the case of *Lost in Translation*, Reitzell worked with Coppola *very* early in the preproduction stage. According to Ross Katz, producer of *Translation*, "Brian got involved at the script stage because he gets what Sofia is trying to relay. It's something that is hard to capture on the page, but Sofia knows exactly how to shoot it and Brian knows how to help find the sounds."[10] Allowing Reitzell such leeway at the preproduction phase indicates the importance Coppola places on popular music for her expressive palette. For Coppola, these musical choices often underscore specifically feminine rites of adolescent passage. At the same time, these musical choices both deliver and enable a significance that comes partially from the extra-diegetic set of discourses that are part of all musical forms. As Susan McClary reminds us,

Like any social discourse, music is meaningful precisely insofar as at least some people believe that it is and act according to that belief. Meaning is not inherent in music, but neither is it in language: both are activities that are kept afloat only because communities of people invest in them, agree collectively that their signs serve as valid currency. Music is always dependent on the conferring of social meaning as ethnomusicologists have long recognized, the study of signification in music cannot be undertaken in isolation from the human contexts that create, transmit, and respond to it.[11]

This is significant as the meaning of popular music often emerges from the many fads, fashions, styles, and creative acts with which it commingles. In other words, a proper understanding of popular music demands an understanding of popular style.

Indeed, discussions of Sofia Coppola's films often begin and end with a focus on their style. An apprentice at Chanel in Paris during high school, Coppola began her career behind the camera as a costume designer for her father's contribution to *New York Stories* and later for Lucas Reiner's *Spirit of '76*.[12] Coppola is often lumped into what Pam Cook calls "a new creative elite that crosses several areas of popular culture," which includes fashion, wine, and music:

> She set up her own fashion label Milk Fed in 1995 with childhood chum Stephanie Hayman and is credited with being the artistic inspiration for fashion designer Marc Jacobs, another of her friends. Francis Ford, who has a successful second career as a vintner, named a range of wines after her, and she now has her own line of sparkling rosé, prettily packaged in pink. Once married to director Spike Jonze (*Being John Malkovich*, *Adaptation*), Sofia is currently with Thomas Mars of the French band Phoenix, who feature on the soundtrack of *Lost in Translation* and perform in her latest film *Marie Antoinette*.[13]

Coppola's instincts cross multiple artistic terrains that also include photography, acting, and boutique fashion. Mark Olsen observes that it is this "diverse background [that] makes her perfectly suited for the role of film director." Speaking about *The Virgin Suicides*, Olsen comments that "perhaps the most impressive thing about her film is the way it's very much a total package. All of its elements—performance, cinematography, sound, art design—combine to illuminate not just a theme or singular idea, but to create a unified feeling and mood."[14]

This specifically intense focus on feeling and mood places Coppola's work squarely in a melodramatic tradition, a mode that prioritizes the pronounced display of emotion. As Thomas Elsaesser explains,

> In its dictionary sense, melodrama is a dramatic narrative in which musical accompaniment marks the emotional effects. This is still perhaps the most useful definition, because it allows melodramatic elements to be seen as constituents of a system of punctuation, giving expressive colour and chromatic contrast to the story-line, by orchestrating the emotional ups and downs of the intrigue. The advantage of this approach is that it formulates the problems of melodrama as problems of style and articulation.[15]

Elsaesser continues,

> Music in melodrama, for example, as a device among others to dramatise a given narrative, is subjective and programmatic. But because it is also a form of punctuation in the above sense (that is, of structural significance) and thematic (that is, belonging to expressive content) because [sic] used to formulate certain moods—sorrow, violence, dread, suspense, happiness.[16]

Elsaesser positions music's melodramatic function as essentially an expressive device, one that has a specific subjective purchase that dramatically underlines specific points in narrative time to create particular aesthetic tensions. This focus on *momentary pressures* is key to melodrama. As Peter Brooks writes in *The Melodramatic Imagination*,

> The narrative voice is not content to describe and record gesture, to see it simply as a figure in the interplay of persons one with another. Rather, the narrator applies pressure to the gesture, pressure through interrogation, through the evocation of more and more fantastic possibilities, to make it yield meaning, to make it give up to consciousness its full potential as "parable."[17]

The melodramatic application and employment of popular music is an essential part of the process, through which Coppola arrests the aims of narrative time for specific psychic exposure. This application of popular music to arrest story time is a trope most closely associated with the oft-maligned popular melodramatic form of film and theatrical musical. The most common criticism of the musical is that the form tends to provide very thin narrative structures, through which specific moments of performance emerge and thrive. Although the form sacrifices narrative momentum to the necessities of spectacle, in return for this sacrifice, the gestural is systematically amplified. Writing about George Sidney's film musicals, Dennis Giles identifies this effect as a specific arrest of narrative time known as "showtime." Giles notes that the presence of showtime in Sidney's musicals aims for "permanent show [as] a cure for the previous drama—its conflict, its agon(y) since the showing arrests the flow of time." Furthermore, "the purpose of the show is to be shown. Any further passage of time is regarded as an evil, since it can only disrupt the harmonies of this moment, only to degrade the beauty so precariously achieved. In sum, by virtue of showing the show, the performers pass to a transcendent state of being."[18] Roland Barthes discusses showtime as a time associated with the music hall, a time that is "by definition interrupted." This time exists in contradistinction to the continuous time of narrative theater. It is a "sidereal time," "the time of the thing itself and not that of its anticipation (tragedy) or its reconsideration (epic)." For Barthes, "the advantage of this literal time is that it can serve gesture best, for it is quite obvious that gesture exists as spectacle on from the moment when time is severed."[19] As Peter Brooks notes, this amplification of the gestural is key to melodramatic modes of expression where "[t]hings cease to be merely themselves, gestures cease to be merely tokens of social intercourse whose meaning is assigned by a social code; they become the vehicles of metaphors whose tenor suggests another kind of reality." In this moral universe, the melodramatic form pronounces that there is an existence beyond "the banal stuff of reality." By charging the narrative with "intenser signifiers," as Brooks puts it, the melodramatic drifts toward a "desire to express all" where "nothing is left unsaid; characters stand on stage and utter the unspeakable, give voice to their deepest feelings, dramatize through their heightened and polarized words and gestures the whole lesson of their relationship. They assume primary psychic roles, father, mother, child and express basic psychic conditions. Life tends, in this fiction, toward ever more concentrated and totally expressive gestures and statements."[20]

This melodramatic shift from the linear story time of history to one that emphasizes the momentous comes with particularly important gender implications. Feminist critic Tania Modleski notes that, "In melodrama, the important moments of the narrative are often felt as eruptions of involuntary memory, to the point where sometimes the only major events are repetitions of former ones."[21] Modleski positions her comments from a feminist psychoanalytic perspective that draws heavily from Max Ophuls's film *Letter from an Unknown Woman* as an example.[22] Ophuls's film explores two gendered modes of time, the masculine time of history and the feminine time of repetition:

> Two conceptions of time here seem unalterably opposed: the time of repetition, which for Lisa [the "unknown woman" of *Letter from an Unknown Woman*] means never entering history, but forever remaining childlike, fixated on the scenes of her youth. And the time of history which Stefan definitively enters at the end of the film when he takes his journey by coach to meet Lisa's husband and his own death.[23]

For Modleski, the issue of time is key to understanding the melodramatic mode, particularly its resonance for women in general and feminism in particular:

> Intuitively we ally melodrama with the feminine insofar as it is a genre quintessentially concerned with emotional expression. Women in melodrama almost always suffer the pains of love and even death while husbands, lovers, and children remain partly or totally unaware of their experience. Women carry the burden of feeling for everyone."[24]

Melodrama's focus on the moments of feeling provides a sense of time and storytelling that makes the mode attractive to Modleski because, "for all the women in melodrama who constantly revisit the scenes of their youth, repetition and return are manifestations of another relationship to time and space, desire and memory, and it is of this difference that the text speaks to me."[25]

Coppola's films fit within this tradition as they construct a relationship to time and space and center on moments of feminine revelation and change.

More specifically, Coppola's moments often focus on what it feels like to be *on the cusp* of specific moments of feminine change. A theme in all her three features and one short film, Coppola focuses on moments of feminine transition such as moments of adolescence, the newlywed period of marriage, and the transition from irresponsible archduchess to a responsible monarch. As mentioned earlier, these films go out of their way to avoid resolution: We never completely understand what drives these characters. The questions "Why did the Lisbon girls take their own lives?," "What is the exact nature of the relationship between the protagonists in *Translation*?," and "How does Marie Antoinette become loyal to Louis Auguste?" are all unanswered, the audience left only with guesses. However, what we are given are opportunities to feel a distinct aspect of all of these protagonists' emotional lives.

Coppola's first cinematic exploration of adolescent temper is her 15-minute short *Lick The Star* (1998). Anna Rogers opines that the film is a "tenuous narrative frame [that] merely sets up the possibility of exploring the construction of adolescent identity and desire."[26] *Lick The Star* consists of the most pedestrian rituals and processes behind adolescent status, such as the pronounced exertion of a hallway presence and the covert passing of classroom notes. Throughout the film, *Star* presents five high school girls and their clique accompanied by seven identifiable pieces of popular music by four different acts: the Amps, Free Kitten, the Go Gos, and Land of the Loops. Of the four, three of the acts are significant women-led rock bands; the other, Land of the Loops, is a sample-heavy instrumental group led by Alan Sutherland. Except for the Go Gos, each of these acts is relatively obscure, and none of them can claim any hit singles or significant commercial success. That said, the Go Gos' guitar-heavy punk/pop aesthetic exists comfortably alongside the film's other selections. For example, Free Kitten, a collaborative duo consisting of Kim Gordon of Sonic Youth and Julia Cafritz of Pussy Galore, emphasizes the staccato rhythms, distorted vocals, and guitars most often associated with the masculinized genres of punk and heavy metal. Indeed, their refusal to accept the musical conventions of femininity is one of the many themes embraced by both musicians and their label, Kill Rock Stars, a label that harbors many of the more important "riot grrl" acts of the 1990s including Bikini Kill and Sleater Kinney. These selections are first put to use when we are introduced to Chloe, "the queen of seventh grade," 45 seconds into the film, with a wide establishing shot. The shot is not so much underscored by 47 seconds of the Amps' "Tipp City" as it seems to be motivated by it.[27] Walking toward the foreground of the shot, Chloe is framed in a slow-motion approach that is edited and defined by the drumbeat, with quick cuts made on emphatic snare accents. Kelley Deal's vocals and guitars do not express a specific idea, but rather

Figure 2.1: *Lick the Star*: Chloe shows a swagger as she walks down the hall to the sound of the Amps' "Tipp City."

an attitude of adolescent yet masculine confidence and bravura. In short, Chloe exhibits a swagger (figure 2.1).

The confluence of rock music and masculinity is a well-worn trope. Numerous authors have noted that rock's "masculinization" is positioned as a liberating force to pop's "femininity." In 1978, Simon Frith and Angela McRobbie wrote that "of all the mass media, rock is the most explicitly concerned with sexual expression."[28] Frith and McRobbie continue:

> Any analysis of the sexuality of rock must begin with the brute social fact that in terms of control and production, rock is a male form. The music business is male-run; popular musicians, writers, creators, technicians, engineers, and producers are mostly men. Female creative roles are limited and mediated through male notions of female ability. Women musicians who make it are almost always singers; the women in the business who make it are usually in publicity; in both roles success goes with a male-made female image. In general, popular music's images, values, and sentiments are male products.[29]

The importance of placing these women-led, guitar-oriented rock bands of the 1990s and 2000s such as the Amps and Free Kitten into the narrative cannot be understated. For example, Mavis Bayton argues that the electric guitar has a strong gendered association with masculinity for a variety of reasons, including its association with technology, the masculine terrain of guitar shops, and the generic convention of rock requiring an electric guitar.[30] Guitar-heavy bands such as the Amps and Free Kitten, as Norma Coates notes, bring "a point of view of female experience and sexuality [and troubles] to the performance of masculinity" in rock music. As Coates argues, "[to think about women and guitars] is to open up the field of male sexuality, a move which I hope would lead to a political rethinking of rock and sexuality and ultimately, masculinity."[31]

The association of Chloe with guitar-oriented rock significantly marks her confidence, as well as the character's attempt to negotiate those specific gender conventions that are formed and hardened in adolescence. It is no coincidence that by the end of the film, Chloe is no longer accompanied by guitars. Her aggressive, masculine cool has been clipped and, in essence, her musical journey follows her feminization from rock to pop, from guitars to keyboards, as Chloe swiftly loses her popularity and status as the clique leader. As Chloe's rank is systematically diminished, her masculine swagger is stripped, and she is transformed from "outward bad girl who leads" to an "inward melancholiac who journals." As the Amps' "Tipp City" marks Chloe's "cool" at the beginning of the film, the Go Gos' "This Town," a song that openly bemoans streets littered with those once-glamorous "chosen toys/of catty girls and pretty boys," marks her decline in status and amplifies the cruel nature of her passage from leader to outcast.[32] Shortly after her downfall, we view a shot of Chloe slowly sliding into a tub of water in what we find out later is a suicide attempt. The slow pace of Chloe's tranquil yet near-deadly descent into the water is accompanied by the staccato, spurting guitars of Free Kitten's "Eat Cake" that provides the non-diegetic excess while Kim Gordon sings, "Feels so good/not to be me."[33] In the words of Anna Rogers, "[the scene is] a type of ritual cleansing of identity. Just as popularity is established through the quasi-tribal markings of makeup and behavior borrowed from popular iconography (such as that of the transgressive femme fatale who smokes), it must be also effaced through ceremonial form."[34] After Chloe writes "everything changes, nothing changes, the tables turn and life goes on," the film ends with an image of Chloe walking across a playground as she clutches a copy of Jean Stein's biography of Edie Sedgwick and we hear the Land of the Loops' percussive yet decidedly unaggressive, quirky electronic pop.

The transition is traumatic partially because such assertiveness was attractive, and the loss of her confidence occurs through the humiliation by her female peers. Unfortunately, this kind of social humiliation is all too often an adolescent rite of passage for many young women. As Coppola's films detail and investigate these particularly significant rites, she consciously applies popular music as a means of melodramatic exposition, a dominant expressive agent throughout her feature films. For Coppola, this means placing a concerted focus on generating a specific cinematic atmosphere:

> I always like to start with the atmosphere and the tone and the look kind of first, and the
> music, and tell the story as much as I can without dialogue. I like just trying to tell the

story as much as you can with the expressions and the emotion; I even thought about doing [*Marie Antoinette*] as a silent film at one point.[35]

This emphasis on atmosphere dominates Coppola's *Virgin Suicides*. This story of the five Lisbon girls and their suicides is narrated from a collective off-screen voice of those five men who are now adults and who, in their youth, idolized the sisters. The prominent moods of the film are melancholy and depression, both of which emerge from a production design and script that emphasize a specific lack of communication. Amplifying this mood, Coppola commissioned a background score for the film by the French electronic duo Air; this would be one of two soundtrack albums released in support of the film:

> I was listening to Premiers Symptomes, an earlier album of theirs, when I was writing the script. I really liked the atmosphere, which fed into what I was doing. Again, I wanted to deal with this idea of memory, because the story doesn't take place in the '70s, per se, but it's being reflected on years later. Also, Air are the masters of a specific kind of melancholy, a good kind of melancholy.[36]

The melancholia that permeates the film also arises from the fact that the Lisbon girls are not allowed to make connections beyond their strict and overbearing home life. Dominated by their mother, Mrs. Lisbon (Kathleen Turner), the girls' social life is strictly regulated, particularly in the case of any sexualized form of communication and contact such as dances and co-ed parties. As a result, the young women's communicative capacities are severely limited, and the Lisbon girls turn to specific pop music records as a communicative strategy to make clear what their lack of dialogue and settings cannot. Early in the film, Coppola places two specific songs that act as premonitory devices in diegetic party music at the Lisbon girls' house. With the intent of lifting the spirits of Cecelia, who has failed at an earlier suicide attempt, Mrs. Lisbon invites a number of local boys over for a chaperoned event. As the scene begins, two light rock songs waft throughout the party: Todd Rundgren's "A Dream Goes on Forever" and the Hollies' version of "The Air That I Breathe."[37] Both songs are reflective of the film's 1974 setting, but they also cast a sense of quiet desperation over the event as they anticipate Cecelia's suicide, which occurs immediately after she excuses herself from the party.

Although this ritual moment of adolescent community curdles as Cecelia crosses that most terminal of boundaries, it also foresees the fiasco that will be the Lisbon sisters' prom night. The lightness of the two songs, as well as those that appear later at the prom, add to the significant tension between the film's imagery of 1970s suburban domesticity and the gravity of the young women's suicides. This is partially due to the feminine associations that songs such as Electric Light Orchestra's "Strange Music," 10cc's "I'm Not in Love," and Styx's "Come Sail Away" have; all three are used in the prom scene.[38] The first two of these songs are keyboard-driven and feature male falsettos who sing about the ambiguous feelings of adolescent desire. "Come Sail Away" is positioned as a crescendo that highlights the transitional moment when Lux Lisbon (Kirsten Dunst) and Trip Fontaine (Josh Hartnett) are elected king and queen of the prom (figure 2.2). "Come Sail Away" also acts as a sort of masculine siren call that tempts the sisters to let loose. In the case of Lux, she will break her curfew and spend the evening with her date Trip. The Lisbon sisters' actions result in Mrs. Lisbon permanently removing the girls from their friends, as well as from high school. Soon thereafter, Mrs. Lisbon returns home from an inspirational sermon and forces Lux to destroy her rock record collection. After this act, Lux begins to meet young men on her roof for seemingly affectionless sex, as if they are substitutes for her album collection.[39]

To be sure, records in *The Virgin Suicides* act as emotional ciphers through which the adolescents communicate. Pop records appear once more in the film's final depiction of affectionate communication between the Lisbon girls and the outside world. Late in the film, the Lisbon girls send a group of local boys notes requesting that they speak over the phone. Their admirers call and the parties have a "conversation" by playing hit pop records through the telephone. The respective light rock records are deployed to announce their presence (Todd Rundgren's "Hello It's Me"), romantic isolation (Gilbert O'Sullivan's "Alone Again, Naturally"), longing (Bee Gees,

Figure 2.2: *The Virgin Suicides*: Trip Fontaine and Lux Lisbon dance at their prom after being crowned king and queen ("Come Sail Away").

"Run to Me"), and distance (Carole King, "So Far Away").[40] All four of these songs are not only love ballads, but each of these singles is a variation of soft rock, a genre in which balladeers often deploy specific musical tropes (e.g., falsettos) and romantic topics (love, relationships, longing, romantic fantasies, etc.) with feminine audiences in mind. The fact that soft-rock records in *The Virgin Suicides* repeatedly intersect at specific ritual moments of transition between opposite-sex adolescents in such a diegetic fashion is a significant motif. It is also the creative work of a music supervisor and director who understands the connotative, reader-dependent powers that popular music records often contain. As I have written elsewhere,

> Because of the ease with which they can be manipulated and circulated, records have always acquired meanings far beyond the control of their creators and/or initial contexts. Even the most casual listener can tell you that the reason that pop records are so effective at evoking memory and social settings is due to their continually repeated use and presence in our daily lives. Thus, records are often loaded with large reserves of social memory, able to spark affections and release intense mnemonic charges.[41]

Coppola's utilization of these soft-rock records adds to *The Virgin Suicides'* "fever dream" atmosphere. As Jessica Winters explains, because "the film similarly hovers between dream and memory, its surreality embodied in the unearthly, untouchable (and superbly backlit) sisters." Coppola herself points out that this disconnect is intentional: "I wanted you to empathize with the girls but not to relate to them because what they do is so heartbreaking, so inexplicable."[42] Indeed, the only items that speak to their desire to connect are these pop songs, records of longing, love, and escape.

Lost in Translation also places its protagonists into a dreamlike setting. In this case, the two protagonists wander in a waking dream due to a combination of jet lag and, as two Americans in Tokyo, an explicit inability to communicate. Indeed, the setting places Bob Harris (Bill Murray) and Charlotte (Scarlett Johansson) in relief so that they are almost forced to find and connect with each other. Separated in age by close to 30 years and numerous rungs on the social ladder (Bob Harris is an American film star of some note), the two strike up a relationship based partially on the questions Charlotte has for Bob about the unspoken mysteries of marriage and personal crises associated with adulthood. Indeed, Coppola later acknowledged a biographical aspect to the film: While writing *Lost in Translation*, she was "trying to figure out that phase of my life [being newly married]."[43] Although the exact nature of Bob and Charlotte's relationship is never clear and often borders on a May-September romance, the two clearly connect as they find themselves in the uncanny environments of Tokyo nightlife. As in the case with *The Virgin Suicides*, Coppola and Reitzell rely upon the aid of contemporary electronic music to give the film an odd sense that is neither completely Eastern nor Western. With an electronic score by Kevin Shields, the legendarily reclusive leader of the hyper-amplified, distorted, and multilayered English guitar group My Bloody Valentine, *Translation* also includes a number of songs from the Jesus and Mary Chain, Air, and the 1970s Japanese pop act Happy End. The resulting soundtrack, as one critic notes, "is almost as dreamily under-stated as the film itself." This lack of statement, this refusal to rely upon the written word in *Translation* is, again, no accident. When Coppola met Shields, reportedly "she had trouble trying to explain to him how she wanted the music to sound." She notes that,

> When we first met, I spent much of the time trying to convey to him what I was looking for. I love music, but I don't really know how to talk about it. It's very abstract to me. Kevin and I worked together by me showing video tapes to him, a musician, and then the result became the way that he responded to it. Brian (Reitzell) also worked with him, as after working on *The Virgin Suicides* he's aware of what's required for a film. But really it was just Kevin's response to the visuals of the film.[44]

Reitzell's interest in sonic environments is one of his most significant contributions: "I always latch onto environments, so for me, one of my biggest roles is to help people be in that place. My job is partially to do sound design, in essence."[45] Reitzell's ability to make audiences feel as if they are part of or alienated from an environment through these particular soundtracks is part of the "understatedness" that saturates Coppola's films. This is particularly true of *Translation*, a film in which the main couple does not actually speak to each other until the 33rd minute. Indeed, the most interesting and intense moments of *Translation* occur between Charlotte and Bob when they leave their American-styled high-rise hotel and enter the Tokyo cityscape. For the most part, Charlotte and Bob are at their most isolated and depressed when they are in their hotel, which is sonically a combination of electrical hums and Western music. This includes classical music in the lobbies and elevators, and an American chanteuse played by Catherine Lambert, an actual lounge singer, who sings pop songs such as Simon and Garfunkle's arrangement of "Scarborough Fair/Canticle," "The Thrill Is Gone," "You Stepped Out of a Dream" (1940), and "Midnight at the Oasis" in the bar.[46] This space of Western-style comforts is essentially a luxurious prison of sorts where very little, including connection, occurs.

It is not until Bob and Charlotte step out of the comforts of the hotel and go to a Japanese bar where they meet several young Japanese men who take them to a private party that something happens. At this time, the music changes to the contemporary sounds of the Chemical Brothers' "The State

We're In," which is mixed in and out of the scene in a diegetic fashion.[47] Quickly, the couple, although limited by language, get involved in the party and start dancing to Phoenix's "Too Young," listening to records, and eventually they find themselves in a karaoke room to sing punk and post-punk singles.[48] While Charlotte sings the Pretenders' "Brass in the Pocket," a song where the singer repeatedly declares "I'm special" and trumpets her sexual swagger, Bob chooses Elvis Costello's arrangement of Nick Lowe's "What's So Funny 'Bout Peace, Love and Understanding" and Roxy Music's "More than This."[49] The performance of these pop hits brings the group together. Despite their inability to communicate through conversation, karaoke acts as a ritual moment of affective pronouncement wherein Bob and Charlotte connect to each other and their Japanese hosts (figure 2.3). Although the karaoke scene hardly resolves their isolation, the relief it provides is prominent, and we do not see a similar energy of connection until the end of the film when we witness the film's most famous moment: the muted exchange between Bob and Charlotte after they have encountered a number of emotional stumbling blocks. While the viewers see the two embrace, they only hear a whisper of what Bob says to Charlotte, and the two finally kiss, embrace again, and separate, at which moment we hear the Jesus and Mary Chain's "Just Like Honey."[50] The song plays out and clearly acts as a melodramatic substitute for what Bob may have said and/or may be thinking. The hazy, overdriven guitars and reverb-laden drums of "Just Like Honey" support the lyrics of "Walking back to you / Is the hardest thing that I can do / That I can do for you / For you." Instead of knowing what Bob said to Charlotte, the audience is left wondering if the song provides the resolution so many seek. In fact, what we witness is the beginning of some sort of relationship, the nature of which we are given no adequate understanding.

Figure 2.3: *Lost in Translation*: Bob Harris performs karaoke to "More than This" as Charlotte looks on.

The Jesus and Mary Chain and other idiosyncratic musical choices is part of a style that places Coppola's work in an unaffiliated, independent movement of American auteurs that include the likes of Wes Anderson, Todd Solondz, David O. Russel, Whit Stillman, and Coppola's former husband Spike Jonze. Claire Perkins writing in *The Velvet Light Trap* argues that what stylistically unites these directors is that they all

> are highly conscious of the way they are positioned as auteurs by those processes that force them to reveal the signatures that, for their European predecessors and their processes of sequelization, have to be deciphered. In these contemporary works, the repetition of characters, actors, themes, and settings is less about the establishment of a signature and more about the narration of that signature. In an approach that often seems more playful than deterministic, authorial remaking becomes a subject as well as a function. In some cases, this is made critically explicit through discussions of the trilogy form itself; in others, this discourse on repetition is left to resonate as a more oblique example of remaking.[51]

As if to repeat and stretch the limits of the melodramatic moment, Coppola's third feature *Marie Antoinette* studiously avoids any chance of being considered "historically accurate." This includes, most notoriously, the soundtrack. Writing for *Variety*, Todd McCarthy notes that, "[t]o her credit, Coppola makes it surprisingly easy to swallow her conceit of laying out momentous history against a backdrop of contempo tunes, largely by not dealing with the history at all."[52] Although these comments may seem a tad excessive, Coppola's intention to eschew history for attitude is directly related to a number of her aesthetic choices, in particular the soundtrack:

> "We started as we always start," explains Brian Reitzell. "She asked me for some music to help her write the script. I struggled with it at first and then put together for her a compilation that included music by the Cure, Aphex Twin and Bow Wow Wow." The Cure and Marie Antoinette? "It seemed kind of natural to us," continues Reitzell. "The whole stage between Punk and the New Romantics seemed to fit what we were doing. Our choices reflected the energy and created an atmosphere. The movie," he explains, "has an arc: innocence, decadence and maturity. I also had to study opera and 18th-century music. I needed three opera arias and I couldn't believe it when I found a very sad aria by Jean-Philippe Rameau. It sounded as though you would really dig this if you were a Bjork fan."[53]

The emphasis on mood and atmosphere over archival accuracy is the kind of peculiar choice befitting any auteur, particularly one who is obsessed with the powers of style. However, the criticism that *Marie Antoinette* pays too much attention to style at the expense of history has been a common one regarding this film. Writing in *The Guardian*, Agnès Poirier is particularly to the point:

> The film is shocking because it is empty, devoid of a point of view, because the person
> who has made it has no curiosity for the woman she is portraying and the time that
> her tragic life is set in. The film director seems as unconcerned by her subject as Marie
> Antoinette was indifferent to the plight of her people and the world she lived in.[54]

Far less cutting, Craig McLean celebrates the soundtrack over the film claiming that "[it] is a brilliant two-CD set, with punk and post-punk classics nestling next to modern, classical-style pieces by Aphex Twin and Squarepusher. In fact, it's more satisfying than the style-over-substance film."[55] In her review of Francis Ford Coppola's *Tetro*, Karina Longworth compares *Marie Antoinette* to her father's film because both "films are so drunk on the melding of disparate cultural references that they read as dewy confessions from the filmmaker, feature-length love letters to their own aesthetics, the specific things they personally think are beautiful."[56] For Coppola, these aesthetic priorities are not simply a question of excess for excess's sake, but are part of a directorial mission to create "believable emotions." *Marie Antoinette*'s focus on style, according to Pam Cook, is part of a "spirit of fashion as creative reinvention, performance and personal style statement [that] informs Coppola's movie, where costume and set design are used in various ways: to capture the essence of the period, to suggest mood, to reinforce and comment on character, to project the state of mind of its heroine, and to visualise the director's concerns." For Cook, "although we witness Marie Antoinette's progress towards maturity, we are not invited to decide whether she is good or bad. Rather, we are encouraged to respond on an *emotional level* to her situation."[57] In this manner, Coppola's selection of Versailles as a location and her emphasis on period dress are less a nod to history than an embrace of style in the attempt to create a particular "visceral effect on the viewer." Anna Rogers explains:

> Through the use of a modern soundtrack, an interpretive approach to costume and
> a strikingly modern vernacular spoken in a variety of accents, Coppola unites what
> Deleuze would term "the sheets of the past" and "the peaks of the present." When time
> is no longer shown through movement and plot resolution, the true character of time is
> revealed: as that which disrupts the traditional concepts of truth and exposes the body
> as, to use Heidegger's term, a "being-towards-death."[58]

Although less theoretically informed, Coppola similarly notes that while "*Marie Antoinette* is not a documentary or a history lesson, I wanted [the film] to be impressionistic and be as close to what it might have felt like to be there at the time."[59] Throughout the film, Coppola's deep investment in style stands out in strong relief against Marie Antoinette's well-known biography. It is in this context that we are given the opening shots of Marie Antoinette beginning with a title in pink, punk-style graphics that is accompanied by the Gang of Four's "Natural's Not In It." The second shot is a lengthy two shot of Antoinette (Kirsten Dunst) on a baby-blue divan with embroidered floral patterns; she is receiving a pedicure from a servant while surrounded by numerous large pink cakes (figure 2.4). As the jagged, staccato rhythms of the song play and the group sings "The problem with pleasure, what to do with leisure," Antoinette stares into the camera, breaking the proverbial fourth wall as if to acknowledge the artifice of the frame in neo-French New Wave fashion. The length of the shot, 15 seconds, combined with the excessive style and accoutrements, invite the audience to luxuriate in the knowing excess of Coppola's *Marie Antoinette*. However, by scoring the scene to the non-diegetic sounds of post-punk's most famous neo-Marxist rock group, this distinctly removed-from-narrative exposure of the excessive material attention that is paid to the Dauphine receives a kind of "cool" dialectical critique, a critique that not only summarizes the many contradictions that populate the film, but also the form that the rest of the film will take.

The collision of "authenticity against inventive remixing" reoccurs time and again throughout the soundtrack. Although "Opus 17" by Dustin O'Halloran is a work of solo piano that feels appropriate to both the period and the melancholic sadness that accompany Marie Antoinette's literal stripping of Austrian significance upon her stepping over to French soil, it is not a period composition. And although classical repertoire was recorded for

Figure 2.4: *Marie Antoinette*: The Dauphine is surrounded by excessive sweets and service as Gang of Four sings "The problem with pleasure, what to do for leisure."

the film, according to Brian Reitzell, it was recorded in a castle, rather than a studio, because "it was important that the sound be right" for the atmosphere of the film.[60] It is this approach to composing a "mood" that allows a remix of Bow Wow Wow's most popular song, their 1982 remake of "I Want Candy," to be used in *Antoinette* as a three-minute music-video-style montage at the 55th minute of the film.[61] Images of silks, wigs, shoes, pug dogs, cakes, and strawberries are positioned against the group's joyful rhythms and Annabella Lwin's teen vocalization of desire as a sort of wry, yet playful thesis that these indulgences stem from the Dauphine's then-lack of wedded consummation that has allowed her adolescent state to persist. As if to reinforce this point, throughout the following scene, we witness Antoinette's decision to go to a masked ball in Paris without her customary formal reception. Upon arrival, we are treated to the melody of "Hong Kong Garden" as played by the courtly instrumentation of strings and harpsichord that will eventually lead to a remix of Siouxsie and the Banshees' version of the song, during which we see multiple couples dance energetically in a round.[62] At the end of the song, "Aphrodisiac" by Bow Wow Wow commences as if in the moment of play the sexual has arisen.[63] This liminal moment of transition from playful flirtation to an erotic engagement with Count Axel von Fersen (Jamie Dornan) from Sweden is marked by music in much the same manner that Lux Lisbon uses the prom as a ritual moment for a night with her paramour.

The masked ball scene and other dances, parties, and the like in Coppola's films have the resonance of John Hughes's depiction of school dances where adolescent youth commingle, beauties flirt, and the socially awkward flounder. Indeed, these ritual dances make the use of relatively contemporary music even more crucial. As Coppola explains in the case of *Marie Antoinette*, "[these choices] came from wanting to show the emotion of the scene as close as I could. I felt like when she goes into a masked ball for the *first time* there would be a feeling of excitement and sort of pick a song that gave that feeling as opposed to . . . I don't think a quartet of that time would give it the same rush. So it was all meant to give the impression."[64] And this is the essence of Coppola's cinema so far: the value that the momentary impression of transition is one that can only be conveyed through a sense of distinct intensities, a feeling that reality has superseded itself, so that the film can become that much more effective at conveying a character's desire and psyche than any pronounced narrative goal he or she may have. Writing about Vincente Minnelli, Thomas Elsaesser once noted that

> what seems to me essential to all of Minnelli's films is the fact that his characters are only superficially concerned with a quest, a desire to get somewhere in life, i.e., with any of the forms by which this dynamism rationalizes or sublimates itself. What we

have instead, just beneath the surface of the plots, is the working of energy itself, as the ever-changing, fascinating movement of a basic impulse in its encounter with, or victory over, a given reality.[65]

And while Coppola's films may never approach the excess of a Minnelli or Sidney musical, Coppola and Reitzell are working with a similar impulse, however understated it may be.

NOTES

1. Ella Taylor, "I Don't Like Being Told What to Do," *Guardian*, October 13, 2003, http://www.guardian.co.uk/world/2003/oct/13/gender.uk.
2. Liz Armstrong, "The Haves: Of jet-setters and 18th-century teenage queens," *Chicago Reader*, October 26, 2006, http://www.chicagoreader.com/chicago/the-haves/Content?oid=923459.
3. Mark Olsen, "The Virgin Suicides," *Sight and Sound*, June 2000, http://www.bfi.org.uk/sightandsound/review/573; Olsen, "Interview: Sofia Coppola Cool and the Gang," *Sight and Sound*, January 15, 2004, http://vnweb.hwwilsonweb.com/hww/results/results_single_fulltext.jhtml;hwwilsonid=NRPLOLMFRVDIHQA3DIMCFF4ADUNGIIV0.
4. Elvis Mitchell, "Film Review; an American in Japan, Making a Connection," *New York Times*, September 12, 2003, http://www.nytimes.com/2003/09/12/movies/film-review-an-american-in-japan-making-a-connection.html?pagewanted=all&src=pm.
5. J. Hoberman, "French Confection; Sofia Coppola pays opulent tribute to the innocent boredom of a teen queen," *Village Voice*, October 3, 2006, http://www.villagevoice.com/2006-10-03/film/french-confection/; Stuart Klawans, "The Queen is Dead," *The Nation*, November 6, 2006, http://www.thenation.com/doc/20061106/klawans/single.
6. Anna Rogers, "Sofia Coppola," *Senses of Cinema*, http://archive.sensesofcinema.com/contents/directors/07/sofia-coppola.html.
7. Pam Cook, "Portrait of a lady: Sofia Coppola," *Sight and Sound*, November 2006, 36.
8. Jeff Smith, "Taking Music Supervisors Seriously," in *Cinesonic: Experiencing the Soundtrack*, ed. Philip Brophy (North Ryde NSW, AU: Southwest Press, 2001), 127.
9. Melinda Newman, "Independent thinking key to smaller scores," *Hollywood Reporter*, November 1, 2007, http://www.hollywoodreporter.com/news/independent-thinking-key-smaller-scores-153961.
10. Anon., *Lost in Translation*, Focus Features (cited April 2, 2010). Available at http://www.lost-in-translation.com/qaPopup.html.
11. Susan McClary, *Feminine Endings: Music, Gender, and Sexuality* (Minneapolis: University of Minnesota Press, 1991), 21.
12. Lucas Reiner, *The Spirit of '76* (film, 1990).
13. Cook, "Portrait of a lady," 36.
14. Olsen, "The Virgin Suicides," http://www.bfi.org.uk/sightandsound/review/573.
15. Thomas Elsaesser, "Tales of Sound and Fury: Observations on the Family Melodrama," in *Home Is Where the Heart Is: Studies in Melodrama and the Woman's Film*, ed. Christine Gledhill (London: BFI, 1987), 50.
16. Elsaesser, "Tales of Sound and Fury," 50.
17. Peter Brooks, *The Melodramatic Imagination: Balzac, Henry James, Melodrama, and the Mode of Excess* (New Haven, CT: Yale University Press, 1976), 1.
18. Dennis Giles, "Show-Making," in *Genre: The Musical*, ed. Rick Altman (Boston: Routledge & Kegan Paul, 1981), 87.
19. Roland Barthes, *The Eiffel Tower and Other Mythologies* (New York: Noonday, 1979), 123.

20. Brooks, *The Melodramatic Imagination*, 3, 4, 9.
21. Tania Modleski, "Time and Desire in the Woman's Film," in *Home Is Where the Heart Is: Studies in Melodrama and the Woman's Film*, ed. Christine Gledhill (London: BFI, 1987), 330.
22. Max Ophuls, *Letter from an Unknown Woman* (film, 1948).
23. Modleski, "Time and Desire in the Woman's Film," 330.
24. Ibid., 331.
25. Ibid., 336.
26. Rogers, "Sofia Coppola," http://archive.sensesofcinema.com/contents/directors/07/sofia-coppola.html.
27. The Amps, *Pacer*, Elektra Records, 1995.
28. Simon Frith and Angela McRobbie, "Rock and Sexuality," in *On Record: Rock, Pop, and the Written Word*, eds. Frith and Andrew Goodwin (London: Routledge, 1990), 371.
29. Frith and McRobbie, "Rock and Sexuality," 373–374.
30. Mavis Bayton, "How Women Become Musicians," in *On Record: Rock, Pop, and the Written Word*, eds. Simon Frith and Andrew Goodwin (London: Routledge, 1988); Bayton, "Women and the Electric Guitar," in *Sexing the Groove: Popular Music and Gender*, ed. Sheila Whitely (London: Routledge, 1997), 37–49.
31. Norma Coates, "(R)Evolution Now?: Rock and the Political Potential of Gender," in *Sexing the Groove: Popular Music and Gender*, ed. Sheila Whitely (London: Routledge, 1997), 58.
32. The Go Gos, *Beauty and the Beat*, IRS Records, 1981.
33. Free Kitten, *Sentimental Education*, Kill Rock Stars, 1997.
34. Rogers, "Sofia Coppola," http://archive.sensesofcinema.com/contents/directors/07/sofia-coppola.html.
35. Todd Gilchrist, "Interview: Sofia Coppola, the *Marie Antoinette* Director Talks About Making a Post-Modern Period Piece," *IGN.COM*, 2006, http://movies.ign.com/articles/739/739308p1.html.
36. Scott Tobias, "Interview: Sofia Coppola, Virgin Territory," *Onion*, May 3, 2000, http://www.avclub.com/articles/sofia-coppola,13656/.
37. Todd Rundgren, *Todd*, Bearsville Records, 1974; the Hollies, "The Air That I Breathe," Epic Records, 1974.
38. The Electric Light Orchestra, *Face the Music*, Jet Records, 1975; 10cc, *The Original Soundtrack*, Mercury Records, 1975; Styx, *The Grand Illusion*, A&M Records, 1977.
39. Tim Anderson, "As If History Was Merely a Record: The Pathology of Nostalgia and the Figure of the Recording in Contemporary Popular Cinema," *Music, Sound, and the Moving Image* 2, no. 1 (2008), 57.
40. Todd Rundgren, *Something/Anything*, Bearsville Records, 1974; Gilbert O'Sullivan, *Alone Again (Naturally)*, MAM Records, 1972; Bee Gees, *To Whom It May Concern*, Polydor Records, 1972; Carole King, *Tapestry*, Columbia Records, 1971.
41. Anderson, "As If History Was Merely a Record," 59–60.
42. Jessica Winter, "Sofia Coppola's Mystery Girls: Dreamlife of Angels," *Village Voice*, April 18, 2000, http://www.villagevoice.com/2000-04-18/film/sofia-coppola-s-mystery-girls.
43. Craig McLean, "Low-Key Queen of Her Own High Court," *Sunday Independent* (Ireland), October 29, 2006, http://www.independent.ie/entertainment/film-cinema/lowkey-queen-of-her-own-high-court-136302.html.
44. Anon., "Kevin's Bloody Great!: Sofia Coppola raves about the cult star's BAFTA-nominated contribution to the soundtrack…," *New Musical Express*, January 20, 2004, http://www.nme.com/news/my-bloody-valentine/15950.
45. Bob Gourley, "Brian Reitzell," *Chaos Control Digizine*, 2009, http://www.chaoscontrol.com/?article=brianreitzell.

46. Art Garfunkle and Paul Simon, *Parsley, Sage, Rosemary, and Thyme*, Columbia Records, 1968; Ray Henderson and Les Brown, "The Thrill Is Gone," 1931; Nacio Herb Brown and Gus Kahn, "You Stepped out of a Dream," 1940; David Nichtern, "Midnight at the Oasis," 1974.
47. The Chemical Brothers, *Come with Us*, Astralwerks Records, 2002.
48. Phoenix, *United*, Astralwerks Records, 2000.
49. The Pretenders, *Pretenders*, Sire Records, 1980; Elvis Costello and the Attractions, *Armed Forces*, Columbia Records, 1979; Roxy Music, *Avalon*, Warner Bros. Records, 1982.
50. The Jesus and Mary Chain, *Psychocandy*, Blanco y Negro Records, 1985.
51. Claire Perkins, "Remaking and the Film Trilogy: Whit Stillman's Authorial Triptych," *Velvet Light Trap*, no. 61 (Spring 2008), 20.
52. Todd McCarthy, "Sofia's Choice Is a Modernist 'Marie.'" *Variety*, May 29, 2006, 31.
53. Allegra Donn, "Sofia's World," *Times Magazine*, October 7, 2006, 30.
54. Agnes Poirier, "An Empty Hall of Mirrors: Sofia Coppola's Latest Film Is a Disgrace and Betrays the Disturbing Trend of Art as Marketing," *Guardian*, May 26, 2006, http://www. guardian.co.uk/commentisfree/2006/may/27/comment.filmnews.
55. Craig McLean, "Pop," *Daily Telegraph*, October 28, 2006, 7.
56. Karina Longworth, "Tetro Review," *SPOUTblog*, 2009. http://blog.spout. com/2009/06/08/tetro-review/.
57. Cook, "Portrait of a Lady," 39; emphasis added.
58. Rogers, "Sofia Coppola," http://archive.sensesofcinema.com/contents/directors/07/ sofia-coppola.html.
59. Gilchrist, "Interview: Sofia Coppola," http://movies.ign.com/articles/739/739308p1. html.
60. Donn, "Sofia's World," 30.
61. Bow Wow Wow, *The Last of the Mohicans*, RCA Records, 1982.
62. Siouxsie and the Banshees, *Once Upon a Time: The Singles*, Geffen/Warner Bros. Records, 1981.
63. Bow Wow Wow, *When the Going Gets Tough, the Tough Get Going*, RCA Records, 1983.
64. Gilchrist, "Interview: Sofia Coppola," http://movies.ign.com/articles/739/739308p1. html.; emphasis added.
65. Thomas Elsaesser, "Vincente Minelli," in *Genre: The Musical*, ed. Rick Altman (Boston: Routledge & Kegan Paul, 1981), 15.

PART TWO

Music and the Image

CHAPTER 3

A Musical Tour of the Bizarre: Popular Music as Fantasy in David Lynch

GENE WILLET

Half the film is picture, the other half is sound. They've got to work together... each piece that ends up in the film supports the scene and makes the whole greater than the sum of the parts.

David Lynch[1]

Lately I feel films are more and more like music.... Music deals with abstractions and, like film, it involves time. It has many different movements, it has much contrast. And through music you learn that, in order to get a particular beautiful feeling, you have to have started far back, arranging certain things in a certain way. You can't just cut to it.

David Lynch[2]

ISSUES OF MUSIC IN THE FILMS OF DAVID LYNCH

Those who see a David Lynch film are almost sure to become transfixed by an image they "cannot get over," as Michel Chion puts it.[3] Viewers are disturbed by his extreme representations, such as the vomiting sculptured faces in *Six Men Getting Sick* (1967)[4]; the grotesque, non-human infant of Henry and his girlfriend in *Eraserhead* (1977); the repulsive, disfigured body of John Merrick in *The Elephant Man* (1980); the sadistic rape of Dorothy by Frank Booth in *Blue Velvet* (1986); and the plastic-wrapped, decomposing body of Laura Palmer in the television series *Twin Peaks* (1990–1991). Not only do such images stretch the limits of interpretation or even go so far as to defy meaning, Lynch's habitual distortion of time, inversion of characters, and complex, nonlinear narrative structures in films like *Lost Highway* (1997), *Mulholland Drive* (2001), and *Inland Empire* (2006) challenge the viewer's ability to follow the plot.

Adding to the confusion is Lynch's refusal to explain his films. When once asked what *Wild at Heart* (1990) was about, Lynch responded, "Well, it's about one hour and [45] minutes."[5] Such rebuffs of explanation have left the door wide open for audiences to propose their own interpretations leading to a variety of contrasting—and even contradictory—readings including postmodern, New Age, conservative, feminist, transcendentalist, psychoanalytical, and post-postmodern.[6] While these readings may differ significantly in their analysis of Lynch's films, they all treat Lynch as an auteur who has something important to say. In particular, Lynch's very ambiguity seems to endow his works with a unique, distinct, and even revelatory perspective on ourselves and the world in which we live, even if that perspective is "weird," "impossible," "strange," "perverse," "nightmarish," or "ridiculous"—to name just a few of the critical responses.[7]

Although these films have been explored from numerous angles, scholars have paid limited attention to Lynch's use of music. This neglect is surprising given Lynch's emphasis on sound and music in the quotes at the beginning of this chapter. Typical discussions of Lynch's use of music point out how it supports the image (delegating music to its usual, secondary role of support), how Lynch's collaboration with composers and sound designers is uncommon in the Hollywood system, or reveal where Lynch got the idea to use a particular piece of music. Such discussions provide important basic information but offer little insight into what work music does in his films.[8] Given the place of music in Lynch's movies, turning an ear toward that music can only help us better understand the workings of his cinematic imagination.

POPULAR MUSIC AS FANTASY

According to Michel Chion, there is nothing more common than an auteur who creates films, but films that create an auteur are rather rare. Such is the case, Chion argues, with Lynch.[9] An auteur is a film director whose films are so distinctive that he or she is perceived as the "author" not only of a particular film, but of a visual style and thematic fixation that runs consistently across a body of work. The very fact that one can refer to a Lynchian style testifies to the fact that Lynch is an auteur, even if that style has yet to be clearly defined. This chapter argues that a significant characteristic of the Lynchian style is his use of popular music to create dreamlike fantasy worlds that function differently than fantasy typically does in film. Specifically, I examine music's relationship to Lacanian fantasy in three of Lynch's films: *Blue Velvet* (1986), *Lost Highway* (1996), and *Mulholland*

Drive (2001). These movies, a sample of Lynch's work from the last three decades, allow us to track his constant employment and development of this particular stylistic device.

The connection of music and fantasy is nothing new to film; the Hollywood musical has always relied on song to help construct an idealized world where characters stage the realization of their desires: Orphans sing about a better "Tomorrow," a day filled with sun and hope; a young girl dreams of a world "Somewhere Over the Rainbow" where all her dreams will come true; and who among us hasn't dreamed of a "White Christmas" with family and friends? But music and fantasy have worked together to construct fantasy worlds in nonmusical films too, and even in the early days of film. For example, Merian Cooper and Ernest Schoedsack's *King Kong* (1933) incorporated relatively little music for the first part of the film and its representation of the cold, drab reality of depression-era New York City; but the soundtrack explodes during the more fantastical part of the film featuring the great Kong. And Michael Curtiz uses music in *Casablanca* (1942) to represent the nostalgic dream of an idealized past where a lover can embrace his love and "a kiss" is still "just a kiss." If such tyings of music to fantasy are nothing new to film, Lynch is new in the *type* of fantasy worlds he creates with the help of music.

Fantasy in the cinematic sense is usually characterized as a type of constructed dream world where the poor peasant becomes rich, the rich celebrity returns to being an average Joe, the shy boy gains the affection of the unapproachable girl, or the unnoticed girl catches the eye of her Prince Charming. In other words, the fantasy world is usually portrayed as one where we can experience the fulfillment and satisfaction of our deepest desires, and the use of music in film as a cue for this type of fantasy is nothing new. The Lynchian relationship between the aural and the imaginary differs, however, in that this filmmaker uses music to generate visions representing fantasies in the more specific, psychoanalytical sense. In psychoanalysis—specifically, in the field of Lacanian psychoanalysis—the primary function of fantasy is to protect us from reality by literally helping to construct our "sense of reality." In doing so, fantasy functions not to stage our desires as fulfilled, but rather to create desire itself. Lynch's *Lost Highway* provides an excellent example of this type of fantasy and shows more particularly how he uses popular music to create an idiosyncratic, distinctly Lynchian fantasy world.

LOST HIGHWAY

Lost Highway is one of the most bizarre and confusing of Lynch's films. It is hardly surprising then that it was one of the least successful, both critically and financially.[10] One reason for the confusion is a split in the film's plot: About a third of the way through the movie, most of the characters disappear and new characters are introduced, even though we seem to be following the same story. *Lost Highway* has been the subject of a variety of readings; however, few have engaged the soundtrack beyond a basic description of how Lynch's blurring of sound effects and music affects the images. Lynch himself has commented that he treats music as just "another sound effect" and loves to "push the pressure" in a scene by sending a lot of stuff to the subwoofer.[11] Greg Hainge comments on Lynch's manner of using soundscapes to intensify the specular spaces in *Lost Highway*, spaces characterized by "frequent use of extremely low lighting or absolute blackness" and impressions that "the image coming from the projector is absorbed by the screen rather than being reflected back to the audience."[12] Beyond such comments, discussions of the film's scoring usually focus on Lynch's specific musical and musical-cinematic influences.

Lost Highway opens with jazz saxophonist Fred Madison (Bill Pullman) sitting on his bed smoking a cigarette. The intercom buzzes, and when he answers he hears someone utter the mystifying, non-sequitur phrase "Dick Laurent is dead." Fred's wife is the brunette Renee (Patricia Arquette), beautiful but cold and unfaithful. Fred and Renee have several problems including an anemic sexual relationship, mysterious videotapes that keep showing up on their doorstep, and a pale-faced Mystery Man (Robert Blake), who seems to be following Fred. Fred eventually kills Renee and is sent to prison, where he suddenly transforms into a different person, a young mechanic named Pete Dayton (Balthazar Getty).

Because Pete is obviously not Fred, he is released from prison, and we see him resume his life as a mechanic at Arty's Garage. It is here that Pete meets a mobster-like character named Mr. Eddy (a.k.a. Dick Laurent, played by Robert Loggia) and his blonde mistress Alice (also played by Patricia Arquette). Pete and Alice start an affair behind Mr. Eddy's back and eventually rob and kill a porn king named Andy to get money that will allow them to escape. Pete and Alice drive to a desert cabin where they make passionate love; when Pete pleads "I want you, Alice," she whispers, "You'll never have me!" and disappears into the darkness. At this moment, Pete transforms back into Fred, who kidnaps and murders Mr. Eddy. Fred returns to the city and delivers the message "Dick Laurent is dead" on the intercom at his own house, and drives back into the desert with the police in hot pursuit.

If this synopsis is confusing, it is because the film itself is confusing; it is nearly impossible to describe a linear narrative. Slavoj Žižek claims, however, that the opposition between the two couples is the key to the film's plot: First, there is the "normal" couple, the impotent Fred and his reserved wife Renee. After Fred kills Renee, or fantasizes about killing her, we are transported into the second part of the film with the younger, virile Pete who is coupled with the sexually aggressive Alice, with Mr. Eddy added as an obstacle to the couple's happiness. According to Žižek, this intervention demonstrates how Lacanian fantasy functions to protect its subjects from reality. In *Lost Highway*, the relationship of Fred and Renee is doomed for internal reasons—Fred is unable to satisfy his wife let alone determine what it is she desires—while the second relationship is doomed for external reasons—Pete and Alice cannot be together because of Mr. Eddy.[13] This creation of an external obstacle to hide an internal impossibility allows the subject to believe that enjoyment would be possible, were it not for the obstacle—and he is thereby saved from confronting his own impotence. According to Žižek, then, the two parts of the film represent the opposition of reality and fantasy. Through the staging of this opposition, Lynch tears apart our "normal sense of reality" where reality and fantasy work together in vertical fashion, with fantasy always supporting and constructing reality. In doing so, he leaves us in a situation where unprotected reality and pure fantasy are separated from each other, laid out in a horizontal relation.[14]

The separation of fantasy from reality, probably not something the average moviegoer would recognize, could explain why audiences dismissed the film. But one does not need to rely on Žižek's psychoanalytical approach to arrive at such conclusions, for Lynch left important clues in the film's soundtrack. Sound and music are so important for understanding *Lost Highway* that it is rumored Lynch snuck back to the projection booth during the premiere and had the projectionist turn up the sound so every little aural detail could be heard, with some scenes even overpowered by the music.

The first sound clue is found in the opposition between Fred and Pete. Pete is exactly the opposite of Fred: Fred is older, impotent, and unable to satisfy his wife, whereas Pete is young, virile, and has women throwing themselves at him. Yet, an examination of the soundtrack suggests that Fred and Pete are the same. Fred has an excellent ear, a fact that becomes apparent during the scene of him virtuosically playing in the high altissimo register of the saxophone. One of the detectives even acknowledges Fred's good ear by stating that he himself could never learn the guitar because he was tone-deaf. Likewise, Pete's ear is so good that he is able to tune Mr. Eddy's Mercedes simply by listening to the engine; and, like the detective, Mr. Eddy confirms Pete's good ear by remarking that Pete has the "best goddamn ears in town."[15] Therefore, both Fred and Pete share the same gift and, even though they are opposite in most ways, the soundtrack suggests that they are in fact the same person. If Fred and Pete are the same person, then Pete is an opposite, dreamlike, or fantasy representation of Fred. In other words, Pete is Fred as Fred sees (or wishes to see) himself, and the split in the film corresponds to the split between the reality of Fred's situation and the fantasy that protects him.

The soundtrack for *Lost Highway* provides a second important clue in that it can be separated into two categories: music represented by actual songs and musical sound effects consisting of various instrumental sounds (i.e., low, almost inaudible pedal tones; ascending string glissandos; short atonal motifs; and various percussive noises). The first half of the film is, with the exception of a few instances of music that are discussed below, completely devoid of music. In fact, in this part of the film, the soundtrack consists primarily of dialogue that is broken occasionally by musical sound effects. These are most conspicuous in those instances where Fred would normally call upon fantasy to act as a defense: the playing of each of the three videotapes, the failed attempt at sex with Renee, and the meeting with the Mystery Man. Musical sound effects, then, are closely tied to these uneasy moments when Fred is confronted with his own impotence, the moments when fantasy is missing. Actual music, on the other hand, is present almost exclusively throughout the second half of the film and most obviously in those instances that are the most fantasmatic. For example, Antônio Carlos Jobim's "Insensatez" plays when we get our first good look at Pete who is relaxing in the backyard complete with swimming pool and white picket fence (see figure 3.1). Lou Reed's version of "This Magic Moment" plays when Pete first sees Alice, and Mr. Eddie, the fantasized external obstacle to Pete and Alice's relationship, has his own cool jazzy themes that accelerate when he gets irritated and slow when he regains his cool. We hear the aggressive "Heirate Mich" and "Rammstein" by the German "dance-metal" band Rammstein when Pete and Alice arrive at Andy's house—the ultimate place of fantasy. Thus, by mapping the presence of musical effects and music onto the Fred-as-real and Pete-as-fantasy dichotomy, we are able to arrive at the same psychoanalytical reading as Žižek, where the film is seen as a split between reality and fantasy (see table 3.1 for the occurrences and timings of music in *Lost Highway*).

Figure 3.1: *Lost Highway*: Pete relaxes in the backyard ("Insensatez").

Table 3.1 MUSIC TIMINGS, MUSIC CUES, AND PLOT EVENTS FOR *LOST HIGHWAY*.

Time	Music	Scene
0:00–2:30	"I'm Deranged" by David Bowie	Opening credits.
6:38–7:26	"Red Bats with Teeth" by Angelo Badalamenti	Fred playing the saxophone at the Luna Lounge.
14:52–15:19	"Song to the Siren" by This Mortal Coil	Fred and Renee attempt sex.
27:04–28:50 and again at 31:20–32:52	"Something Wicked This Way Comes" by Barry Adamson	Fred and Renee at Andy's house. Music stops when Mystery Man enters, begins again when he leaves.
48:13–48:48	"Song to the Siren" by This Mortal Coil	Fred begins to turn into Pete.
50:18	Film splits, Fred turns into Pete.	
54:56–56:50	"Insensatez" by Antônio Carlos Jobim	Pete in the backyard.
57:47–58:40	"Eye" by The Smashing Pumpkins	Pete dancing with Sheila.
1:00:02–1:07:44	"Mr. Eddy's Theme 1" and "Mr. Eddy's Theme 2" by Barry Adamson	Mr. Eddy takes Pete for a ride.
1:08:16–1:11:33	"Dub Driving" by Angelo Badalamenti	Pete and Sheila make love.
1:11:33–1:11:59	"Red Bats with Teeth"	Pete changes radio in the garage.
1:13:22–1:14:48	"This Magic Moment" by Lou Reed	Pete sees Alice for the first time.
1:14:48–1:21:00	"Hollywood Sunset" by Angelo Badalamenti	Alice picks up Pete after work; they make love at several hotels.
1:20:03–1:24:07	"Apple of Sodom" by Marilyn Manson	Pete rushes to have sex with Sheila.
1:31:32–1:34:03	"I Put a Spell on You" by Marilyn Manson.	Alice is forced to perform for Mr. Eddy.
1:42:03–1:42:33	"Heirate Mich" by Rammstein	Pete enters Andy's house.
1:46:27–1:47:26	"Rammstein" by Rammstein	Pete after Andy is killed.
1:52:59–1:55:23	"Song to the Siren" by This Mortal Coil	Pete and Alice make love.
2:01:09–2:02:20	"Rammstein"	Fred kidnaps Mr. Eddy.
2:04:09–2:04:57	"Heirate Mich"	Fred kills Mr. Eddy.
2:08:17–2:09:34	"Driver Down" by Trent Reznor	Police chase Fred into the desert.
2:09:46–2:13:30	"I'm Deranged" by David Bowie	End credits.

Once one accepts the split in the film as the opposition between reality and fantasy, we can fine- tune, through an investigation of the soundtrack, our reading of several instances where reality and fantasy try to work together (as they normally would) but are pulled apart by Lynch. The first takes place at a jazz club where Fred improvises a saxophone solo against a steady groove played by a small jazz ensemble (Badalamenti's "Red Bats with Teeth," see figure 3.2). The solo starts out as a kind of modern jazz solo, and it is here that we see Fred fantasizing about Renee leaving the club with another man (Andy).[16] As Fred fantasizes, he quickly shifts to the highest altissimo register of the saxophone, and the music becomes so disjointed—tonally blurred and out of tempo—that the ensemble stops

Figure 3.2: *Lost Highway:* Fred plays "Red Bats with Teeth" at the Luna Lounge.

playing. But Fred, seemingly oblivious to the fact that he is playing alone, continues to squawk out an intense solo. In this scene, music (fantasy) is seemingly trying to break through, but Fred literally destroys the music, turning it into a kind of sound effect, returning the scene back to the world of reality. This reading of the scene is strengthened when, later in the fantasy half of the film, Pete hears the same squawking saxophone from "Red Bats with Teeth" being played on the radio in the garage where he works. He slowly gets up, goes over to the radio, and changes the station to softer music after exclaiming that he "just didn't like it." With this, Pete (from the fantasy world) effectively chooses the protection of fantasy over lived reality, and it is at precisely this moment that Alice appears.

These are not the only instances when one of the two worlds tries to invade the other. Pete's fantasy world begins to fall apart when Alice calls to inform him that they cannot meet because Mr. Eddy is getting suspicious. At that moment, we get the typical Lynchian glimpses of a spider crawling up a wall and moths dying in a light fixture. The sound accompanying this scene is dominated by musical sound effects and, once again, it is Pete who effectively holds back reality by rushing out and having sex with his old girlfriend Sheila. Once he does, the musical sound effects are replaced by Marilyn Manson's "Apple of Sodom," and the fantasy world is restored.

Another instance of music in the reality world occurs when Fred and Renee attempt sex. We begin to hear This Mortal Coil's "Song to the Siren," but the song is cut off and replaced by musical sound effects when Fred is unable to perform sexually. This use of "Song to the Siren" at the film's splitting point, to start the transformation from Fred in the reality world to Pete in the fantasy world, confirms that the song is tied to fantasy.

The final instance of actual music in the reality world occurs when Fred and Renee attend a party at Andy's house. Here, Barry Adamson's "Something Wicked This Way Comes" is heard playing diegetically at the social gathering, suggesting that the scene is tied to fantasy. As Andy's house represents the furthest extent of fantasy in the second part of the film, it is understandable that the presence of music here should foreshadow the fantasy world. Moreover, the music stops at the precise moment when the Mystery Man confronts Fred; at that point, the music is replaced by musical effects, and picks up again only when the Mystery Man leaves Andy's house.

Lost Highway, then, provides a perfect example of how Lynch aligns his films more with a psychoanalytical notion of fantasy than with a conventionally cinematic one. In *Lost Highway*, we see fantasy functioning to protect the Fred/Pete character by providing an external excuse for the failure of the relationship; the relationship would be possible if it were not for Mr. Eddy, and Fred is thus saved from confronting his own impotence. We also see how fantasy functions not to fulfill desire, but rather to produce it, to stage desire as something unsatisfied rather than fulfilled. Pete, for example, is unable to satisfy Alice even though he is the idealized version of Fred: Mr. Eddy is in the way; Alice always wants more and, just before she disappears, tells Pete that he will never have her. In other words, this fantasy world is not the kind of perfect world where Pete and Alice can run off together and live happily ever after; it is a world that stages Alice as unattainable and reproduces desire rather satisfying it.

Lost Highway demonstrates music's fundamental role in the construction of Lynchian fantasy. This filmmaker uses popular music not simply as a cue for fantasy; he makes music function as a screen upon which fantasy itself is projected. Additionally, Lynch's use of popular music and musical sound effects to separate reality and fantasy creates an unmediated experience of each. Unprotected reality and pure fantasy are extremes that most viewers find discomfiting, yet they are major components of the Lynchian style. His combination of popular music and fantasy makes up one of his most identifiable, fundamental characteristics, and although this aspect of his style is most clearly demonstrated in *Lost Highway*, it is a relationship that he experiments with in nearly all of his films. This characteristic of the Lynchian style makes its first notable appearance in *Blue Velvet*.

BLUE VELVET

Lynch's *Blue Velvet* takes place in the ostensible utopia of Lumberton, USA. The film tells the story of Jeffery Beaumont (Kyle MacLachlan), a young student who arrives home from college to visit his father, who is in the hospital after suffering a severe stroke. As Jeffery walks home from the hospital, he comes across a rotting human ear covered with ants and sets out—in Hardy Boys fashion—to discover the ear's owner.

Jeffery, with help from Sandy (the girl next door, played by Laura Dern), learns that a woman named Dorothy Vallens (Isabella Rossellini) may be involved with the discarded ear. Dorothy is a torch singer at a local establishment called the Slow Club where her signature song is a rendition of "Blue Velvet." Jeffery spies on Dorothy and learns that a man named Frank Booth (Dennis Hopper) has kidnapped Dorothy's husband Don (owner of the discarded ear) and her son Don Junior. Frank, a sadistic sociopath with an appetite for drugs and violence, extorts sadomasochistic sexual favors from Dorothy by threatening to kill her family if she does not comply.[17] Jeffery is drawn deeper and deeper into Lumberton's dark underbelly where blackmail, illegal drugs, unrestrained violence, and sadomasochistic sexual forces run rampant, but he is rescued by Sandy's love just as these dark forces threaten to consume him. The film ends with the restoration of Lumberton as a utopian vision.

Blue Velvet was Lynch's first movie to draw extensively on rock, pop, and contemporary music to create and define his cinematic vision.[18] Before *Blue Velvet*, Lynch claimed he was musically "frustrated" by the traditional practice of directors not being able to "sit down with the composer until late in the game."[19] Lynch's use of popular music is heavily inspired by the deceptively simple and naïve lyrics of the songs in question, but the "message" of the song tends to be less significant in Lynch's work than how it is delivered within the larger context of the film. Any filmmaker can use pop music, but for Lynch, "It's gotta have some ingredients that are really digging in to be part of the story. It could be in an abstract way or it could be in a lyric way. Then it's really, like, you can't live without it. It just can't be another piece of music."[20]

Discussing the music in *Blue Velvet*, Michel Chion goes so far as to suggest that Lynch may have even "written parts of the script from free associations triggered by the lyrics."[21] Lynch borrows three 1960s American love songs for *Blue Velvet* and juxtaposes them with images of extreme violence in order to twist their meanings (or reveal meanings otherwise submerged). He uses Bobby Vinton's "Blue Velvet" (1963), Roy Orbison's "In Dreams" (1963), and Ketty Lester's "Love Letters" (1962).

At first, it seems Lynch might be using these early 1960s love songs to evoke a kind of nostalgia for an earlier, simpler America. For example, the wholesomeness of Lumberton is established in the opening shots of the film (see figure 3.3). Accompanied by Vinton's "Blue Velvet" playing non-diegetically on the soundtrack, we see images of a sunny day, white picket fences, uniform green lawns, robust flower beds, a bright shiny fire truck complete with friendly firemen, and children walking home from school. This utopian vision of Lumberton is suddenly dispelled, however, when Mr. Beaumont falls to the ground from a stroke while watering his lawn.

Figure 3.3: *Blue Velvet:* The opening utopian image of Lumberton, USA ("Blue Velvet").

The seriousness of the situation conflicts not only with the slow-motion shots of a little dog happily playing with the water from the hose that Mr. Beaumont is still holding even as he lies unconscious in the mud, but also with the Vinton tune that continues to play over the scene.

Later in the film, the song occurs diegetically when Jeffery visits Dorothy at the Slow Club and she sings a tearfully sentimental rendition. This scene occurs just after Jeffery has snuck into Dorothy's apartment and witnessed a bizarre, fetishistic sex scene between her and Frank involving a blue velvet robe, drugs (amyl nitrate), physical abuse, and apparent rape—all of which Dorothy masochistically seems to enjoy.[22] At this point, any ordinary association between the song "Blue Velvet" and innocent love has been distorted. The song no longer just represents pure, youthful love; it also becomes a metaphor for all that is wrong with Dorothy's life, and all that is wrong with Lumberton.[23]

Frank eventually suspects that Jeffery and Dorothy are having an affair, and this compels him to kidnap Jeffery. He takes him to Ben's house, where he is also holding Don and Don Junior. As soon as he appears, it becomes clear that the suave and pale Ben (Dean Stockwell) is under the influence of drugs. In a bizarre scene, Ben gives in to Frank's insistence and sings Roy Orbison's "In Dreams," another nostalgic love song. In Lynch's world, the lyrics "A candy-colored clown they call the sandman / tiptoes to my room every night" and "I close my eyes then I drift away" no longer suggest a young man dreaming of his love, but take on very different meanings when placed in the scenario of Ben and Frank popping pills as they discuss drug deals, kidnapping, and murder.

Frank leaves Ben's place and takes Jeffery out to the country where he beats him nearly to death while "In Dreams" continues playing on Frank's cassette machine. Before this brutal assault, Frank gets high once again on amyl nitrate, smears lipstick on his own face, and begins kissing Jeffery (see

Figure 3.4: *Blue Velvet*: Frank warns Jeffery that he doesn't want to receive a "love letter" ("In Dreams").

figure 3.4). As Frank kisses him, he recites the lyrics from a third nostalgic love song, Ketty Lester's "Love Letters." The lyrics of the song are ostensibly about a young woman finding comfort by reading her boyfriend's love letters, but Frank asks Jeffery, "Do you know what a love letter is? It's a bullet from a fucking gun, fucker! You receive a love letter from me, you're fucked forever!" Here the top-ten love ballad "In Dreams" has not only become associated with extreme violence, narcotics, and mental instability, the lyrics of a third romantic song ("Love Letters") are distorted in such a way that love becomes inseparable from murder. Moreover, Frank's utterance of the "Love Letters" lyrics while "In Dreams" continues playing diegetically over the scene suggests that he "dreams" of killing Jeffery—and nearly accomplishes this with the beating that follows.

We finally hear "Love Letters" as an actual song, with music as well as words, in the penultimate scene of the film. This is the final denouement where Jeffery rushes off to Dorothy's apartment and finds her husband Don tied to a chair—missing an ear and shot in the head—as well as a crooked cop named Detective Gordon, who has also been shot in the head but remains alive, standing, and bleeding. The nostalgic love song "Love Letters" is heard here, at the point when Jeffery discovers that Detective Gordon and Don have both received "love letters" from Frank.[24]

Returning to the issue of fantasy in *Blue Velvet*, we run up against the question: Which aspect of Lumberton is fantasy, the dark, grotesque underworld or the naïve, idyllic surface? The answer, according to Žižek, is actually found in the later film *Lost Highway*. The idyllic surface of Lumberton in *Blue Velvet* is found in the fantasy world of *Lost Highway*—evident in the scene when we get our first good look at Pete (see figure 3.1). In this scene, we get idyllic suburban images of a white picket fence, swimming pool, green grass, and a pet dog, images that could have come from *Blue Velvet*. Additionally, there is a shared naïveté between Pete's old girlfriend Sheila from *Lost Highway* and Jeffery's girlfriend Sandy from *Blue Velvet*. The dark side of Lumberton also shares similarities with the fantasy world of *Lost Highway*, for example, the sadomasochistic sexuality of both Dorothy and Alice and the over-the-top outbursts of rage and violence from Frank and Mr. Eddy. In Žižek's analysis, both worlds of *Blue Velvet* are therefore revealed as fantasy. The film shows us fantasy in its two extremes: idyllic, naïve, and beautiful, as well as dark, grotesque, and obscene.[25]

Lynch's use of music confirms this reading in that he uses the same nostalgic love songs to represent both aspects of Lumberton, the bright and dark extremes of fantasy. Vinton's "Blue Velvet" accompanies the idyllic images during the opening scene and also becomes a metonym for all that has gone wrong with Dorothy. Orbison's "In Dreams" fits perfectly into the idyllic suburban world of Lumberton and takes on additional distorted meaning when associated with drugs and kidnapping. And Lester's "Love Letters," a third nostalgic love song originally associated with the comfort of love, is distorted and takes on a second meaning of murder. The meanings of all three songs, naturally associated with the idyllic side of Lumberton, are subverted to also represent the opposite grotesque Lumberton underworld. Lynch, by using the same songs to represent both aspects of Lumberton, musically signifies both worlds as fantasy. This suggestion that an entire film is fantasy—or a dream within a dream—is a common theme for Lynch, but he uses his connection of music with fantasy to make an important revelation in the later film *Mulholland Drive*.

MULHOLLAND DRIVE

Lynch constructs an especially powerful relationship between music and fantasy in *Mulholland Drive*. He originally shot this film as a two-hour pilot for an ABC drama. After viewing the pilot, however, the producers at ABC passed on the project but retained control of the footage. A number of years went by before Lynch was able to put together a group of financiers to buy back the pilot so that it could be released as a dramatic feature. The actors were called back to shoot some additional footage, and *Mulholland Drive* was released theatrically in 2001.

Mulholland Drive is the story of Betty (Naomi Watts), a blonde, beautiful, energetic, and extremely talented young woman who comes to Hollywood direct from Deep River, Ontario, in order to realize her dream of becoming a famous actress. Betty's career, however, is held back by anonymous men who make backroom deals to get the girls they want regardless of talent.

Arriving at her aunt's home, she discovers a mysterious brunette with amnesia (Laura Elena Harring) who has wandered into the apartment after being in a car accident on Mulholland Drive. The two women set out to find the true identity of Rita—the brunette's interim name—and hope in the process to discover where she obtained a purse full of money and a small blue triangular key that she carries with her.

Betty and Rita eventually begin a passionate love affair, but just as they get closer to finding Rita's identity, the film splits and—much as in *Lost Highway*—we suddenly seem to be watching a different story in which the personalities of Betty and Rita are inverted and their names are changed: Betty is now Diane (Watts), and Rita becomes Camilla (Harring). In a series of flashbacks presented in twisted chronological order over the last 30 minutes of the film, we learn that Diane (a failed actress) and Camilla (the most successful actress in town) were romantically involved until Camilla became engaged to Adam (a Hollywood director). Diane, enraged and humiliated by this rejection, hires a hit man to murder Camilla. The hit man tells Diane that she will find a small blue key on her coffee table when the job is done. Once Diane gets confirmation that Camilla is dead, she runs into her bedroom screaming and commits suicide by shooting herself.

Two scenes are crucial to understanding the film, and they both rely heavily on music. The first occurs at the opening of the movie. A non-diegetic jazz band plays a swinging riff tune (à la Gene Krupa) that accompanies images of dancers jitterbugging to the beat. In the shot, at least five different images of the same few dancers are superimposed over one another. Images of Betty begin to bleed through the layers of dancers, and it appears that she is standing before a large crowd that is showering her with applause (see figure 3.5). As the song ends, the camera zooms in on a pillow.

As the pillow might suggest, the segment at first seems as if it could have all been a dream. For Hitchcock fans, however, the scene takes on added meaning. In *Shadow of a Doubt*, Hitchcock and his composer Dimitri Tiomkin create what Royal S. Brown calls a "musicovisual metonymy" for the main character (Uncle Charlie) by associating him from the very beginning with Franz Lehár's "Merry Widow Waltz." The movie opens with a non-diegetic visual of couples dancing to the "Merry Widow Waltz" in turn-of-the-century dress. In his book *Overtones and Undertones*, Brown observes that

> [i]t quickly becomes evident that the waltz stands not just for Uncle Charlie's peculiarities [he likes to seduce and murder rich widows for their money] but for the very nature of his psychology. The screenplay quickly establishes a major element of Uncle Charlie's psychology as a loathing of the present day in favor of an idealized past.... Within this perspective both the "old-fashioned" waltz and the "old-fashioned" couples dancing

Figure 3.5: *Mulholland Drive*: An image of Betty, presumably in front of a large crowd, bleeds through the images of the dancers.

become a metonymical expression of Charlie's nostalgia and a warning of his inability to relate to the present world.[26]

This musicovisual metonymy from *Shadow of a Doubt* parallels the opening scene of *Mulholland Drive*. Lynch, in addition to telling us that Betty is a dreamlike fantasy representation of Diane, establishes Diane's psychology from the very beginning of the movie—her inability to deal with reality—even though Diane doesn't enter until the last 30 minutes of the film. This connection of Diane with the opening is confirmed when she, speaking as Betty, announces that she had "always wanted to come here [Hollywood]....I won this jitterbug contest...that sort of led to acting...you know, wanting to act." Thus, the jitterbugging scene becomes a stand-in for Diane's nostalgic, utopian past—a time before her dreams of acting were crushed by the oppressive Hollywood system with its unseen power mongers. A kind of naïve nostalgia pervades the entire first two hours of *Mulholland Drive*, before the film's split.

Most of the narrative in the first two hours can be read as a dreamlike fantasy world where Diane imagines herself as a strong, daring, and talented actress named Betty in a much simpler time (the name Betty comes from the name of the waitress in the diner where Diane hires the hit man). Betty's lover Rita is a scared and weak individual who depends on Betty for survival; she even starts trying to look like Betty by donning a blond wig. In reality (i.e., in the post-split section of the film), it is Diane who depends on Camilla: From Diane's perspective, Camilla Rhodes is an actress who conspires with mysterious forces to ensure that she gets the lead roles in the best films. Thus, similar to the Fred/Pete characters in *Lost Highway*, Betty is Diane as Diane sees herself (or as she would like others to see her), and the split in the film is the split between Diane's fantasy world and her reality, a Lynchian recognition of fantasy's function as protective screen against reality. *Mulholland Drive*, however, adds a significant twist through a scene at Club Silencio, another crucial scene that involves music, just before the film's split.

Betty and Rita are drawn to the club late one night when Rita begins talking in her sleep, repeating over and over again the phrase "*Silencio…No hay banda. Silencio…No hay banda.*" Upon arriving at Club Silencio, Betty and Rita find the magician Bondar already onstage, and it seems that everyone has been waiting for them. As they take their seats, Bondar begins his performance:

> *No hay banda!* There is no band! *Il n'y a pas d'orchestre.* This is all a tape recording. *No hay banda,* and yet, we hear a band. If you want to hear a clarinet, listen. [clarinet plays] *Un trombon en coulisse.* [trombone plays]. *Un trombon con sordina.* [muted trombone plays] *J'aime le son d'une trombone en sourdine. J'ame le son!* A muted trumpet.

A musician steps out from behind the curtain playing a muted trumpet. Suddenly, he pulls the trumpet away from his mouth, holding out both arms as the sound of a muted trumpet continues. Bondar continues, "It's all recorded. *No hay banda!* It is all a tape." Bondar throws his hand to the left and a trumpet sounds on the left, then to the right and back to the left. "*Il n'y a pas d'orchestre.* It is an illusion. Listen!" Bondar throws his hands into the air creating thunderclaps and blue lightning. Betty begins to shake and Bondar disappears in a cloud of smoke.

It is at this moment that we first see the Blue-Haired Lady sitting stoically in an upper box, a critical character that we discuss shortly. As the smoke settles, the Emcee enters the stage to introduce the next act: "*la llorona de los Angeles…*Rebekah Del Rio," who sings "*Llorando*"—a solo version of Roy Orbison's "Crying" in Spanish (see figure 3.6). In Mexican folklore, *La Llorona*—Spanish for "the Weeping Woman"—is the ghost of a woman crying for her children, whom she has murdered after being abandoned by her lover; her appearance is interpreted as a foreshadowing of death. Similarly, the lyrics to Orbison's "Crying" tell the story of an encounter with a lover who no longer reciprocates. The abandoned lover believes he or she has gotten over the old flame; nevertheless, the encounter results in crying.

During the song, there are extreme close-ups of the singer and of Betty and Rita who, moved by the song, begin to cry. At the climax of the song and precisely on the lyric "now you're gone," Del Rio collapses without warning as the song continues. Her body is carried off the stage and, as the song finishes, Betty and Rita discover a small blue box in Betty's purse. The

Figure 3.6: *Mulholland Drive*: Following the magician's act, "*La Llorona de los Angeles*...Rebekah Del Rio" takes the stage to perform "*Llorando*" ("Crying").

two women rush home with the blue box to get the blue key that will open it; at the moment the box is opened, the film splits to its alternate "reality" narrative and scenario.

This scene helps us confirm that the first two hours of the film are fantasy, "an illusion"—and Lynch uses music to underline this point, much as he does in *Lost Highway*. In other words, songs are the points where Lynch actually invites viewers to think of each film as a juxtaposition of two worlds. As Bondar uses it, the Spanish word "banda"—which can mean both "musical ensemble" and "tape"—can refer, like the film *Mulholland Drive* itself, to either a state of reality or a state of unreality. Betty's physical reactions to "*Llorando*"—she shakes and cries—are likely the result of her world being exposed "as illusion," especially because the fantasy world ends almost immediately after the two women leave the club. However, this scene is significant not only because it helps establish the fantasy/reality split, but also because it sets up the final pronouncement of the film. The critical figure in this scene is not Betty, Rita, Bondar, or Rebekah del Rio, but the Blue-Haired Woman who sits high above in the box watching the scene. Her pronouncement of the word "*Silencio*" in the final shot of the film, is a crucial event.

One could easily interpret this concluding pronouncement as a wish of peace for Diane, who has killed herself at the end of the film. The Blue-Haired Woman could be saying something like "*Silencio*, silence, poor Diane...your torment is no more...rest in peace." But to accept this interpretation is to forget the messages Lynch gave us at Club Silencio. In that scene, Bondar told us that it was all an illusion, yet we perceive the musician as authentically playing the trumpet and are surprised when we discover it is an illusion. Once Bondar disappears, Rebekah del Rio takes the stage, and even though it is a different act, even though we get completely pulled into her performance, we learn that it too is an illusion. Therefore, the Blue-Haired Woman at the end of *Mulholland Drive* is not saying *"Silencio,"* but referring to Silencio (the club where everything is an illusion). She thereby signifies that even the final 30 minutes, the part of the film we had thought represented reality, is in fact yet another layer of fantasy, an additional illusion. This is different from *Blue Velvet* where we were enveloped in a world of fantasy and from *Lost Highway* where there was a clear reality/fantasy split; with the final pronouncement of *Mulholland Drive*, Lynch is telling us that reality is just another layer of fantasy, that fantasy constructs reality.[27] The significance of this revelation is that it corresponds precisely to what Lacan refers to as the final step in the psychoanalytic process, the moment when the subject is finally able to let go of the hope of finding enjoyment in fantasy (in the Lacanian "Other") and construct their own enjoyment. In other words, once subjects realize that reality is constructed, they are free to construct their own realities where enjoyment is possible, rather than relying on the "Other" to provide it.

POSTMODERN IRONY AND FANTASY

As seen in the three films discussed, music is a critical aspect of Lynch's cinematic style; music and fantasy are tied together so closely that it even becomes part of the narrative in *Mulholland Drive*. However, most of the fantasies in these films are of an extreme and violent nature, which gives rise to an apparent contradiction between Lynch's use of nostalgic music and scenes of brutal violence. These scenes are typically read as examples of postmodern irony, and Lynch himself has clearly suggested that his juxtapositions of music and violence are meant to be ironic when, in an interview about *Blue Velvet*, he claimed that what inspired him to use Orbison's "In Dreams" was the possibility for the main character to twist the meaning. In Frank's hands, a song about love "becomes putrefied to the opposite degree."[28] In fact, moments like this are so easily read as ironic that critics barely take the time to mention them except to point out the multiplicity of meanings that their juxtapositions with violence invoke.[29]

Treating these moments as ironic suggests that Lynch opens gaps between what the songs say and what the film means: He juxtaposes how things are made to appear with how they "really" are. These ironic juxtapositions call attention to themselves to such an extent that they come to be seen as creative strategies, rather than ways of being. In this sense, an ironic work no longer represents something "real," but becomes a critique of such "reality." This creates the impression that there is a position outside of that reality. In other words, reading the juxtaposition between music and violence in Lynch's films as ironic ultimately lets us off the hook: We can view and interpret his dystopian worlds without having to confront them as in any sense "real," as part of our own "reality" (*except* in an ironic sense).

Recall, however, that the role of fantasy is to protect the subject and to produce desire rather than stage it as fulfilled. Characters like Frank Booth in *Blue Velvet* and Mr. Eddy in *Lost Highway* function as external obstacles to enjoyment, forbidding the main characters to enjoy; enjoyment would be possible for those main characters if not for people like Frank and Mr. Eddy. But the elimination of these obstacle characters at the ends of the films is not an actual elimination of the external obstacle, but rather a fantasized staging of the removal of the obstacle. This reading is confirmed by the fact that the enjoyment at the end of *Blue Velvet*, Jeffery and Sandy's happy ending, is constructed—as false as the mechanical robin that appears at the end of the film, robins representing love in Sandy's dream. The reading is also confirmed by the delivery of the message "Dick Laurent is dead," which starts the loop all over again in the later film *Lost Highway*. Thus these violent characters protect the protagonists not by staging desire as satisfied but by reproducing desire, in this case the desire to eliminate these violent characters and obtain their access to enjoyment. And from what do these characters offer protection? In discussing these types of obscene characters, Žižek poses these rhetorical questions: "[Are these characters] not, in spite of [their] horrifying features, the ultimate guarantee that there is somewhere full, unconstrained enjoyment? And, consequently, what if the true horror is the lack of enjoyment itself?"[30] In other words, these violent characters not only represent external obstacles to enjoyment, but also represent the ones who can enjoy, the ones who have access to pure, unrestrained enjoyment and satisfaction of desire. They provide proof that enjoyment does exist, that satisfaction of one's desire is possible.[31]

Music in Lynch's films is so associated with fantasy and violence that one could say characters like Frank and Mr. Eddy are only able to experience pleasure through an engagement with music. But irony becomes a strategy that produces denial. Reading the juxtapositions between music and violence as an example of postmodern irony may act as a defense that keeps us from having to confront these violent characters as real; but by reading them ironically, we lose our signifier of enjoyment in the Other, the one who would guarantee enjoyment in the face of crisis. This loss creates a situation more horrible than any encounter with a character like Frank and Mr. Eddy—it does this by eliminating fantasy's protective function, forcing us to confront the realization that the satisfaction of desire may not be possible, that enjoyment does not exist! This is why the pronouncement at the end of *Mulholland Drive* is so critical: It shows that our sense of reality itself is constructed, thus, enjoyment exists, but it too exists as a construct. This frees us to let go of trying to find enjoyment in characters like Frank and Mr. Eddy—the Lacanian Other—and instead, construct our own enjoyment without the Other.

Understanding popular music's role in the production of fantasy, then, not only exposes one of the primary characteristics in Lynch's style, but also shows how Lynch's seemingly incoherent narratives can be illuminated by an examination of the musical score. Lynch's fantasy worlds are not so much cued by popular music, as they are generated by it. These fantasy worlds provide protection from reality and are presented in an unmediated, pure form that often overwhelms the audience. The dismissal of these protective fantasies, however, as is the case with most postmodern readings of Lynch, negates fantasy's protective function, creating a situation even more unbearable than the fantasy worlds themselves. Thus, even though Lynch's techniques may be postmodern, *Mulholland Drive* shows that he is at the same time beyond postmodernism. This confirms David Lynch as an auteur, a filmmaker who—in addition to taking his audiences on a musical tour of the bizarre—elevates music's role in film.

NOTES

1. *The City of Absurdity, Lost Highway* Soundtrack, available at http://www.thecityofabsurdity.com/losthighway/lhsound.html; accessed April 21, 2007.
2. Mark Kermode, "Weirdo," *Q Magazine*, September 1997; posted on *The City of Absurdity, Lost Highway* Interviews and Articles; available at http://www.thecityofabsurdity.com/losthighway/intlhqmag.html; accessed April 21, 2007.
3. Michel Chion, *David Lynch*, trans., Robert Julian (London: BFI, 1995), 3.
4. *Six Men Getting Sick* is a short one-minute film completed by Lynch while studying painting at the Philadelphia Academy of Fine Arts. The film is continuously looped and projected onto a three-dimensional sculptured screen.
5. Chris Rodley, ed., *Lynch on Lynch* (London: Farber and Farber, 1997), 54.
6. For a postmodern reading of Lynch, see James Naremore, *More Than Night* (Los Angeles: University of California Press, 1998). An exemplary New Age reading is Martha P. Nochimson, *The Passion of David Lynch* (Austin, TX: University of Texas Press, 1997). An excellent reading of Lynch as a Reagan-esque conservative is Jeff Johnson, *Pervert in the Pulpit: Morality in the Works of David Lynch* (Jefferson, NC, and London: McFarland, 2004). For a feminist reading, see Kelly McDowell, "Unleashing the Feminine Unconscious: Female Oedipal Desires and Lesbian Sadomasochism in *Mulholland Drive*." *The Journal of Popular Culture* 38, no. 6 (2005): 1037–1049. For a reading of transcendental irony in Lynch, see Eric G. Wilson, *The Strange World of David Lynch: Transcendental Irony from Eraserhead to Mulholland Dr.* (New York: Continuum, 2007). The consummate Lacanian reading is Slavoj Žižek, *The Art of the Ridiculous Sublime: On David Lynch's Lost Highway*, Walter Chapin Simpson Center for the Humanities Short Studies (Seattle: University of Washington Press, 2002), 28–31; other philosophical readings include Todd McGowan, *The Impossible David Lynch* (New York: Columbia University Press, 2007); and William J. Devlin and Shai Biderman, eds., *The Philosophy*

of David Lynch (Lexington, KY: University of Kentucky Press, 2011). For an argument of Lynch's work as moving beyond postmodernism, see Nicholas Rombes, "*Blue Velvet* Underground: David Lynch's Post-Punk Poetics," in *The Cinema of David Lynch: American Dreams, Nightmare Visions*, eds. Erica Sheen and Annette Davison, Directors' Cuts Series (New York: Wallflower, 2004), 61–76.

7. These descriptions can be found in some of the more recent books on Lynch's films.

8. John Richardson, "*Laura* and *Twin Peaks*: Postmodern Parody and the Musical Reconstruction of the Absent Femme Fatale," in *The Cinema of David Lynch: American Dreams, Nightmare Visions*, eds. Erica Sheen and Annette Davison, Directors' Cuts Series (New York: Wallflower, 2004), 77–92, is an exception; he draws parallels with Otto Preminger's noir classic *Laura*, which uses music and sound to fill in for the missing title character. Annette Davison, "'Up in Flames': Love, Control and Collaboration in the Soundtrack to *Wild at Heart*," in *The Cinema of David Lynch: American Dreams, Nightmare Visions*, eds. Erica Sheen and Annette Davison, Directors' Cuts Series (New York: Wallflower, 2004), 119–135, is unusual in that she not only considers the musical and sonic codes of the film, but explores the "concept of 'music' as a code in itself"; and Colin Odell and Michelle Le Blanc, *David Lynch* (Harpenden, UK: Kamera, 2007), 157–162, is a good chapter on Lynch's use of diegetic, non-diegetic, and sound effects. These articles are important first steps in uncovering the crucial role music plays in Lynch's films.

9. Chion, *David Lynch*, 3.

10. *Lost Highway* opened on February 21, 1997, and had fallen off the radar by April with a final U.S. gross of $3.57 million. This was devastatingly disappointing given that October Films reportedly paid $10 million for the North American distribution rights. David Hughes, *The Complete Lynch* (London: Virgin, 2001), 221.

11. Rodley, *Lynch on Lynch*, 242, 227.

12. Greg Hainge, "Weird or Loopy? Specular Spaces, Feedback and Artifice in *Lost Highway*'s Aesthetics of Sensation," in *The Cinema of David Lynch: American Dreams, Nightmare Visions*, 138.

13. Žižek, *The Art of the Ridiculous Sublime*, 16.

14. Ibid., 21.

15. Additionally, Fred and Pete share headaches, and their love interests (Renee/Alice) are played by the same actress.

16. This tying of fantasy with Fred's solo actually occurs a few scenes later when we see images of Fred's soloing mixed with images of Renee leaving the bar with another man (Andy).

17. Frank Booth ranks number 36 on AFI's list of the top 50 film villains of all time. AFI's 100 Years...100 Heroes and Villains; available at http://www.afi.com/tvevents/100years/handv.aspx; accessed April 21, 2007.

18. In an interview with Chris Rodley, Lynch mentions that his passion for music began as a child on a warm, twilight summer night in Boise, Idaho. His friend came running toward him from down the street and said, "You missed it!" What Lynch had missed was "Elvis on Ed Sullivan!" Lynch says that this "just, like, set a fire in my head." Elvis, then, became "a bigger event in my head because I missed it." Rodley, *Lynch on Lynch*, 126–127.

19. Ibid., 127.

20. Ibid., 130.

21. Chion, *David Lynch*, 89.

22. Frank actually rapes Dorothy with a piece of blue velvet that he wraps around his fist.

23. The inclusion of an actual piece of blue velvet in subsequent acts of violence and murder reinforces these twisted connotations throughout the remainder of the film.

24. Lynch blurs the line between diegetic and non-diegetic music in this scene. There is a radio on in the apartment, but at first, the only thing we can hear is static (Jeffery stops and notices

the radio static before entering the room). "Love Letters" begins to play just as Jeffery hears on Detective Gordon's police radio that there is a police raid on Frank's apartment. There are close-ups of the radio both with static coming out of it and while the song is playing. Next, we see several images of the police raid on Frank's apartment as the tune continues to play non-diegetically over the montage. After a cut back to Dorothy's apartment, the song continues to play and stops only when Jeffery leaves and shuts the door behind him.

25. Žižek, *The Art of the Ridiculous Sublime*, 45, note 16.

26. Royal S. Brown, *Overtones and Undertones: Reading Film Music* (Los Angeles: University of California Press, 1994), 71–72 (bracketed material added).

27. *Inland Empire* (2006) is the follow-up film to *Mulholland Drive* and continues Lynch's experimentation with the construction/manipulation of reality.

28. Rodley, *Lynch on Lynch*, 130.

29. For example, in talking about the three love ballads from *Blue Velvet,* Charles Drazin remarks, "[T]he way these once-innocent love ballads were refashioned into messages of violence and obsession offered a musical expression of man's dual nature." Charles Drazin, *Charles Drazin on "Blue Velvet,"* Bloomsbury Movie Guide No. 3 (New York: Bloomsbury, 1998), 103. And in the scene of Jeffery's beating, Frank's recitation of Orbison's lyrics, "In dreams I walk with you / In dreams I talk to you / In dreams you're mine," is for Chion simultaneously read as terrifying, homoerotic, and paternal: "We are alike, you belong to me, you resemble me," and "whatever happens, I will love you and I will never leave you." There is a deleted scene that was to take place after Jeffery's beating by Frank that shows Jeffrey coming to, with his pants around his ankles, and "FUCK YOU" written in lipstick on his legs, implying that he has been raped by one or more of Frank's gang. This deleted scene undoubtedly would have confirmed the homoerotic connection between Frank and Jeffery. Chion, *David Lynch*, 96.

30. Žižek, *The Art of the Ridiculous Sublime*, 28–31.

31. Moreover, these forces are not eliminated in *Mulholland Drive*; rather, the main protagonist commits suicide. It is only with the final pronouncement of "Silencio" that a breakthrough is made.

CHAPTER 4

Songs of Delusion: Popular Music and the Aesthetics of the Self in Wong Kar-wai's Cinema

GIORGIO BIANCOROSSO

It's nighttime in the Boca neighborhood of Buenos Aires, the main locale of the Hong Kong cult film *Happy Together* (1997). Yu Fai, played by the former matinee idol and now-consecrated international star Tony Leung, is biting nervously into what looks like a hastily-put-together dinner. He stands at a corner opposite the tourist trap into which, in his Cantonese-accented Mandarin, he shepherds with near-comic regularity busloads of Taiwanese visitors who are taken by their predatory agents to see the quintessential expression of local folklore: a tango performance. The image is drenched in charcoal grays, the frame unstable. Visibly shivering, Yu Fai is waiting for Po Wing, his former lover, to leave the premises to avoid seeing him. The two have just consummated the last, and most painful, in a long series of breakups. Po Wing is played by the languorously beautiful Leslie Cheung—singer, entertainer, actor, and at the time of filming an even bigger star than Leung. As Po Wing rushes out in the company of a small group of young, local men, Yu Fai feigns indifference. His gaze barely meets Po Wing's in the penumbra of the poorly lit street; they sense each other's presence without the benefit of actually seeing one another. Po Wing enters a car and leaves.

The quasi-encounter is over; yet its aftermath is just as intense. As Yu Fai walks back toward the tavern, the beginning of Frank Zappa's guitar jam "Chunga's Revenge" bursts onto the soundtrack.[1] The music has a jolting effect in that it launches a coda at the point when the episode seems to have come to an end. Yu Fai momentarily stops near the spot where the car was parked as if to catch a last glimpse of Po Wing or perhaps claim vicarious

Figure 4.1: *Happy Together*: Po Wing creates his own image as beautiful and vindicated lover ("Chunga's Revenge").

and belated possession of him by occupying the space previously taken up by the vehicle. Inside the car, Po Wing savors, in slow motion, his triumph as vindicated lover (figure 4.1). Zappa's opening riff repeats at a higher volume. As the street corner where the two had last seen each other vanishes behind the moving car, Po Wing lights up a cigarette. A sudden, intense beam of light directs our gaze toward his face, carving it out against the moving, blurry background. He looks defiant, self-assured, and evidently conscious of his own beauty. The second strain of the music, a subdued call and response between reeds and guitar over an ostinato bass pattern, folds within its regular rhythms the frictionless, slow motion of the car. Compared to the abrasive collages that marked Zappa's style as early as the Mothers of Invention's first release *Freak Out!* (1966), "Chunga's Revenge" is a more conventional track in that it sounds like a single take with minimal tape editing. This is in keeping with the musician's goal of exploring, within a rock context, sustained improvised solos. Drowning out all ambient sound, the music detaches the car and its cargo from the here and now of the narrative, completing a portrait in images and sound that originates within Po Wing himself and is meant, as a form of rebuke, for a lover who cannot possibly see it.[2]

The lengthy, unedited shot inside the car is the materialization of an impossible vantage point, a biased "take" on oneself that bypasses reflection to give way to self-mythologizing of a sort. Knowledge that no one will actually gain access to the self-images conjured in our daydreaming stimulates the creative instinct and frees one from inhibitions: The irrepressible narcissistic impulse toward implausibly flattering self-representations is thus given free rein. Music is often a constitutive element of such fantasizing.

In the person of Leslie Cheung, Po Wing looks photogenic, to be sure; but a simple image or a mirror would merely remind him of his appearance. A different kind of image is needed for the restorative narcissism of the soul at work here, a multimedia concoction inspired by movies, popular music, and advertising. The cigarette lighting gesture alone conjures up dozens of cinematic precedents in world cinema. Far from uncovering for us an invisible, "truer" layer of Po Wing's psyche, the music too partakes of the construction of a cool, cosmopolitan, artsy, and winning self. These are moving images, to paraphrase Bogart's misremembered quote from *The Tempest*, as the stuff delusional self-portraits are made of. We, the spectators, literally bask in the glow of such luminous and resonant images of beautiful stars, our ears and eyes irresistibly drawn to their magnetic power, our egos melting with theirs; all of which makes Wong's cinema deeply sensual and manipulative but also an apt elaboration of the very idea of "the image" in an era of constant motion and near omnipresent music—be it piped in all manner of public spaces, deployed as sound effect in video and virtual reality games, or synched to the everyday through mobile devices.[3]

When reality hits back, the music is either cut or faded out. After a brief countershot of Yu Fai lingering alone in the middle of the street, a straight cut takes us to a completely different milieu, where we see him showering in his depressing lodgings.[4] Heightened subjectivity in Wong's cinema often occurs precisely at the point of maximum visibility of the work of the filmmaker (be he the cinematographer, editor, set designer, or all of them as subsumed under the persona of the director). Slow motion and a recognizable musical intertext are interventions that call attention to a sphere outside the characters' world proper. What is more, viewers familiar with other films by the same director will recognize in the slow motion image of Po Wing a returning stylistic motif. In *Fallen Angels*, for instance, the killer's "agent" (Michelle Reis) is memorably caught proudly walking the streets of Hong Kong in a glorious close-up—once again in slow motion—to the all-enveloping sound of Massive Attack's "Karmacoma" (here sampled by Robison Randriaharimalala). This image, too, is a nexus of multiple, or shared, agency. Not only do the distinctive features of the shot intimate the presence of an intelligence above and beyond the immediate on-screen reality, but their recurrence as familiar stylistic tropes points more specifically to Wong Kar-wai himself, the film's director-author. Yet this is not incompatible with viewing that very moment of the film as "authored" by the fictional character. As inflected by the combined effect of music and slow motion (i.e., the very features betraying a recognizable Wong Kar-wai signature), the shot may be said to express the agent's desire to project a glossy, attractive, and exemplary look for the benefit of the absent hit man (with whom she is in love).[5]

But to see the agent imagining what she wishes she looked like is also to see the former Miss Hong Kong, media celebrity, and sometime actress Michelle Reis herself. Like preexisting music, stars bring their own personas and histories into play. Their adoption means that they speak through the director as much as he through them: another significant instance of the diffusion of agency.[6] And yet in something like the way Hitchcock worked the presence of his stars into a recognizable style, so Wong Kar-wai too has been able to boldly reassert a frankly auteurist approach to filmmaking by, as it were, "riding" the power of the glow and personas of his star actors. This is all the more remarkable as he was not only working under the strictures of a ruthlessly, unrepentantly commercial movie industry, but also one that was defined by a very small handful of actors and pop stars to begin with. Though hardly the most felicitous of Wong's casting choices, Reis is symptomatic of the productivity of Wong's compromise. It's not just that stars are key to sourcing the funds for his projects, though that too has undoubtedly been the case; it is also that they have become the vehicle for endless elaborations and variations around recurrent themes and, as we have seen, forms of image-making—all of which have contributed to strengthen his authorial signature despite embracing faces, types, and voices that were, so to speak, "in the public domain" for at least two generations of Hong Kongers.

NITRATE MEMORIES

The close-ups of Po Wing (aka Leslie Cheung) and "the agent" (aka Michelle Reis) are points of image-making that stand outside the narrative trajectories of the films in question; yet they capture their essence to an extent that is beyond the reach of any critical summary. From where do these images come? Like the subjects of Cindy Sherman's haunting portraits in her celebrated photographic series *Untitled Film Stills*, many of the most memorable characters in Wong Kar-wai's oeuvre are suffused with a distinctly multimedia sensibility and filtered through recollections of popular films. As an artifact of film production and marketing, a still bears a direct existential relationship with a specific feature film. As a photograph, however, it can only capture a singular moment, no matter how suggestive it is of a temporal arc or chain of events. And yet it is precisely through this process of temporal compression, dictated by the very nature of the photographic medium, that a still opens up for the viewer a space filled with allusions. Sherman's own stills further titillate the projective powers of the viewer and thus brim with even greater symbolic possibilities, as her evocative setups refer to films that were never made and call up memories of long-gone genres (if not whole periods of film history).[7] Wong Kar-wai's portraits, in contrast, are themselves cinema and this, along with the ingrained habit of reading moving images as an unmediated representation of reality, may obscure their roots in the world of movies.[8] It is at this critical juncture that preexisting music comes to our rescue as either explicit reference or allusion, helping us see Wong's characters as celluloid fantasies, a gallery of jigsaw puzzle cuts seamlessly blended out of the memories of countless faces, poses, sounds, and props of films of the recent or distant past.[9]

A production still is only rarely taken directly from the released film itself; rather, it is staged in such a way as to appear exemplary (of the protagonist's character, the film's locale, its genre, and so forth). Capturing locales, situations, and characters that are twice removed from the world as both past and fictional, a still relinquishes over time its documentary value to function as an emotional device, a concentrate of the image's emotive power. Its ability to distill the essence of a film, and with it a historical moment, therefore resonates with a distinctly elegiac tone. Telling stories of frustrated or unrequited loves from a point in time at which their loss is inescapable, Wong's cinema, too, is elegiac through and through; and because his characters are imbued with reminiscences of older actors, the elegy ends up being for the latter as much as the former.

This is made explicit in *Hua Yang De Nian Hua* (*When Flowers Were in Full Bloom*, 2000), his own private homage to a number of iconic—mostly female—figures of Chinese cinema. Prefaced by the dedication "To those who we remember fondly," the delightful two min./20 sec. film consists of a series of short excerpts of old Chinese-language nitrate movies, chosen by Wong himself, capturing props, locales, and above all the faces and figures of Chinese divas of the 1930s and 1940s.[10] Whether the film is meant to celebrate the characters or the actresses impersonating them is a moot question. Their confusion is both deliberate and poignant. The extreme flammability of nitrate is at once a reference to the physical fragility of archival footage, the phantasmagoric status of fictional characters, and the Chinese practice of cremating the bodies of the deceased (including, one surmises, those of the very actresses we see paraded on the screen). The indexical nature of the archival footage, its status as trace of flesh and blood individuals—deceased actresses in actual locales, a long-disappeared China—is key to its emotional surplus. The fears and attachments we experience for fictional characters and those we feel for real people spring from the same source, Wong seems to be saying. *Hua Yang De Nian Hua* thus reminds us that, no matter how chopped up, scattered, and endlessly reproducible in different formats and venues, films are for Wong a collective site of remembrance.

As befits such a ritualistically conceived work, appropriate music accompanies the nitrate film excerpts from beginning to end. In keeping with the criteria that guided the selection of the visual excerpts, the director chose a song from the soundtrack of an older movie, *Chang xiangsi* (*All-Consuming Love*, 1947). This is the eponymous song "*Hua Yang De Nian Hua*" performed by the legendary singer-actress Zhou Xuan (1918–1957), who also stars in the same film. The text of the song runs as follows:

> The years slipped past like flowers in full bloom / glowing at the light of the bright moon / wise as glacier snow / our beautiful life, my affectionate spouse / this happy and fulfilled family made suddenly gloomy / clouds and fog loom across this solitary island / clouds of gloom and melancholy / Ah, my lovely native country / when will I be able to run into your arms / and see these fogs dissipate / and behold you shine again / as in those flower-like years, years of the bright moon. . . .

A representative example of *shidaiqu* scored for a small jazz combo capped by a string ensemble and sung in Mandarin, "*Hua Yang De Nian Hua*" is more than just the appropriately contemporaneous soundtrack to the images seen on-screen; nor is it simply Wong's way of honoring Zhou's voice (the aural equivalent, in other words, of the visual elegy instantiated by the archive footage).[11] The song, rather, inspires the choice of excerpts and dictates their placement and length. As the clarinet intones a literal quotation of the first line of "Happy Birthday to You" by way of introduction, the music box-like accompaniment inspires images of a young ballerina twirling around like a light, mechanical creature. This is followed by film titles in quick succession and finally images of clocks marking the time. Over the second statement of the theme in rallentando, played by the trumpet, we then see, at an increasingly slower speed of projection, the image of a girl blowing out the candles of a birthday cake: a fine example of synchronization between music and the moving image obtained not through staging and mise en scène but rather the simple manipulation of the number of frames per second. What eventually turns out to be a miniature "pre-title sequence" comes to an end with a blue-ish close-up of Zhou Xuan herself, held long enough for her striking, severe beauty to capture the viewer's attention (figure 4.2).

The song proper begins with the first verse synched to images of Zhou's on-screen performance of it in *All-Consuming Love*. The Chinese subtitle, added as a matter of course for the benefit of the dialect-speaking members of the audience, cleverly doubles as the title of Wong's own film. There follows the most memorable section of the short, a series of shots of famous divas—"the flowers in full bloom, glowing at the moonlight"—interrupted by images of doom and eventually war ("suddenly gloomy clouds and fog loom across this solitary isle"). The climax of the song—and Wong's short

Figure 4.2: *Hua Yang De Nian Hua*: close-up of Zhou Xuan.

movie—comes with a high, long-held note on the verbal image of a warm, all-encompassing embrace with the motherland ("Ah, my lovely native country / when can I go back into your arms"). This is movingly echoed by Wong and his loyal collaborator, editor William Chang, through the insertion of brief shots of lovers' embraces. As the text expresses the hope that the "fogs" of war and occupation give way to a rebirth, joyful images fill the screen until the shots of a filmed pageant literalize the final verbal reference to blooming flowers that end the song and, with it, the short film.

The pace of the cutting is such that one is barely able to register a face or locale before the next one sets in; the images come across rather like ghostly presences flickering on the blank wall of memory. One wonders if the fast tempo is meant to distract the viewer from the otherwise all-too-recognizable Wong Kar-wai's motifs nested therein: the languid faces of slightly resigned lovers, the radiant smiles of the hopeful ones, the large clocks, and the cheongsams, as well as the slim, stocking-clad calves of leading ladies striking precarious balances on their well- appointed high-heeled shoes. There is even the fleeting appearance of two lovers beside a bus— the latter a major recurring element in the one film seemingly untouched by the influence of pre-war cinema, Wong's first release, *As Tears Go By* (1988). The impression of familiarity with these visual motifs takes on a slightly delusional, even oneiric, character. In which direction should one read the exquisitely paced frenzy of quotations? By a marvelous inversion of standard chronology, the nitrate films' excerpts might just as well seem as if they were quotations from Wong Kar-wai's films, which in a sense they are because the director, by insisting on certain images in his own films, has made them more prominent and given them a new lease of life.

WHAT'S IN A TITLE?

As always symptomatic of the thrust of Wong's projects, the title sharpens the equivocation. The short film was released around the time of the award-winning *In the Mood for Love*. Both films, moreover, are titled after the same song.[12] Via the title, the short film echoes the portrayals and thematic threads of the 2000 feature as much as the original context of the song—so much so that it would not be a stretch to view it as a trailer for it (and we know that Wong, ever the shrewd marketer, may have conceived of it that way too).

As heard in Wong's short homage, the song *"Hua Yang De Nian Hua"* is postdated. A paean to the motherland expressed in tenderly oblique metaphors, the song hints at the brutal Japanese occupation of Shanghai during the 1937–1945 war, respite from which could only be found in the city's foreign concessions, where many films were set and produced. Yet, folded inside this primary historical frame of reference, there are other, equally significant, allusions to events that took place after its putative 1947 appearance and whose memories, too, can now be said to be attached to its mellow sounds: the fading of *shidaiqu* itself, precipitated by the decline of gramophone technology on the one hand and the forced eradication of the genre by the Communist Party in the early 1950s; the resulting diasporic character of popular songwriting in the Chinese-speaking world until at least the 1980s, the effects of which persist to this day; the tragically early death of Zhou Xuan in 1958; and, of course, the unfulfilled promise of a Republican China on the mainland.

In the 1947 film, Zhou Xuan, who performs the song, plays the love interest of two men in Japanese-occupied Shanghai. The impromptu performance is occasioned by her birthday and is accompanied by a phonograph, which her husband has given her as a gift (the gramophone ostensibly provides the instrumental accompaniment). It is while hearing her sing that Mr. Gao, a visiting family friend, realizes with amused bafflement that he has bought her the same gift her husband bought—an oblique manner of introducing the theme of the love triangle. Set in Shanghai but shot, significantly, in Hong Kong, the film parallels *In the Mood for Love* in ways not yet explored: Japan as the harbinger of unhappiness; the gift of a state-of-the-art piece of technology (a phonograph in the older film, the Japanese rice cooker in Wong's counterpart); the doubling of gifts; and the protagonists' social and political seclusion, whether escaping from the Japanese in the foreign concessions of wartime Shanghai, or experiencing exclusion from the Cantonese majority and the ruling British elite in early 1960s Hong Kong (and eventually, too, escaping the instability provoked by the 1966 riots: Hong Kong itself being a "foreign concession" of sorts vis-à-vis what was perceived as Mao's encroaching China). Most important, both films tell the story of a great passion that is repressed against the background of a betrayal (marital in the new film, political in the older one).

The parallels between *In the Mood for Love* and *All-Consuming Love* would be obvious to anyone who knew both films well; but it is Wong's decision to title his 2000 feature after the song that seals the bond between them. The adoption of the song's first line is not a mere clue to the genesis of the film; nor is it just a tribute, though one is undoubtedly meant too. As intertext, the title is a messenger of echoes, an invitation to ponder textual and thematic similarities between the two films. As paratext, it stresses the significance of the song in its new environment, guiding our attention to the sequence in which it is embedded, and creating a degree of suspense as to when and how it will be introduced, and what kind of image-making it will invite.

MOVING PORTRAITS

The sequence during which the two protagonists of *In the Mood for Love* hear the radio broadcast of *"Hua Yang De Nian Hua"* has justifiably become a locus classicus of Wong Kar-wai lore and a focal point of interpretation.[13] Here, the characters are both the subjects and—in my reading—the *authors* of a memorable, if fleeting, cinematic self-representation, one that deploys the full arsenal of the director's "tools of the trade." Like a virtuosic storyteller, Wong vibrates in sympathy with the plight of Mo-wan (Tony Leung) and Li-zhen (Maggie Cheung) by temporarily impersonating them in his own register of voice, that is, by lending his audio and visual language to the representation of their response to the broadcast: yet another form of authorial imprinting in the form of the abdication of narrative agency. It is one of the most enduring sources of fascination of Wong Kar-wai's cinema that these moments of self-representation, and the preexisting songs that so often either prompt or underscore them, have inspired maximum virtuosity and ingenuity on the part of the director and his collaborators—to wit, the securest marks of his own authorship.

The song's appearance is elaborately woven into the narrative and opens up a rich field of dynamic relationships. The broadcast scene follows, significantly, Mo-wan's decision to leave for Singapore. The two lovers have just enacted a heartbreaking rehearsal of their separation. Mo-wan, pretending to bid farewell to Li-zhen with a simple stroke of his hand on hers, walks away from her down the out-of-the-way alley that has thus far been the site of their clandestine night conversations. But Li-zhen breaks down, and the two return home together to the familiar sound of Umebayashi's

"Yumeiji's Theme."[14] For the first time, Mo-wan's attempt to hold her hand is not met with a rejection; she rests her head on his shoulder and whispers to him, "I don't want to go home tonight." For the first time in the film too, "Yumeiji's Theme" is synchronized to the action in the manner of a standard Hollywood score, poignantly underscoring Li-zhen's words and heightening the impact of the action as it takes place in the immediate present of the image (rather than projecting a sense of pastness, as it does practically throughout the entire film, onto slow-motion images of the protagonists' comings and goings).

Just as they have become lovers, however, their romance has already come to an end. It is as if Mo-wan could declare his love to Li-zhen and ask her to leave her husband only in the context of his decision to leave Hong Kong, while Li-zhen allowed herself to act on her feelings only when she had ascertained once and for all the impossibility of ever seeing Mo-wan again. A dissolve takes us from night to day, from one music to another, and from the expression of love to its repression. The change of locale and the different sound world, characterized by new acoustics, voice, and musical style, signal not only an ellipsis in time—it's presumably the day after—but also a more quotidian setting. "Yumeiji's Theme" plunged the audience into a sphere separate from the everyday, a sphere shared presumably by the lovers themselves, oblivious to their surroundings and entirely absorbed by their sense of an absolute present. The radio broadcast initially appears to deliver us back to chronological time instead—indeed, the painful awareness of time passing resulting from the discharge of a boring task or the longueurs of an eventless, confined life. After the cut, in other words, we are in the rather prosaic world of the Suen household in the morning of yet another typical day of the week. Li-zhen and Mo-wan are engaged in routine activities segregated by the literal and metaphorical walls of their living quarters. Water is being brought to a boil in the kitchen, where Li-zhen, sitting on a stool, is drinking some tea; Mo-wan too is sitting on a stool in the other side of the divided flat, ostensibly holding a rice cooker (figure 4.3). It is at this point that "*Hua Yang De Nian Hua*" strikes them—and the audience—with all its equivocal force. Introduced by the radio host as a caller's request for his wife's birthday, the song is a gift for Li-zhen from her adulterous husband (who is in Japan for business).[15] Simultaneously, it sets the stage for yet another replaying of the protagonists' "all-consuming love." The leisurely dissolve to the shot of the radio, in smoothing over the contrast in styles and sonority between the end of the previous sequence and the beginning of the new, suggests continuity as much as rupture. The radio is shown in a close, caressing panning shot moving from left to right at a speed consistent with that of the taxicab delivering Mo-wan and Li-zhen home after their mock farewell the night before. With title and dedicatee

Figure 4.3: *In the Mood for Love*: Mo-Wan, separated by a wall from Li-Zhen, interrupts routine activities as he hears a radio broadcast of *"Hua Yang De Nian Hua"*.

announced, the song begins. The "panoramic" shot of the radio gives way to an image of Li-zhen's silhouette, slightly off-center, sitting at the edge of the light-drenched kitchen. She is framed by the walls of the corridor leading to the kitchen, increasingly darker as they approximate our vantage point. Her head is reclined as if to suggest pensiveness while her torso and arms appear to be gently rocking to and fro in time with the music.

As Zhou Xuan intones the first line of the song, Li-zhen raises her head and leans with her back on the wall, thus not only responding to the beginning of the song proper but also betraying the signs of reverie, absorption, or reminiscence (or perhaps all). Unimpeded by the wall, which apparently turns near the darkest area of the shot, the bottom left-hand corner of the frame, the camera begins to track laterally toward the left, moving adjacently to what appears to be a thick portion of the concrete structure separating the two corridors of the divided apartment. As Li-zhen is pushed to the right of the frame until she is no longer visible, the dark wall takes over the screen. Despite being foregrounded in this way, it nevertheless remains unlit and out of focus, which deprives it of the presence and hard materiality it would otherwise exude. Indeed, the blurry appearance of the wall's edge as it moves out of the frame to the right reminds one of a "wipe" to black as much as the crossing of the camera into a dark area. The time it takes to see light at the wall's other end, moreover, further contributes to the ambiguity: Is this a moving shot, or has the camera come to a halt? Put another way: Is the camera tracking along an actual portion of the apartment, or is the black screen simply an extended fade? Our inability to tell whether we are looking at an unlit wall or merely a black screen, and a moving versus a static shot, effectively neutralizes our sense of space, rather like an oblique invitation to stop looking and share with Li-zhen a moment of absorbed listening, unencumbered by visual distractions.

The visual ambiguities are temporarily dispelled as light enters the frame from the left along the same axis. The steadily moving camera unveils the presence of Mo-wan at the end of the other corridor, sitting alone. As we begin to register his presence at the threshold of his own kitchen, the camera quietly stops to allow us a leisurely look. We soon realize he is at the exact same distance from the camera as his female counterpart, occupying a similarly configured portion of space and striking almost the same exact pose as she is, the two of them standing in perfect symmetry with respect to the central wall. Like Li-zhen, moreover, Mo-wan duly takes notice of the song and begins to listen. Having thus shown both characters engrossed by the sounds of the same song, in a sort of telepathic communication with one another, the camera proceeds to reverse its course, moving from left to right, and crossing the same unlit passage along the same axis as before, until light enters the frame through the edge on the right and we discern an immobile Li-zhen leaning against the wall, her head slightly tilted toward the camera. Her pose conveys a state of either reverie or resignation.

The completion of this perfectly symmetrical shot structure clarifies its logic. Its goal is to underline the two protagonists' separation despite their physical proximity—the sustained black screen renders their distance both metaphorical and unquantifiable—while at the same time, it demonstrates the convergence of their states of mind toward a point of absolute equivalence. This is fleshed out, as we have seen, through a set of almost comically neat visual symmetries: their position in the divided flat in relation to the wall, their similarity in demeanor, and their place within the frame. But it is the sounds of *"Hua Yang De Nian Hua"* that synchronize their behavior and choreograph their moods so that Li-zhen and Mo-wan become attuned, literally, with one another. The broadcast fills the air with the sounds of Zhou's voice and in so doing offers them an unhoped-for chance to silently communicate: Instead of exchanging silent yet revealing glances, as is the norm with clandestine lovers who are in each other's presence but can't betray their feelings, Mo-wan and Li-zhen reach out to one another "around corners," as it were, riding the field of sound waves in the cramped quarters of the house. They meet halfway in the "meta-space" of absorbed listening. Those seemingly interminable seconds of black screen are a rapturous representation of the gradual disappearance of the visible world: the exquisite visual metaphor for gazing into nothingness or, perhaps, closing one's eyelids. The symmetry of the camera movement is justified as much more than just a visual ploy: It indicates that Mo-wan's attention follows the exact same course as Li-zhen's.

Despite the fact that the music is justified realistically, the sequence as a whole stretches the limits of what is plausible; its almost excessive precious-ness and all-too captivating symmetries defy the impression that it is an unmediated rendering of reality, suggesting instead the productive—and beautifying—filter of memory, fantasy, or worse, self-fulfilling prophecy. It is a creative embellishment of reality, spurred by the music, on the part of the characters themselves—an embellishment of the more mundane happenings of that run-of-the-mill morning. Fittingly, as if to reaffirm the centrality of the song in eliciting their state of reverie, a jarring aural intru-sion—a phone ringing—takes us to another time and another place. The sequence ends.

Whether or not we can allow that Mo-wan and Li-zhen have authored the images unfolding on-screen, there is another sense in which they are agents of the cinematicization of their own lives. I am referring to their response to the broadcast of *"Hua Yang De Nian Hua"* itself and their iden-tification with the two protagonists of *All-Consuming Love*, which the song inevitably calls up. Literally unable to define their situation in words due to their physical separation, Mo-wan and Li-zhen seize on the song to perform that role on their behalf or, put another way, the song reveals to them an aspect of their relationship they had not yet contemplated. In letting the song address them as a (frustrated) couple, they allow it to define the scope and nature of their predicament in the terms laid out by its text and genre and, by implication, the tone set by the film from which it is drawn. *"Hua Yang De Nian Hua"* is for the protagonists an ennobling affirmation of love and an escape into some kind of "melodramatic grandiosity," away from the constraints of their mundane circumstances; as such, it is also a rational-ization of their inaction. For in *All-Consuming Love*, it is in vain that Mr. Gao waits for the opportunity to marry his beloved. Zhou's husband does eventually return from the Japanese front, just as Li-zhen's does from his frequent trips to Japan, and she proves unable to break free of her marriage vows. Such thematic parallels are certainly not lost on Mo-wan and Li-zhen as they listen to the broadcast. The song's text provides a skeleton of sorts to their own narrative, and possibly a foreshadowing of its foreclosed end-ing: It becomes a poignant reminder of how traditional songs and their texts can cause inhibition by providing models of behavior.[16]

The film *All-Consuming Love*, and the song that has come to symbolize it, are thus both source and vehicle of the characters' inner motives and impulses, desires and fears, and hopes and anxieties. This has little to do with a superficially rehearsed postmodern narrative of infinite regression away from social reality. Rather, it reflects the more sensible, and more interesting, fact that films and their songs provide the characters—and us— with a fund of images and concepts that, like latter-day urban bricoleurs, we use to create images of ourselves. The dynamics of the quotation are highly productive in that on the one hand, the song heightens our sense that Li-zhen and Mo-wan, in contrast to their "merely fictional" counterparts in *All-Consuming Love*, are deeply etched, full-blown human characters; on the other hand, such a heightened sense of a protagonist's depth shows the power of movies in suggesting imagery and ideas that ordinary people use to recast their own experiences outside the movie theater. Mo-wan and Li-zhen are not cinephiles; they are, one assumes, mere moviegoers. But that is exactly what seems to interest Wong: the grip of movies, and the songs that herald their enduring presence, on the culture at large. And that is why Wong's film citations do more than just impart a layer of "movieness" to his characters; the cine-musical references reflect the feedback loop that exists between experience and its audiovisual representations on the silver screen, with preexisting songs acting as "ambassadors" across the permeable boundary that divides the two realms, the undeniably objective manifestation of a "world out there" shared by characters and audience alike.

PRESENTATION AND THE AESTHETICS OF THE SELF

Mere "movieness" is instead a charge frequently leveled against Wong's contemporary, and champion in the American market, Quentin Tarantino. That the latter saw in Wong something of a kindred spirit is understandable: The two directors share a love for action flicks and oldies that they endlessly scavenge for ideas and characters. Think of Tarantino's strategy of introducing his characters, before they engage in the action proper, by way of multimedia "capsule" bios—itself a throwback to a number of beloved action flicks and spaghetti westerns (many of whose stylistic markers Tarantino both refined and parodied). Take, for instance, Shosanna in *Inglourious Basterds*. Her arrival on the scene is announced by her name printed on-screen and a brief montage of her most "representative" features and deeds. This is the presentational mode of spectatorial address of the wrestling or boxing circuit, TV variety show, and the circus: a world of heroes, freaks, virtuosos, and exotic creatures.

Tarantino's portraits are symptomatic of his attempt to recruit the tools of an unabashedly popular aesthetic, drawn from comic books and all manner of so-called "B-movies." Clearly marked as breaks from the flow of the narrative, the brief montages or title sequences that introduce his characters hold a clear and unambiguous association with the music employed therein; the musical choice completes the portrait, placing the character in a gallery of types, a place where narrative time is temporarily suspended. It's a gallery filled with complex, multifaceted characters (one need only think of Jackie Brown [aka Pam

Grier] in the eponymous film). In the *Kill Bill* diptych, however, the association between music and character has a different kind of import than it does for Wong Kar-wai. There, the characters seem to be conceived as bi-dimensional figures to begin with: vehicles of action devoid of narrative agency. In *Kill Bill*, Tarantino comes as close to being Hollywood's Roy Lichtenstein as Wong is to being Cindy Sherman; instead of following the journey of preexisting materials into the reflexive depths of consciousness, all the while charting their appropriation and sometimes surprising transformations, the director rejects depth altogether, reducing mental life to a token of the simple psychology embedded in the musical selections—and iconography—he deploys. As an aesthetic project, it is just as significant, notwithstanding the negative reactions it has been known and continues to provoke.[17] But it entails that the question of whether the music may be issuing from within the character's mind as part of a hopeful, flattering, or delusional self-portrait, so critical to the understanding of Wong's ruminating characters, loses its urgency.

In all of Wong's films, in contrast, the drama essentially lies in the recovery from a love's loss and the process of self-(re)definition that such a loss entails. In this context, it is of great moment to know whether the portraits in sound, music, and moving images that dot his rambling narratives are the expression of an omniscient, objective perspective, the spectacular vignettes by a director-trickster reveling in his virtuosic mastery of the medium, or self-representations by the characters for their own use. The fluidity with which the narration shifts in and out of a reliably objective narrative register creates a state of almost perpetual imbalance in Wong Kar-wai's films, one that the frequent voiceover narrations not only fail to acquiesce to but to in fact often exacerbate. It has been my contention in this chapter that preexisting songs be heard as a symptom that we've entered a zone in which desire, fantasy, or delusion reign supreme. Whether used as source or score, the music does not merely project subjectivity; rather, it is an element of an image-in-the-making whose roots are traceable to the world of cinema.

Purely presentational action-less sequences pepper Wong's cinema throughout his oeuvre. Think of the slow-motion shots in *Happy Together* surveyed at the beginning of this chapter; the notorious sequence in *Fallen Angels* in which the female agent curls provocatively over a jukebox playing Laurie Anderson's "Speak My Language"; or, going further back chronologically, the magnificent portrait of playboy/gambler Tony Leung, complete with a resplendent version of Xavier Kugat's "Jungle Drums," that ends *Days of Being Wild*. At these junctures, the songs are not merely heard or simply embraced: They are literally worn by the characters as an essential element of their apparel. The transmutation of musical sounds into elements of an iconography, and the coalescing of the latter back into the former, is of the essence to Wong's characterizations and points to a long-overdue redefinition of portraiture as a multimedia construct.

ACKNOWLEDGMENT

My deepest thanks go to the editor, Arved Ashby, for the inspiration and generosity he bestowed upon this project. Jean Ma and my student Chen Chih-Ting shared ideas and offered precious feedback on the penultimate version of this chapter. My thanks also go to Kiki Leung, Kelvin Lee, Gordon Fung, and Estela Ibañéz-Garcia, all of whom attended my Wong Kar-wai seminar at HKU's Music Department in the fall semester of 2011. Earlier versions of this chapter were read at Seoul National University on the occasion of the IMS conference "Current Musicological Scene in East Asia" presided over by Professor Suk Won Yi; Institut für Musikwissenschaft, University of Leipzig, at the kind invitation of Dr. Beate Kutschke; and National Chiao Tong University, Hsinchu (Taiwan), where Professor Kam Lap Kwan not only played the gracious host but also exchanged ideas on the topic. Research for this chapter was partly funded by a grant administered by the University Grants Committee, Hong Kong S.A.R. (Ref. no. HKU 740610H).

NOTES

1. *Happy Together* is a trove of preexisting musical materials. An exhaustive analysis of the film's soundtrack lies well beyond the scope of this chapter. The film's title quotes a famous song by The Turtles (featured at the end in a live cover by Danny Chung). The Turtles' two lead singers, having famously rechristened themselves as Flo and Eddie, are featured in some of the vocal tracks of *Chunga's Revenge* (as well as other Zappa titles). Whether Wong arrived at Zappa via The Turtles, or vice versa, it seems sensible to assume that one musical selection led to the other. The film features another Zappa song, "I Have Been in You" (*Happy Together*, DVD. MEI HA, at 1:11:06 and 1:16:58, respectively).

2. Though the same defiant self until the end, Po Wing is the loser in the two lovers' game of to and fro. The last images of him crying in utter desperation at the sound of Piazzolla's doleful music, alone and destitute, strike one as having an almost unbearable documentary value in light of Leslie Cheung's suicide on April 1, 2003 (the actor jumped to his death from the 24th floor of the centrally located Mandarin Hotel in Hong Kong).

3. I first discussed the "aesthetics of the self" in relation to Wong's cinema in "Global Music/Local Cinema: Two Wong Kar-wai Pop Compilations," in *Hong Kong Culture: Word and Image*, ed. Kam Louie (Hong Kong: Hong Kong University Press, 2010), 229–245.

4. "Chunga's Revenge" returns two more times in the course of the film, delivering the image of Po Wing rather like an involuntary memory. First, it haunts the image of a pensive Yu Fai as he gathers strength for a new beginning (*Happy Together*, at 1:07:25); then, the music (i.e., the memory of Po Wing) strikes him again as he washes away blood in the abattoir where he has a night job (1:20:36).

5. The hit man himself, as I have argued in "Global Music/Local Cinema," indulges in multiple, spellbinding forms of self-portraiture. As noted by Yeh and Hu, during a hilarious sequence set on a minibus, he resents being recognized for who he actually is by a former schoolmate (see Emilie Yueh-yu Yeh and Lake Wang Hu, "Transcultural Sounds: Music, Identity, and the Cinema of Wong Kar-wai," *Asian Cinema*, 19/1, Spring/Summer 2008: 38. Albeit in a different vein, in *Fallen Angels* too, He Zhiwu makes an impromptu video of himself lip-synching "Simu De Ren" ("Missing You," as sung by Taiwanese star

Chyi Chin). The song will then become the soundtrack to a memorial, in the form of a home video, to his recently deceased father.

6. On the fuzzy boundaries between the "being" and "making" of a star, see Richard Dyer, *Heavenly Bodies: Film Stars and Society*, second ed. (New York and London: Routledge, 2003).

7. For influential interpretations of Sherman's early work, see Laura Mulvey, "A Phantasmagoria of the Female Body: The Work of Cindy Sherman," *New Left Review* 1/188, July/August 1991: 137–150; and Rosalind Krauss, *Cindy Sherman 1975-1993*, with an essay by Norman Bryson (New York: Rizzoli, 1993).

8. Because of their angst, lack of irony, and certain adolescent air of self-importance, the protagonists of Wong's films do not give away their "sources" upon contriving images of themselves. For an instructive contrast, see the explicitly mocking yet ultimately endearing vignettes, inspired by old films, in Fellini's *Amarcord*.

9. For a brilliant montage of texts chronicling the use of preexisting images in 20th-century art, see David Evans, ed., *Appropriation* (London: Whitechapel Gallery; Cambridge, MA: MIT Press, 2009).

10. The film is available in the Criterion Collection DVD release of *In the Mood for Love* (2002). The nitrate prints of several films, long thought lost, were found in a California warehouse in the 1990s.

11. For a study of the emergence of the genre in interwar Shanghai, see Andrew F. Jones, *Yellow Music* (Durham, NC: Duke University Press, 2001).

12. The Chinese title of *In the Mood for Love* is *Hua Yang Nian Hua*, an only slightly abbreviated version of the original "Hua Yang De Nian Hua" (i.e., without the preposition "de). The change imparts the title of Wong's film a somewhat abstract and poetic character lacking in the original song title. In the interest of space, I refrain here from exploring the allusions implicit in the film's English title, also crafted after that of a well-known song, Brian Ferry's "I'm in the Mood for Love." I note in passing that Hong Kong films are normally released with both a Chinese title and a—usually idiomatic, often ingenious—English one. Only rarely is one the literal translation of the other. This creates ample room for punning and intertextual references.

13. Most recently in Hsiu-Chuang Deppman, *Adapted for the Screen: The Cultural Politics of Modern Chinese Fiction and Film* (Honolulu: University of Hawai'i Press, 2010), 119–122.

14. The theme, heard many times throughout the films, warrants a treatment of its own. It was written for *Yumeiji*, directed by Japanese cult-auteur Seijun Suzuki (1991), where it appears only once. In recontextualizing it for *In the Mood for Love*, Wong has considerably transformed its identity.

15. Hsiu-Chuang Deppman notes how the song, in the context of the rapidly changing 1960s, is symptomatic of Li-zhen's "out-of-date vision of life" (*Adapted for the Screen*, 119).

16. Though he does not explore the parallels with *All-Consuming Love*, Stephen Teo has written at length about the didactic intent of romantic melodramas in Chinese-language cinema(s). See, for instance, S. Teo, "Wong Kar-wai's *In the Mood for Love*: Like a Ritual in Transfigured Time," *Senses of Cinema*, 13 (April 10, 2001), http://www.sensesofcinema. com/2001/13/mood/, accessed March 25, 2012. Teo has also explored the unmistakable thematic allusions to the famous 1947 film *Springtime in a Small Town*, yet another tale of repressed love, as well as the literary model that inspired *In the Mood for Love*, namely Liu Yichang's *Tête-bêche* ("Wong Kar-wai's *In the Mood for Love*").

17. See, for instance, Daniel Mendelsohn, "It's Only a Movie," in *How Beautiful It Is and How Easily It Can Be Broken* (New York: HarperCollins, 2008), 150–160.

PART THREE

Music as Instrument of Irony and Authenticity

CHAPTER 5

O Brother, Where Chart Thou?: Pop Music and the Coen Brothers

JEFF SMITH

I watched a lot of movies on TV—mostly my exposure to movies is from TV. There was a guy in Minneapolis, where I grew up, who had a show called "Matinee Movies." It was a very eclectic program. It would show Hercules one day, then the next.... I also watched a lot of Doris Day movies.[1]

Joel Coen

To those familiar with the Coen brothers' work, Joel Coen's reminiscences of growing up in suburban Minneapolis might go a long way toward explaining the postmodern bent of much of their filmmaking. Growing up as the children of academics and as the only Jews in their St. Louis Park neighborhood, the Coen brothers began their filmmaking career by remaking some of the films they had seen on television with a Super-8 Vivitar camera. In this way, Cornel Wilde's *The Naked Prey* (1966) became *Zeimers in Zambesi* featuring a neighborhood teen named Mark Zimering. *Ed...A Dog* was the boys' reinterpretation of the 1943 MGM classic *Lassie Come Home*. The Coens even remade films that they had not actually seen, as in the case of their reinterpretation of Otto Preminger's political potboiler *Advise and Consent* (1962).[2]

For some critical biographers, television's mediation of the Coens' early experience of cinema was an important formative influence on their work. Josh Levine, for example, writes, "Their first experiment was simply to film a television screen—a hint perhaps, of their later tendency to make postmodern, self-referential films?"[3] Whether or not one grants significance to these early Super-8 experiments, it is certainly true that much of the scholarship and critical reception of the Coen brothers' films treats the duo as exemplary practitioners of postmodernist cinema. For these critics, the Coen brothers' films re-present already-familiar Hollywood tropes and styles in a way that calls attention to the artifice of the originals and rejects cultural nostalgia in favor of a pleasurable, yet calculated deconstruction of classical codes and conventions.[4]

For their critics, however, it is precisely this solipsism and refusal to engage social reality that marks the Coen brothers' work as problematic. Todd McCarthy, for example, described *The Hudsucker Proxy* (1994) as "one of the most inspired and technically stunning pastiches of Old Hollywood pictures ever to come out of New Hollywood." McCarthy also griped, though, that *Hudsucker* was nothing more than a pastiche and lacked both "emotion and humanity."[5] For McCarthy and other critics, the Coens lack both sentiment and sincerity, qualities found in abundance in the work of their older, Jewish, suburban doppelganger, Steven Spielberg.

This notion of postmodern cynicism is one that I wish to critically interrogate in this essay through an examination of the Coen brothers' use of popular music, which both supports and problematizes the broader characterization of them as cinematic postmodernists. Although I do not wish to suggest that notions of postmodernism are baseless in critical analyses of the Coens' films, I intend to argue that the rubric of postmodernism does not completely capture the complexity of the Coens' relation to cinematic and musical traditions. This difficulty might be traced to the notorious incorrigibility of definitions of postmodernism, which are loosely applied and also rather capacious. My own sense of the critical reception of the Coens' work, though, is that the term postmodernism functions as a descriptor of aesthetic features, rather than as a reference to the economic, political, and epistemological conditions present within late capitalism. With this in mind, my conception of the term postmodernism will be closer to the definitions circulated by literary critics like Linda Hutcheon and Brian McHale than the definitions promulgated by philosophers and sociologists.[6]

Moreover, in my analysis of the Coens' work, I use the concept of intertextuality as a hermeneutic tool to explore their use of allusion, quotation, and citation. For Hutcheon and McHale, intertextuality is a central component of postmodern aesthetics, but literary or cultural critics do not all share this particular understanding of the concept. Julia Kristeva, for example, sees the concept of intertextuality as a more general relation between one text and other texts. Kristeva writes that because every text "takes shape as a mosaic of citations, every text is the absorption and transformation of other texts."[7] Viewed this way, the Coens' penchant for cross-referencing popular culture might be seen as an especially prominent example of this more general property of texts.

Beyond its conceptual limitations, however, the emphasis on postmodernism also obscures other, perhaps more salient, features of the way in which music functions in the Coen brothers' films. For example, the Coens frequently use music as a resource for making allusions to various forms of popular culture, and these allusions might be seen as aspects of their postmodernist film practice. Yet though this is true, I argue that these allusions enhance, rather than negate, the music's more traditional narrative and narrational functions. Indeed, one might view this interplay between intertextual irony and narrative significance as something related to composer Carter Burwell's assertion that his music provides warmth, humanity, and emotional weight to the Coens' cool visual style and misanthropic stories. Moreover, in arguing for the complexity of the Coens' relation to postmodernism, I also focus on their selection of artists and styles that embody notions of cultural authenticity. This latter aspect of the Coens' work is evident in their designation of T-Bone Burnett as "music archivist," a title that seemingly treats the films as virtual museum pieces and preserves the soundtrack as a space for lost or neglected moments in American musical history.

While composer Carter Burwell's contributions to the Coens' cinema have been well documented, relatively little has been written about the Coens' use of popular music in film. Of the extant work, the lion's share of attention has been devoted to the music of O Brother, Where Art Thou? (2000) because of the unexpected success of its soundtrack album. Although the status of O Brother as both a commercial and cultural phenomenon has encouraged critics to treat it as a singular sensation, I contend that the dramatic and stylistic organization found in O Brother is entirely consistent with broader patterns of storytelling and signification evident in the Coens' oeuvre. More specifically, in O Brother, as in other Coens films, there is a tension between the playful allusiveness evident in the selection of particular songs by the Coens and Burnett and the dramatic purposes that these songs serve within their respective narratives. Although popular music certainly contributes to the winking, ironic tone of the Coen brothers' films, it also serves very conventional storytelling functions by reinforcing particular settings, underlining character traits, and establishing mood and tone for specific scenes. The tension between these two aspects of the Coens' use of pop music was already evident in their first feature film, Blood Simple (1984). Like the Coens' other early films, Raising Arizona (1987) and Miller's Crossing (1990), Blood Simple contains, in nascent form, elements that will emerge more fully in the two Coens films that make the most extensive use of popular music: *The Big Lebowski* (1998) and *O Brother, Where Art Thou?*

BLOOD SIMPLE

A tale of blood, lust, and duplicity, *Blood Simple* is the first of several Coens films that owes a deep and frequently acknowledged debt to the hardboiled literature of James M. Cain. As R. Barton Palmer notes in his monograph on the Coens, "Like Cain's *The Postman Always Rings Twice, Blood Simple* opens with a romance born of necessity, dissatisfaction, and opportunity."[8] The film begins with Abby (Frances McDormand), a young woman seeking to escape from an unhappy marriage, riding to Houston with her new boyfriend Ray (John Getz). The couple is trailed, though, by Visser (M. Emmett Walsh), a private detective hired by Abby's jealous and violent husband Marty (Dan Hedaya). After Marty fails in his attempt to abduct Abby from her new apartment, he hires Visser to kill the couple. Visser, however, double-crosses Marty by doctoring photos to fake the deaths of Abby and Ray. Operating in a manner analogous to the "servant of two masters" plots found in novels and films, such as Dashiel Hammett's *Red Harvest,* Akira Kurosawa's *Yojimbo* (1960), and Sergio Leone's *A Fistful of Dollars* (1964), Visser accepts payment from Marty, but then shoots the man who hired him in an effort to frame Abby and blackmail her for the crime that he has committed.[9] Visser's plan goes wrong, however, when Ray discovers Marty's body and assumes that Abby is responsible for the shooting. In an effort to dispose of the body, Ray hauls Marty to the desert only to discover that the ostensible murder victim is not quite dead. In the film's most notorious sequence, Ray then buries Marty alive, thereby performing an even more heinous act than the one he believes Abby has committed. More important, though, Visser's mistake in leaving Marty alive is now magnified by the fact that he left his lighter at the scene of the crime. Concerned that Abby and Ray have figured out his blackmail scheme, Visser decides he must kill them instead in order to cover up all of his previous misdeeds. Visser shoots Ray with a hunting rifle, but is thwarted by Abby in the film's climactic confrontation. Abby initially forestalls Visser's attack by impaling the detective's hand to the windowsill with a hunting knife. She then shoots Visser through the door using the same pistol that the detective had earlier used to shoot Marty. In the film's bitterly funny denouement, Visser realizes his tragic miscalculations when Abby, who remains ignorant of much of the plot action performed by Visser and Ray, says, "I ain't afraid of you, Marty." Lying at death's door, Visser laughs and replies, "If I see him, ma'am, I'll sure give him the message."

For much of the film's 97-minute running time, the popular music that appears in *Blood Simple* functions in a very conventional fashion. The music is diegetically motivated as "source music" and is used to reinforce the realism of the film's settings, particularly the bar owned by Marty that serves as the locus for some of the film's most important action. This music consists of oldies and contemporary country songs that are heard in brief snatches coming from the bar's jukebox. As reinforcement of the film's Texas roadhouse setting, these pop songs are largely subordinate to Carter Burwell's score, which plays a far more prominent role in communicating the characters' emotional turmoil and heightening the film's suspense.

Yet while Burwell's score bears the burden of the music's most significant storytelling functions, the pop music in *Blood Simple* plays an important symbolic role within the film. Because the music is of a contemporary idiom, these pop songs subtly but insistently mark the distance between the modern-day, rural Texas settings of the Coens' film and the Depression-era, urban California settings of James M. Cain's most famous novels. In this respect, the pop music of *Blood Simple* underlines its status as neo-noir rather than as a more explicit pastiche of hardboiled literature and films noir. To understand this difference, one might briefly compare the music in *Blood Simple* with that of the Coens' later Cain homage, *The Man Who Wasn't There* (2001). While the latter makes use of preexisting music, these cues are linked to Birdy (Scarlett Johannson) and are motivated by her aspiration to become a concert pianist. The substitution of classical music for popular music is telling. In the later film, the Coens opt for music that is more universal and less specifically coded in terms of its temporal and geographical origins. In contrast, the rhythm and blues and country artists that comprise *Blood Simple*'s source music cannot help but feel more contemporary.

The emphasis on popular music as source music, however, is reversed in the final scene. The film concludes with an overhead shot of Visser lying on the floor staring at the pipes under the bathroom sink. The final shot is marked as Visser's point of view, and shows a medium close-up of a drop of condensation on the pipes that hangs and then falls, a morbidly humorous indication that the detective's last moments will involve an impromptu version of water torture. Under these last shots, the Four Tops' recording of "It's the Same Old Song" fades in to provide a transition to the end credits. As R. Barton Palmer notes, the use of the Four Tops' number comments quite self-consciously and reflexively on the Coens' own borrowing of narrative material. Although the song maintains the character of the source music heard earlier in Marty's bar, it also utilizes the viewer's awareness of popular music history to acknowledge the Coens' reworking of hardboiled and noir conventions. "It's the Same Old Song" was the Four Tops' follow-up to their

big hit "I Can't Help Myself," and it showed the adeptness of Motown producers in churning out hits by creating a new single out of a thinly veiled
rewrite of the earlier tune. Just as "Same Old Song" seems to reflexively comment on Motown's status as a hit factory, its use in *Blood Simple* comments
on the Coens' appropriation of generic traits and their ability to "transform
these inherited elements into something different and unexpected."[10]

What is perhaps most significant about this particular musical reference
is that it comes during the end credits, a point in the film where more overt,
self-conscious narration is expected. In later Coen brothers' films, the allusions to popular music are more frequent and more clearly interwoven with
the overall texture of the film.

RAISING ARIZONA AND O BROTHER, WHERE ART THOU?

In his monograph on the Coen brothers, R. Barton Palmer pairs *The
Hudsucker Proxy* with *O Brother, Where Art Thou?* in a chapter that explores
each text's relation to classical Hollywood conventions. More specifically,
Palmer discusses these films in relation to the Hollywood auteurs who
inspired them, Frank Capra and Preston Sturges, respectively. Although
there is ample evidence from each film to support Palmer's editorial decision, I wish to propose a slightly different take on *O Brother*, one that examines its relation to the Coens' second feature film, *Raising Arizona*.

At first blush, it would appear as though *Raising Arizona* and *O Brother,
Where Art Thou?* have relatively little in common:

- *O Brother* is a period piece set in southern Mississippi during the
  Depression; *Raising Arizona* is set in present-day Arizona.
- *O Brother*'s visual style resembles the "social problem" films of the 1930s;
  Raising Arizona borrows its look and iconography from George Miller's
  Road Warrior series and from Chuck Jones's series of "Road Runner"
  cartoons.
- *O Brother* is a very loose adaptation of Homer's *The Odyssey* that mixes
  narrative elements from the road movie and backstage musical; *Raising
  Arizona* is an original screenplay that mixes elements of romantic com-
  edy with the caper film.

Although the differences between these two films are quite significant, they
obscure a set of core similarities that suggest that *Raising Arizona* might be
considered a sort of "trial run" for some of the ideas and themes that are
developed more fully in *O Brother*.

- Both films star Holly Hunter as the female lead, who functions as the morally upstanding romantic partner of each film's disreputable hero.
- The plots of both films hinge on the actions of escaped convicts. In *Raising Arizona*, Hi offers refuge to the Snopes brothers, a pair of escapees from Hi's old prison. In *O Brother*, Ulysses Everett McGill escapes to try to prevent his wife from remarrying, but convinces Pete (Tim Blake Nelson) and Delmar (John Turturro) to assist him by holding out the promise of stolen loot that he had hidden before going to prison.
- Both films are also centrally concerned with the constitution of the family. Hi and Ed try to build a family by kidnapping one of the Arizona quintuplets while McGill tries to restore his position as the pater familias for the singing Wharvey Gals.
- Both films make extensive use of folk and bluegrass music on their soundtracks.
- Both films also reflect the influence of Preston Sturges, one of the Coens' favorite filmmakers. *O Brother* makes overt reference to *Sullivan's Travels* (1941), whereas *Arizona* is very loosely inspired by *The Miracle of Morgan's Creek* (1944).

As I noted earlier, because of its phenomenal commercial success, the soundtrack for *O Brother* has received much more attention than that for *Raising Arizona*. That seems all the more regrettable insofar as *Arizona* appears to be something of a stylistic template for the music in *Brother*. Like *Brother*, *Arizona* derives at least some of its droll, offbeat tone from the use of folk music, in this instance, several sections of Pete Seeger's "Goofing-Off Suite."[11]

Raising Arizona is a very stylized romantic comedy that charts the relationship between Hi (Nicolas Cage) and Ed (Holly Hunter). Supporting the axiom that opposites attract, Hi and Ed meet as she photographs and fingerprints him after he is arrested for robbery. Because Hi is a habitual criminal and repeat offender, the couple continues their flirtation each time he is arrested. After Hi boldly declares his love for Ed during one arrest, the couple marries and sets up a household in a trailer in the middle of the desert. Yet Hi and Ed's inability to conceive a child places a strain on their marriage. Unable to have their own, the couple plots to kidnap one of the Arizona quintuplets, justifying their actions by appealing to a television interview with Nathan, the kids' father, who says that they have "more than they can handle." After Nathan Jr. is kidnapped, his father hires a rogue bounty hunter known as the Lone Biker of the Apocalypse to recover his missing child. Meanwhile, Nathan Jr. is taken from Hi and Ed by the Snopes brothers (John Goodman and William Forsythe), who hope to collect reward money offered by the Arizonas. Hi recovers Nathan Jr., but only after an epic battle with the Lone Biker of the Apocalypse. Hi and Ed decide to return Nathan Jr. to his family, a gesture that seems to restore harmony to the couple as illustrated in an epilogue in which Hi dreams of growing old and meeting his grandchildren.

The association of folk music and childhood seems especially apt for *Arizona*, which pays homage to Charles Laughton's classic cinematic fable *The Night of the Hunter*. Mimicking the earlier film's famous river sequence, the Lone Biker's journey across the desert landscape is punctuated by shots of small animals (rabbits and lizards) that get caught up in the cyclist's destructive path. Moreover, at one point in the film, Hi pensively looks out the window of his trailer and remarks, "Sometimes it's a hard world for little things," paraphrasing a line previously uttered in *Hunter* by Lillian Gish's character Rachel in response to the off-screen cry of a rabbit as an owl snares it.

Some of the film's childlike perspective is reflected in the Coens' visual style, but a good deal of it is also reflected in Pete Seeger's music. After achieving early popularity with the Weavers, Pete Seeger became an icon of the emerging folk music scene of the 1950s and 1960s. Seeger's interest in folk music was nurtured by an early stint working at the Archive of American Folk Song in the Library of Congress. In fact, Seeger dropped out of Harvard in 1939 in order to assist Alan Lomax in making field recordings in the American South. While Lomax became the era's most famous collector and archivist of folk music, a fact frequently mentioned in reviews and discussions of the *Brother* soundtrack, Seeger used this formative experience to build a repertoire as a performer, popularizing many of the field songs, hollers, and ballads he heard during his travels.

Seeger's "Goofing-Off Suite" was first recorded in 1954, and it consists of several short pieces arranged for banjo and voice. The suite combines original music composed by Seeger with banjo renditions of folk songs, themes from the canon of Western classical music, and Tin Pan Alley tunes, such as Irving Berlin's "Blue Skies." *Raising Arizona* incorporates three pieces from the suite into its soundtrack: the "Opening Theme," the chorale melody from Beethoven's Ninth Symphony, and a track entitled "Russian Themes and Yodel" that features the music of Igor Stravinsky. On the original recording of the "Goofing-Off Suite," all three tracks feature Seeger's inimitable banjo and whistling. The last of the three also incorporates Seeger's yodeling, a sound that itself presaged the "coyote yelps" found in Ennio Morricone's landmark score for *The Good, the Bad, and the Ugly* (1967).

The film's rather elaborate and extended prologue offers an indication of the way that Seeger's "Goofing-Off Suite" will be used throughout *Arizona*. "Russian Themes and Yodel" appears at the start of the film under Hi's narration about his first prison stretch. The suite's "Opening Theme" follows shortly thereafter playing under Hi's second arrest and his speech berating Ed's inconsiderate boyfriend. Hi's third arrest—once again outside the Short Stop convenience store that plays an important role later on in the film—incorporates the third theme from Seeger's suite, the chorale melody from Beethoven's Ninth. This theme accompanies Hi's walk to his cell and the subsequent fantasy image of Ed and Hi getting married. In a slight variation on Seeger's original, in Carter Burwell's score, the vocalized melody of the chorale is hummed rather than whistled. The banjo portion of the chorale returns for the montage of Hi's proposal, the couple's marriage ceremony, and Hi's first days at his new job. The chorale comes back a third time under Hi's narration of the couple's efforts to conceive. The suite's "Opening Theme" also comes back under shots of Hi and Ed's failed attempts to adopt, and the "Russian Themes and Yodel" returns to conclude the film's exposition as it plays under the film's credits.

Besides Pete Seeger's "Goofing-Off Suite," two other pieces of music play a prominent role in the film's soundtrack. As Hi and Ed bring Nathan Jr. to their trailer for the first time, they play a recording of "Home on the Range" to commemorate the occasion (figure 5.1). The recording's arrangement prominently features the banjo, and is thus aurally matched to the style of Seeger's suite. The other musical theme in *Arizona* employs a synthesized orchestral sound that is quite different in style from the rest of the score, but it is nonetheless linked to the Seeger suite and "Home on the Range" in terms of its origin. The theme is introduced in a cue for Hi's nightmare about the Lone Biker of the Apocalypse, and it subsequently serves as an aural tag for the grungy bounty hunter. The cue returns for the Biker's entry into Nathan Arizona's furniture store and for his climactic showdown with

Figure 5.1: *Raising Arizona*: Hi and Ed put on a record of "Home on the Range."

Hi. Although associated consistently with the Biker, the theme's psychic and historical origins are revealed just after Hi's nightmare when he awakens to hear Ed singing the tune as a lullaby to Nathan Jr. Heard in this version, the viewer might recognize the song as "Down in the Willow," a southern gothic murder ballad of the type favored by many of the artists associated with *O Brother, Where Art Thou?*[12]

The latter film expands upon the musical concept employed in *Arizona* in a couple of ways. First, the *O Brother* soundtrack features a much wider variety of artists and styles, although all of these are still subsumed under the rubric of folk and bluegrass that is exemplified by Burwell's score for *Arizona*. Second, the score for *O Brother* serves a broader range of textual functions, some of which are linked to the music's tendencies toward intertextual allusions. In some instances, the music works to reinforce the Coens' play with historicity by referring either to specific personages or to fictional versions of real-life historical figures. Near the end of *O Brother*, the Soggy Bottom Boys provide impromptu musical accompaniment for Pappy O'Daniel's political stump, a scenario that seems inspired by the real-life Texas governor and flour magnate's populist campaigns, which featured the musical offerings of his self-styled "Dough Boys." Similarly, as Everett leads Delmar and Pete to the radio station where they will first perform "A Man of Constant Sorrow," the trio encounters Tommy Johnson, a thinly veiled counterpart of legendary delta blues singer Robert Johnson. Tommy Johnson recounts his experience of meeting the devil at the crossroads, thereby incorporating the narrative of Robert Johnson's most famous song into the Coens' cornpone version of Homer's *Odyssey*.

Besides its allusions to historical figures, the soundtrack for *O Brother* also showcases its penchant for intertextual referentiality through the use of popular songs in the service of musical puns. In his analysis of the music for *O Brother*, Daniel Goldmark argues that Allison Kraus and Gillian Welch's recording of "I'll Fly Away" functions as a musical pun in aurally reinforcing the three fugitives' escape from the law. Although the music is foregrounded during a montage that shows the characters making their way toward Everett's home (figure 5.2), Goldmark notes that the song's "old-timey" sound remains appropriate to the film's setting and style.[13] Goldmark also points out, though, that it is here that the Coens' manipulation of historicity is most acutely felt. In a prototypically postmodern fashion, the song hails from the 1950s and is sung by contemporary artists to accompany a narrative that is set in the 1930s. Although "I'll Fly Away" could not realistically be motivated within the film's diegesis, it trades upon the old-timey sound of bluegrass music to recreate the ethos of its historical setting, regardless of the song's actual origins.

Figure 5.2: *O Brother Where Art Thou?*: The prisoners' escape is accompanied by "I'll Fly Away," a musical pun that expresses the Coens' wry sense of humor.

Of course, in the liner notes to the *O Brother* soundtrack, Robert K. Oerrman gleefully acknowledges the Coens' irreverent treatment of historical factoids and the film's "mishmash of periods and styles." More important for my purposes, the Coens' playful treatment of historicity related to *O Brother*'s music makes it—along with *The Big Lebowski*, which is also "curated" by T-Bone Burnett—one of their most postmodern soundtracks. But because the soundtrack itself nostalgically invokes the musical style of bluegrass pioneers like Jimmie Rodgers and Harry "Mac" McClintock, the emphasis on "roots" music not only serves to minimize the soundtrack's postmodern qualities, but it also enables these songs to play several more conventional narrative functions. Indeed, while "I'll Fly Away" functions as a musical pun, it also works quite conventionally to accompany the visual montage and to reinforce the film's temporal structures. Similarly, the musical performances of the Wharvey Gals and the Soggy Bottom Boys serve to initiate and resolve important subplots within the film's narrative. In fact, one might argue that the soundtrack's massive commercial success is largely due to the music's combination of placement and narrative saliency. Fans remembered *O Brother*'s music largely because of its obvious dramatic functions, not in spite of them.

THE BIG LEBOWSKI (1998)

From the perspective of their fans, the Coen brothers' *The Big Lebowski* is undoubtedly the most important film of their career. Although the film was a financial flop earning less than $18 million in domestic box office revenue, it found a huge cult audience through its sales on home video.[14] Indeed, fan fervor finds expression each year in a rolling Lebowski festival where devotees dress like their favorite characters from the film, spout dialogue, engage in bowling marathons, and ingest copious quantities of marijuana and White Russians. Although *The Big Lebowski* exudes less ambition than other Coen films, like *Barton Fink* or *The Man Who Wasn't There*, it nonetheless is the film that most strongly resonates with audiences. At first blush, it seems like an unlikely candidate for such adulation insofar as the film's plot is little more than an elaborate "shaggy dog" story. Yet, the film's lack of narrative drive seems to work in its favor by encouraging audiences to focus more squarely on the film's quirky characters and comic set pieces. The latter include the hero's bowling duel with a Latino sex offender, his sufferance as thugs urinate on his throw rug, his tryst with a Hepburn-ish performance artist, and his drug-addled hallucinations that combine bowling with Busby Berkeley, Wagnerian opera, and Kenny Rogers and the First Edition.

The Big Lebowski is the Coens' "Raymond Chandler" movie in much the same way that *Blood Simple* was their "Cain" film and *Miller's Crossing* was their "Hammett" film. Like Chandler's Philip Marlowe novels, *The Big Lebowski* features a convoluted and episodic plot that involves its hero's movement through several different segments of Los Angeles society. Through a case of mistaken identity, Dude, the film's protagonist, becomes involved in the kidnapping of Bunny, the young wife of his namesake, an elderly millionaire by the name of Jeffrey Lebowski. When Dude visits the "Big Lebowski" seeking compensation for his soiled rug, the latter recruits him to serve as a courier for the ransom demanded by the kidnappers. Dude loses the ransom, however, when his car is stolen before he can return the money to its rightful owner. With the ransom missing, the situation becomes further complicated when Lebowski's daughter Maude promises Dude a $100,000 reward for recovering the money. Meanwhile, the "Big Lebowkski" surmises that Dude must still have the ransom, and sends a group of German nihilists to recover it. Seemingly beset on all sides, Dude is also pressured for the money by mobster and pornographer Jackie Treehorn, who seeks it to pay off Bunny's gambling debts. The plot comes to a tentative resolution when Dude realizes that there never was a million dollars in the briefcase, and that the "Big Lebowski" was attempting to use Dude as a patsy who could take the fall when the ransom was never received.

Inspired by Robert Altman's *The Long Goodbye*, *The Big Lebowski* represents the Coens' attempt to update Raymond Chandler's detective fiction to a contemporary Los Angeles setting. Whereas Altman treats Chandler's most famous fictional character, Philip Marlowe, as a kind of historical anachronism, the Coens avoid making direct references to Chandler's fiction, but develop a similar type of "man out of time" in Dude, an aging pot-smoking hippie who seems unfashionably out of place in Los Angeles circa 1991. Dude's temporal dislocation is partly conveyed by the character's costume and hairstyle, but it is also suggested by the film's music, which plays with the concept of historicity much as *O Brother* did. As Carter Burwell noted of the concept behind the film's compilation of '70s pop songs, Dude "kind of scores his own life with his [eight]-track collection."[15] Not surprisingly, several '70s artists provide a kind of aural signature for Dude, including Bob Dylan, Creedence Clearwater Revival, Santana, Elvis Costello, Captain Beefheart, and the Eagles.

Yet the music in the film reinforces its characterizations beyond that of Dude. As Ethan Coen noted in the press notes for *Lebowski*, the music "was an important part of the movie, we had this collection of characters, and it was always in our mind that each one would have their own musical genre to identify them."[16] Examples of musical genre as an aspect of characterization abound in the film. Consider, for example, the pastiche of early '80s electro pop that Carter Burwell composed for the German nihilists, whose earlier incarnation as the band Autobahn functions as a direct reference to the German synth-pop pioneers Kraftwerk. Or consider the Coens' selection of the Gypsy Kings' cover version of the Eagles' "Hotel California" to underline the flamboyance of rival bowler Jesus Quintana.

The introduction of Jesus proves to be one of the more memorable moments in the film. The Gypsy Kings' recording begins over the last shot of the previous sequence in which Brandt asks Dude if he will deliver the ransom money to Bunny's kidnappers. As a sound bridge featuring a flamenco-styled acoustic guitar solo leads us into the next shot, the Coens cut to a close-up of Quintana's hands tying the laces of his purple bowling shoe and pulling up his matching purple sock. This is followed by a medium close-up of the bowling lane hand fan. Quintana's left hand enters the frame from off-screen right, ornamented by three large rings. His pinky is adorned by an unusually long fingernail, which is covered in purple nail polish. As the long instrumental introduction to "Hotel California" continues, the Coens cut to a side view of Jesus preparing to roll his bowling ball. Dressed head to toe in purple, the more distant camera position allows us to see that the rest of Quintana's clothing matches his shoes, socks, and nail polish. Shot in slow motion at 48 frames per second, the cinematography adds a subtle gracefulness to the other bowlers as they pass by Jesus. A cut to another close-up of Jesus shows him holding the ball up near his face. He rather perversely extends his tongue to lick the bowling ball before rolling it.

After Jesus rolls a strike, the next image shows him framed in a long shot with his back to the camera, his arm extended, and his right leg curled behind the rest of his body, an almost textbook display of proper bowling form. As the final notes of the song's introduction play out, Jesus turns back to the camera, still in slow motion. After a couple seconds of silence, the song's first verse begins with a faster tempo and percussion laying down

Figure 5.3: *The Big Lebowski:* The introduction of pedophile bowler Jesus Quintana is accompanied by the Gypsy Kings' recording of "Hotel California."

a strong, insistent rhythm. To celebrate his strike, Quintana does something akin to a kind of "end-zone dance," taking four steps backward as his arms move vigorously from side to side (figure 5.3). He finishes his move by lifting his right leg behind him and pointing directly at the camera. At this moment, the frontal camera position, the 28-mm wide-angle lens, the change in the music, and the slow-motion cinematography all evoke the style of older song and dance numbers. Indeed, the Coens' stylistic filigrees endow Quintana's movement with a dance-like quality, seemingly presented directly to the audience solely for their enjoyment. The reverse angle, though, shows Quintana's bowling partner O'Brian pointing back at the camera, a gesture that retrospectively marks the previous shot as one from O'Brian's optical point of view, a device that somewhat naturalizes Quintana's display and contains its potential excess.

Both Burwell's and Coen's comments on the film's musical concept are illuminating in the degree to which they foreground characterization as a foundational principle for the selection of pop songs in *Lebowski*. Each of the musical styles deployed on the soundtrack carries certain cultural associations that are used to underline or emphasize certain traits of each character while ignoring others. In the case of Jesus Quintana, for example, the use of flamenco music underscores his ethnicity, rather than his background as a convicted sex offender. This matching of music and character is, of course, a common principle of classical scoring, and suggests that the Coens seek to adhere to conventions as much as deviate from them. Yet it is also worth noting that the historical dimensions of *Lebowski*'s pop music function in a manner that is much different from the songs in *O Brother, Where Art Thou?* In *O Brother*, historical anomalies are glossed over by the music's old-timey sound, which furnishes a sense of stylistic unity to the music even though it was recorded over a period of several decades. In contrast, *Lebowski*'s music depends for its effect on much more specific and concrete associations between music, history, and culture. To understand the music's role in suggesting that Dude is a character out of time, one must have a general awareness of the music's typicality as late '60s and early '70s American rock and roll. This is hardly surprising as the pattern is representative of the kinds of hierarchies of knowledge between characters and spectators that are established through film narration, but it is also a far cry from the "loss of historicity" commonly attributed to the postmodern subject.

Moreover, like *O Brother*, *The Big Lebowksi* offers a similar complementarity between conventional musical function and intertextual referentiality. Consider the sequence in which Dude goes to the doctor to have his jaw examined. In an earlier scene, Dude had been knocked cold by one of Maude Lebowski's henchmen. Although Dude believes that Maude has arranged the appointment to atone for the assault, we later learn that the purpose of the doctor visit is to check Dude's fitness as a prospective sperm donor. Dude is initially puzzled by the doctor's request to remove his shorts, protesting that he had been hit in the jaw. But Dude apparently complies with the doctor's seemingly strange request, and as he does so, the familiar intro of Creedence Clearwater Revival's "Lookin' Out My Back Door" sneaks onto the soundtrack and provides a sound bridge to the next sequence in which Dude sings along to the song on his car radio. Of course, the sequence offers an elaborate pun that works at a couple of different levels. On the one hand, the song's title seems to comment on Dude's frequent glances at his rearview mirror and his realization that he is being followed. On the other hand, the song functions as a pun on the more scatological implications of the term "back door," by recasting the literal back door of John Fogerty's song as a metaphor for the orifice probed in Dude's elided prostate exam.[17]

As in the previous example, this musical pun depends on a bisociative play on the song's title for its effect. However, if we focus solely on this aspect of the song's function, we also ignore other aspects of the song's placement within the sequence, namely its function as a sound bridge smoothing the ellipsis between sequences and its role in expressing Dude's emotional state. While the song's function as pun devolves on its linguistic features, its other formal elements—its fast tempo, rollicking skiffle rhythms, ascending melody line—all capture Dude's "devil may care" spirit, his joie de vivre, his copious use of alcohol and psychoactive drugs. Viewed in this way, the song's contribution to the Coens' postmodern aesthetic is inseparable from its fulfillment of highly conventional dramatic functions.

MILLER'S CROSSING

Miller's Crossing is a characteristic pastiche of the characters, plot patterns, and language of '30s pulp fiction, especially the work of Dashiell Hammett. Like *Blood Simple*, the film features a complex narrative that involves several characters attempting to double-cross one another. The film begins with a brief homage to *The Godfather* (1972) as mobster Johnny Caspar (Jon Polito) explains the importance of business ethics to rival boss Leo (Albert Finney), in an effort to gain the latter's permission to kill Bernie Birnbaum (John Turturro). Caspar complains that Birnbaum, nicknamed the "Schmata," has been foiling his attempts to cash in on fixed boxing matches. Upset at the Schmata's double-dealing, Caspar informs Leo that he intends to kill Birnbaum despite the fact that the latter has been paying Leo protection money. Unbeknown to Caspar, though, Leo has begun an affair with Bernie's sister Verna. Verna, it seems, has no real love or affection for Leo, but has been trading sexual favors to protect her brother's safety.

Although Leo firmly resists Caspar's entreaties and threats, his consiglieri Tom Reagan suggests that his boss has made "a bad play," and that Birnbaum is not worth risking a gang war that would disrupt business for both sides. After Leo physically removes Tom from his nightclub in an extremely public dispute, Tom infiltrates Caspar's gang and uses his newfound influence to undermine the organization from within. Sowing seeds of discontent and distrust among various members of the gang, Tom plays one against the other until Caspar, Bernie, and Caspar's right-hand man Eddie Dane all end up dead. In a final irony, Tom himself pulls the trigger on Birnbaum, committing an act that Caspar desired, that Leo resisted, and that Tom proved incapable of doing in the killing fields that give the film its name.

The film's centerpiece is undoubtedly the scene in which two of Caspar's goons attempt to assassinate Leo in his suburban home. The sequence took several weeks to shoot, partly because of the way it mixes footage taken in several locations, as well as studio interiors.[18] Leavening its bounty of violence with dashes of grisly humor, the sequence is described by Steven Levy as "tour de force filmmaking." The Coens built the sequence around something they called the "Thompson jitterbug," which refers to the horrific "dance" performed by stuntman Monte Starr as his character's body is riddled with bullets. The scene also features the most famous—and most queried—musical selection in all of the Coens' work: a recording of "Danny Boy" by contemporary Irish tenor Frank Patterson.

The sequence begins with a shot that matches the lace curtains in Leo's home to the curtains that appear in the last shot of the previous scene. This editing transition links Caspar's assassination attempt, both physically and metaphorically, to Tom and Verna's rekindling their affair. As the pastoral strains of "Danny Boy" begin to play on the soundtrack, the camera pulls back from the curtains, tracks left, and tilts down past a small table showing an unattended gun and a cup of coffee. The camera continues its downward trajectory until it reveals Leo's bodyguard lying on the floor, his chair tipped over, his head bleeding, and a lit match in his hands. The match lights some newspapers underneath his lifeless body, and the fire spreads throughout the house. In the background plane of the shot, a gunman is barely visible walking away from the camera toward Leo's front door.

In this brilliantly constructed opening shot, the Coens rather economically provide the viewer with almost all of the essential information they need to grasp the unfolding situation. As the camera begins to glide over the room, the lilting melody of "Danny Boy" seems oddly appropriate to the introduction of this new space. Moreover, given its prominence in the sound mix, the song initially appears to be non-diegetic. However, almost as quickly, a new element in the soundtrack initiates a tonal shift from the understated elegance of the sequence's introduction. As the camera makes its way past the bodyguard's table, the muffled, off-screen sounds of a man being beaten mix with the strains of "Danny Boy." When the camera finally reveals the results of this brutality, the muted sounds of footsteps and the match flame mix with the music. This additional aural data complicate our initial impression of "Danny Boy" by suggesting that the song may be acousmatic rather than non-diegetic.

After this opening tracking shot—a leisurely 39 seconds, which is considerably longer than the 2.8 second average for the sequence—the Coens then cut to a closer view of the gunman opening the door for his partner and receiving a Thompson machine gun. Having established the threat to Leo's safety in these first two shots, the scene suddenly shifts to Leo's bedroom, which is introduced with an overhead close-up of a Victrola playing a recording of "Danny Boy." The space of the scene then shifts to the staircase with a tracking shot of the two assassins' feet as they walk to the second floor. The muzzles of their tommy guns stick down into the frame, which endows this shot with a certain ominous tone that seems to counter the melancholy singing emanating from Leo's Victrola. Interestingly, whereas the song is introduced without any consideration of its fidelity within the space of Leo's home, it is lowered in the mix in this shot so that it mingles with the sound of the fire spreading through the downstairs of Leo's home. The shift in sound space also plays an important role in the narrative by suggesting that the off-screen sounds of "Danny Boy" are leading the assassins to Leo's location. Shots six through18 in the sequence are keyed to Leo's POV and enable the audience to recognize Leo's quick diagnosis of the situation. Not surprisingly, the function of "Danny Boy" shifts accordingly.

Whereas it earlier suggested a role in Leo's nightly routine, it now serves to underscore Leo's grace under pressure as he rather calmly puts out his cigar and slides his bare feet into slippers in preparation for the assassins' attack.

Shots 19 through 31 of the sequence show the assassins' initial assault on Leo's bedroom. As the two men burst through the door (shot 19) and walk toward the middle of the room (shot 22), the Coens intercut Leo's quick reactions as he grabs the gun (shot 20) and rolls under his bed (shots 23 and 24). It is worth noting that the camerawork earlier in the sequence has primed us for this perspective with its earlier shots of the assassins' feet (shots six, eight, and 13). As bullets riddle the floor in front of Leo and the bedding above him, he carefully takes aim and fires into the shin of one of the gunmen. When the man falls, the top of his head comes into Leo's view, and he responds by firing a second shot into the man's skull. When his partner withdraws, Leo rolls out from under the bed, picks up the tommy gun, and exits his bedroom.

Shots 32 through 36 show Leo escaping from his house through the window of his spare bedroom. In shot 38, the fedora of the second assassin becomes barely visible in the distance through the same window through which Leo had escaped. As Leo begins to fire his tommy gun, a swift crane down toward him expressively heightens the fury of his actions. Throughout the attack, "Danny Boy" continues as accompaniment to the action, but now its function is almost anempathetic. Rather than enhancing the sequence's emotional shifts, it plays on, seemingly oblivious to the violence and bloodshed that surround it.

Shots 40 through 58 depict the aforementioned Thompson jitterbug as Leo's ammunitions rip through the body of the assassin. As his body convulses and spasms from their impact, the gunman begins discharging his tommy gun wildly and involuntarily, spraying the room with gunfire. Shot 50 even shows the assassin accidentally shooting off toes from his right foot. The soporific strains of "Danny Boy" persist, but now they take on a comically macabre tone, almost seeming to mock the grisly demise of the hit man. Whereas the song's lilting rhythms seemed to initially underscore the stylish glide of the Coens' camera in shot one, those same rhythms seem to counter the rapid montage of wild gesticulations and exploding viscera. The contrast produces an affective dissonance that seems to heighten the absurdity of the gunman's "dance" of death.

The remaining 22 shots of the sequence depict Leo's exchange of gunfire with the riders of an automobile that attempts to flee the scene (figure 5.4). With the driver apparently wounded, the automobile runs headlong into a tree, catches fire, and then explodes. "Danny Boy" continues as spatially displaced diegetic music to underscore these final actions. The recording concludes with a final cadential progression and vocal flourish for the sequence's final three shots. These show Leo finally halting as he watches

Figure 5.4: *Miller's Crossing*: Leo fights off two assassins, all to the tune of "Danny Boy."

the car burn in the distance. In a final gesture of bravado, Leo pulls the unlit cigar seen earlier from the pocket of his robe and plunks it squarely in his mouth.

Throughout the scene, the recording of "Danny Boy" works on several levels in order to achieve its rather unusual emotional impact. On the one hand, the song seems to function as a bit of stock music used to reinforce character. The song's association with "Irishness" certainly reinforces the ethnic background of Leo, but it does so as an obvious musical cliché.[19] By explicitly using "Danny Boy" as stock music, the Coens effectively render the song an empty signifier of Irishness, a gesture that is little different from their use of characters borrowed from other cinematic traditions (i.e., Jennifer Jason Leigh's fast-talking reporter from *Hudsucker*, Michael Lerner's manic studio boss in *Barton Fink*) or the pastiche of '30s and '40s "tough guy" slang that figures in *Miller's Crossing*.

Yet the song also functions in a more conventional fashion by indicating hitherto-unseen emotional depth in Leo. "Danny Boy" shows a streak of sentimentality in Leo that seems to belie his tough exterior and speaks to the personal warmth and affection he later shows for both Tom and Verna. Leo may be a ruthless gang boss, but his obvious enjoyment of "Danny Boy" implies a soft spot evident in his willingness to wallow in the melody's bathetic strains.[20] Indeed, the Coens' depiction of Leo might seem to reflexively comment on their own engagement with film audiences insofar as they display Leo emotionally connecting with an artwork in a manner that the brothers themselves seem to deny their viewers.

Furthermore, "Danny Boy" also plays an important role in the film's narration by underscoring Leo's eerie calm among the furor. While "Danny

Boy" functions anempathetically through the Thompson jitterbug that is the sequence's raison d'être, the Coens can't resist the temptation to use "Danny Boy" to match the scene's concluding "hit point," namely the fiery crash of the escaping automobile into the tree. As Carter Burwell has recounted in several interviews, the sequence had been temp-tracked to a recording of "Danny Boy" by contemporary Irish tenor Frank Patterson. However, once the sequence had been edited, Burwell and the Coens brought in Patterson to re-record the song for the film's final cut. According to Burwell:

> ... [W]e didn't want to use the song *exactly* how it was on the original recording. We needed certain actions to sync to key moments in the song. For example, just prior to the car hitting the tree and bursting into flames, there is a long note held by Frank in the new recording that perfectly matches the timing of the edit. When we pointed out to Frank these moments of synchronization, he was amazingly game about the process and wrote down notes about what words went with which visual actions.[21]

Although the song starts out as simple source music and becomes a more complex form of emotional counterpoint, it finishes as a wholly conventional piece of underscoring, its formal and dramatic peaks coinciding in a manner that perfectly matches music to action and mood. It is also perhaps the most conclusive evidence that the Coens' tendency toward intertextual allusionism and their play with historicity are inextricable from their use of classical storytelling techniques. The cue's jokiness and its status as a musical cliché do not negate its essentially classical function. The use of "Danny Boy" serves largely to represent important traits of Leo's character and to align the spectator with his knowledge and emotions.

POP MUSIC AND AUTHENTICITY IN THE FILMS OF THE COEN BROTHERS

Although film music's traditional dramatic functions complicate the role of popular music as an aspect of the Coens' postmodernism, another issue arises in relation to T-Bone Burnett's credit as "music archivist" on *The Big Lebowksi*. While Burnett's role in the musical design of *Lebowksi*, *O Brother*, and *The Ladykillers* (2004) is similar to that of a music supervisor, the special designation of "archivist" carries some important implications regarding the Coens' attitudes toward the place of popular music within their films. The term "music archivist" is thus significant in at least three different senses: (1) It implies a mastery of popular music history; (2) it portends an archeological function of the cinema in uncovering buried musical treasures; and (3) it suggests that films and filmmakers play a role in preserving and displaying popular culture artifacts. Let me speak briefly to each one of these aspects of Burnett's function as musical archivist.

First, whereas the term "music supervisor" carries with it the clear connotations of middle-level corporate management, the term "music archivist" implies a somewhat different type of knowledge and skills. Rightly or wrongly, music supervisors are sometimes viewed within the industry as bureaucratic functionaries, people whose jobs entail licensing arrangements, contract negotiations, and soundtrack packaging.[22] A "music archivist," on the other hand, occupies a different institutional niche, one whose mission is educational rather than commercial and preservationist rather than promotional. An archivist is more or less a public servant, one whose role involves safeguarding our shared cultural heritage.[23] In contrast, the music supervisor is frequently characterized in industry discourse as a cog in a much larger system of corporate synergies, a system designed to maximize the economic value of those intellectual properties that comprise that same cultural heritage.

In adopting the mantle of the music archivist, T-Bone Burnett and the Coen brothers accomplish two goals that bear upon the way popular music functions within their films. On the one hand, the notion of the archivist serves to motivate the selection of unusual or unconventional material for the Coens' soundtracks; this itself serves as a sign of the filmmakers' mastery of popular music history. Only a self-proclaimed music archivist would include an arcane Bob Dylan track, such as "The Man in Me," over the credit sequence of *The Big Lebowski*. Or consider the inclusion of the Gypsy Kings' recording of "Hotel California," a track that—at the time of *Lebowski*—appeared only on *The Rubaiyat*, a pseudo-tribute album celebrating Elektra Records 40th anniversary. On the other hand, by identifying Burnett's role in their productions as that of music archivist, the Coens reinforce their position outside of mainstream Hollywood. Like the archivist, the Coens' institutional niche is situated outside the nexus of commercial entertainment. Instead, the Coens align themselves with a culture in need of preservation, and thus embrace the values of marginalized folk cultures rather than corporatized mass culture.

By using folk musics like bluegrass and gospel to reinforce their position outside of Hollywood, the Coens buy into a discourse of authenticity that has structured the relationship between popular music and the culture industries throughout its history. As Marion Leonard and Robert Strachan have said, "Notions of authenticity have been positioned around issues related to historical continuity, artistic expression and sincerity, autonomy from commercial imperatives, technology and production, and the expression of and engagement with the cultures of certain audiences, communities, or localities."[24] These specific articulations of the concept of authenticity have proven especially important to aesthetic judgments and evaluations of popular music among both fans and critics. The concept of authenticity may take several different forms related to popular music's aesthetic precepts, but the varied meanings of authenticity are typically mobilized to highlight the ways in which a particular artist is positioned outside of the matrix of commercial entertainment. Authenticity thus serves as a kind of guarantor of a particular artist's ambition, sincerity, importance, and insight into everyday life or social experience. In the past, particular expressions of authenticity have been used to valorize rock artists rather than pop performers, African American originators rather than white copycats, world music rather than American top-40 radio, albums rather than singles, music of the past rather than music of the present, and folk and roots music rather than slickly produced, radio-ready teen fare.

Having briefly sketched this discursive positioning of authenticity, we can see how the concept informs the Coens' work at several levels. The Coens' films, for example, furnish several examples of music that embraces the values of authenticity as it has been constructed in fan and critical discourses. Their use of songs and artists from earlier historical periods, such as Bob Dylan, the Four Tops, and the Stanley Brothers, evinces a sense of authenticity rooted in tradition that exists in opposition to contemporary superstars like Justin Bieber or Maroon 5. Likewise, in *Blood Simple* and *The Ladykillers*, the Coens make use of African American styles of music that are, in themselves, racially coded as more authentic than white pop music. In both of these films, the Coens make use of vernacular music that, because of its relation to folk art, is seen as a more genuine expression of working-class and rural values. The marketing of the soundtrack album from *O Brother* supported the music's location in this sort of habitus, as the album was frequently featured on National Public Radio rather than more mainstream venues. Last, by selecting bluegrass and country artists, the Coens embrace the aesthetic of "high lonesome," a concept that summarizes several markers of country music tradition. Indeed, the narrative of *O Brother, Where Art Thou?* is virtually a catalog of the themes and images explored by Cecelia Tichi in her landmark work on country music.[25] These themes and images include such things as home, family, the road, loneliness, rootlessness, and nature.

Yet although it is almost inevitable that the Coens' selection of artists would carry some of the discursive baggage entailed in the concept of authenticity, their use of the appellation "music archivist" suggests that their soundtracks participate in some aspect of auteurist self-definition. In this respect, the Coens' desire to elevate the cultural status of their soundtracks is not unlike the way fans use musical tastes as a marker of identity within particular subcultures. Teddy Boys, Mods, Hippies, Punks, Goths, and Riot Grrls all use their tastes in music and fashion to communicate their rejection of mainstream culture. Although it is manifested in a different way, the Coens display the same impulse to link taste, culture, and identity in a manner that embraces the space of the margins. Viewed critically, the term "music archivist" might thus seem to be little more than a fancy way to describe the Coens as "fanboy" record collectors who, of course, are known for their cataloging and taxonomic tendencies. Though they aspire to the cultural capital of a music archivist, the Coens are probably closer to the real-life counterparts of Nick Hornby's record-store geeks in *High Fidelity* (1995).

Besides implying a shift in the music producer's institutional status and mission, the term "music archivist" suggests that films may serve an "archeological" role by unearthing long- forgotten or neglected recording artists. This aspect of the aural design of *Lebowski*, *O Brother*, and *The Ladykillers* is supported by a symptomatic reading of some of the critical scholarship on the so-called *O Brother* phenomenon. For example, in two separate articles included in *Echo*'s roundtable discussion of *O Brother*, the authors situate T-Bone Burnett's soundtrack in relation to the pioneering work of Alan Lomax and his extensive body of ethnographic recordings. In fact, Rachel Howard began her essay by asserting:

> When Alan Lomax died in July 2002 at the age of 87, nearly every obituary mentioned the *O Brother, Where Art Thou?* soundtrack, which includes both a recording by Lomax and a song he arranged. I find it fitting that Lomax's epitaphs tie him directly to this platinum-selling package of roots music. Both Lomax's work and the *O Brother* soundtrack have exposed time-tested music to contemporary audiences.[26]

Yet if Howard is correct in contending that Lomax's legacy and the *O Brother* phenomenon deserve to be mentioned in the same breath, isn't the reverse also true? If *O Brother*'s commercial success casts a reflected glow on Lomax's legacy, doesn't Lomax's legacy suggest something about the cultural ambitions of both the Coens and T-Bone Burnett? Howard writes, "Lomax's noble impulse to preserve and present vernacular music was long intertwined with his desire to popularize and profit from it." Might the same be said of the Coens and Burnett?

Besides articulating a cultural synergy between cinema and music, the success of *O Brother, Where Art Thou?* and, to a lesser degree, *The Ladykillers* suggests that film could play an even greater role in the preservation and dissemination of vernacular music than it has in the past. As Anthony Seeger notes in his discussion of Alan Lomax's field recordings, anthologies and compilation albums may soon be things of the past. File-sharing, MP3s, and other technological advances have drastically altered consumption and listening habits, and companies like Rounder and Folkways that specialize in anthologies of vernacular music have been especially affected by these shifts. As Seeger puts it, "Is the age of compilations over in a time when individual files are shared, often without any text, and often without neighboring tracks?"[27]

Yet if Seeger is right, then films may well be one of the last places where audiences can hear vernacular music in a holistic, rather than atomistic, fashion. Clearly, a film typically does not offer the kinds of background information that appears in the annotations and liner notes of compilation albums. That said, films nonetheless preserve some of the anthology's virtues insofar as music can be selected and sequenced in ways that indicate the depth, diversity, and richness of vernacular music history. This potentiality of film is implicitly inscribed in the Coens' collaboration with T-Bone Burnett under the guise of "music archivist."

POP MUSIC IN THE COENS' FILMS AFTER *O BROTHER, WHERE ART THOU?*

As the film that seemed to provide the Coens with their commercial breakthrough, *O Brother, Where Art Thou?* has a central place in any account of their career. For this reason, the film seems to divide the Coens' career into two distinct parts: pre-*Brother* and post-*Brother*. While space does not allow for a complete survey of pop music in the films the Coens made after *O Brother*, a few remarks are in order to illustrate the way that they continue to display, albeit in somewhat piecemeal fashion, the tendencies that I have already highlighted.

Intolerable Cruelty (2003) and *True Grit* (2010) show both the Coens' archival leanings and their penchant for intertextual allusionism. *Intolerable Cruelty* features Big Bill Broonzy's "The Glory of Love," a Smithsonian Folkways recording that seems to hark back to the roots music of *O Brother*. Yet the Coens' inclusion of four Paul Simon songs in *Intolerable Cruelty* proves to be a far more meaningful musical gesture, as the frequent professional separations and reunions between Simon and Garfunkel seem to parallel the marriages and divorces that inform the film's plot. *True Grit*, on the other hand, includes several Protestant hymns that appear both as source music in the film and that are incorporated into Carter Burwell's score for the film. The inclusion of these hymns is motivated by *True Grit's* treatment of biblical themes of retribution and grace; yet they also recall the inclusion of gospel music in the soundtracks for both *O Brother* and *The Ladykillers*. More to the point, though, the inclusion of "Leaning on the Everlasting Arms" also serves as an allusion to a Coens favorite, *The Night of the Hunter*. Once again, the

Coens' allusion goes well beyond a simple reference to the Charles Laughton classic. The inclusion of "Leaning" draws parallels between the two films' pre-adolescent heroes: *Hunter's* John Harper and *Grit's* Mattie Ross.

Like *The Big Lebowski* and *O Brother*, the Coens' 2009 film *A Serious Man* exhibits their interest in playing with ideas of historicity. In the same way that *O Brother* glosses Homer's *Odyssey*, *A Serious Man* is a tongue-in-cheek reworking of the Book of Job updated to a more contemporary setting. The Coens' play with historicity also extends to the film's treatment of popular music. A running gag in the film involves the protagonist's dispute with the Columbia Record Club. Larry repeatedly tries to return copies of Santana's *Abraxis* and Creedence Clearwater Revival's *Cosmo's Factory*. It is worth noting that both of these musical artists were featured on the soundtrack of *The Big Lebowski*, but here they function more explicitly to create a kind of historical anachronism in *A Serious Man*. Both albums were released in 1970, even though the film itself is set in 1967. A similar anachronism is created by the use of Jimi Hendrix's song "Machine Gun" to accompany the story told to Larry by Rabbi Nachtner about Dr. Sussman's discovery of letters engraved on the teeth of a "goy" patient. Like the Santana and CCR albums, "Machine Gun" was released in 1970.

Although all of these examples offer further evidence of the Coens' interests in musical archivism and intertextuality, the film that is perhaps their biggest critical success notably departs from these tendencies. *No Country for Old Men* cleaned up at the 2008 Academy Awards, winning Oscars for the Coens for Best Directing, Best Adapted Screenplay, and Best Picture. One mark of the Coens' seriousness in their dramatic treatment of the material is their very faithful adaptation of Cormac McCarthy's acclaimed novel. Another is the film's rejection of any kind of conventional music. As Carter Burwell put it, "[T]he entire film takes place without songs or identifiable score...."[28] Burwell composed 13 minutes of music for *No Country*, but the music consists of sustained tones that more or less merge with the film's sound effects. By avoiding conventional harmonies, melodies, and rhythms, Burwell tried to preserve the sense of raw quiet that characterizes the film's Texas landscapes. Despite the Coens' reputation for postmodern jokiness, their decision to play it straight in *No Country* brought them Hollywood's biggest prize. It is perhaps telling that they achieved it by appearing to avoid the use of music altogether.

CONCLUSION

These two aspects of the Coens' use of popular music in their films—as a form of postmodern referentiality and as a quasi-archival presentation of folk, country, and gospel music—might seem to be at cross purposes. Yet, if we accept these as two legitimate, if distinct, tendencies within the Coens' work, we can also see the way they are correlated with the narrative, visual, and aural regimes of their films. The narrative elements and visual style of the Coens' films is often grotesque, caricatured, ironic, satiric, and highly intertextual. Yet such playful postmodernism does not always extend to the music of the Coen brothers' films. Rather, the Coens' use of popular music displays their deep investment in notions of musical expressiveness and cultural authenticity, even as they manipulate that music's historicity in their placement of it within a narrative context. When the Coens borrow the title of director John Louis Sullivan's fictive social problem film, *O Brother, Where Art Thou?* the gesture reinforces the playful allusiveness of their storytelling. When, however, the Coens also play Harry McClintock's 1928 recording of "Big Rock Candy Mountain" over the film's title card, their inclusion of this little-known chestnut practically begs to be taken seriously.

NOTES

1. Quoted in James Mottram, *The Coen Brothers: The Life of the Mind* (London: BT Batsford, 2000), 11.
2. Josh Levine, *The Coen Brothers* (Toronto: ECW, 2000), 5–7. See also Eddie Robson, *Coen Brothers* (London: Virgin, 2003), 5–7.
3. Levine, 5.
4. For more on the Coens as exemplary postmodernists, see Joseph Natoli, "Ethan and Joel Coen," *Postmodernism: The Key Figures*, Hans Bertens and Joseph Natoli, eds. (Malden, UK: Blackwell, 2002), 88–92; and R. Barton Palmer, *Joel and Ethan Coen* (Urbana, IL: University of Illinois Press, 2004). In contrast to this characterization, Michael Z. Newman acknowledges the importance of postmodernism to the Coens' work, but expresses interest in the way academic definitions of postmodernism have "trickled down" into pop culture discourse, situating the Coens' application of postmodernist ideas within this vernacular sphere. Commenting on the question of postmodernist originality, Newman says, "What might appear to be a simple failure of originality—one critic upon seeing *Miller's Crossing* wrote that Dashiell Hammett's estate should sue for plagiarism—is actually a point of interest. The Coens have an original way of being unoriginal. This is what people mean when they say that the Coens play with genre: genres are among their influences, and the way these influences are repurposed and inhabited in the Coen brothers' work is a central appeal of their aesthetic." See Michael Z. Newman, *Indie: An American Film Culture* (New York: Columbia University Press, 2011), 147–148.
5. Todd McCarthy, "Review of *The Hudsucker Proxy*," *Variety*, January 31, 1994. Reprinted in Paul A. Woods, ed., *Joel & Ethan Coen: Blood Siblings* (London: Plexus, 2000), 117–119.
6. See, for example, Hutcheon's *A Poetics of Postmodernism: History, Theory, Fiction* (New York: Routledge, 1988); and McHale's *Postmodernist Fiction* (New York: Methuen, 1987).
7. Quoted in Jonathan Culler, *Structuralist Poetics: Structuralism, Linguistics, and the Study of Literature* (Ithaca, NY: Cornell University Press, 1975), 139.
8. Palmer, 17.

9. For more on the "servant of two masters" plot, see Christopher Frayling's *Spaghetti Westerns: Cowboys and Europeans from Karl May to Sergio Leone*, second edition (New York: I. B. Tauris, 2006), 141–153.

10. Palmer, 32.

11. Parts of the "Goofing-Off Suite" are reprinted in Pete Seeger's *Where Have All the Flowers Gone: A Singer's Stories, Songs, Seeds, Robberies* (Bethlehem, PA: Sing Out Corp., 1999).

12. The Coens use this interplay between source music and non-diegetic score elsewhere in the film. For example, when Hi tries to steal some Huggies from the Short Stop midway through the film, the soundtrack alternates between iterations of the various themes from Seeger's "Goofing-Off Suite" with muzak versions of those themes that are motivated as originating from the sound systems of the convenience and grocery stores that Hi passes through during the chase that follows his attempted robbery. For example, the "Russian Themes and Yodel" is rearranged as Brazilian-styled samba heard inside the Short Stop.

13. Daniel Goldmark, "*O Brother, Where Art Thou?*: A Musical Appreciation," *Xavier Review* 23, no. 2 (Fall 2003): 31–41.

14. Box office figures provided in Mottram, 135.

15. Robson, 182.

16. Quoted in Levine, 143. Erica Rowell argues that the choice of music becomes an important way of drawing a sharp distinction between Dude and millionaire Jeffrey Lebowski. In contrast to the rock and roll that helps to characterize Dude, classical music—excerpts of Mozart's *Requiem* and Erich Wolfgang Korngold's opera *Die Tote Stadt*—is used for the scenes in the Lebowski mansion. Thus, whereas rock and roll is life-affirming for Dude, classical music carries associations of death for Jeffrey, a widowed man who has amorous feelings for a woman who resembles his dead wife. See Rowell, *The Brothers Grim: The Films of Ethan and Joel Coen* (Lanham, MD: Scarecrow, 2007), 234–235.

17. For more on this example as musical pun, see my essay "Popular Song and Comic Allusion in Contemporary Cinema," *Soundtrack Available: Essays on Film and Popular Music*, Arthur Knight and Pamela Robertson Wojcik, eds. (Durham, NC: Duke University Press, 2002), 407–430.

18. Steven Levy, "Shot by Shot," *The Coen Brothers Interviews*, William Rodney Allen, ed. (Jackson, MS: University of Mississippi Press, 2006), 39.

19. For an incisive analysis of the song's historic association with Irishness, see Malachy McCourt, *Danny Boy: The Legend of a Beloved Irish Ballad* (New York: New American Library, 2002).

20. McCourt's book also discusses the longstanding association of "Danny Boy" with sorrow and mourning. In fact, McCourt points out that the song has commonly been performed at funeral ceremonies since 2001. He cites the rendition performed at Carroll O'Connor's funeral mass and at memorial services for the fallen heroes of the New York Fire and Police Departments after 9/11.

21. Quoted in Philip Brophy, ed., "Music for the Films of Joel and Ethan Coen: Carter Burwell in Conversation," *Cinesonic: The World of Sound in Film* (Sydney, AU: Australian Film, Television and Radio School, 1999), 32. See also Carter Burwell, "Composing for the Coen Brothers," *Soundscape: The School of Sound Lectures, 1998-2001*, Larry Sider, Diane Freeman, and Jerry Sider, eds. (London: Wallflower, 2003), 195–208.

22. For more on the role of music supervisors, see my essay "Taking Music Supervisors Seriously," *Cinesonic: Experiencing the Soundtrack*, Philip Brophy, ed. (Sydney, AU: Australian Film, Television and Radio School, 2001), 125–146.

23. Michael Z. Newman makes a similar point about the Coens' fondness for allusions to film texts and genres: "The Coens' pastiches do a critical job of selecting, collecting, foregrounding, curating, preserving, archiving, interpreting, and reimagining the media that have been significant in their lives and in the lives of the community that shares their cultural literacy." See Newman, *Indie: An American Film Culture*, 154.

24. Marion Leonard and Robert Strachan, "Authenticity," *The Continuum Encyclopedia of Popular Music of the World*, volume 1, John Shepherd, David Horn, Dave Laing, Paul Oliver, and Peter Wicke, eds. (New York: Continuum, 2003), 164–166.

25. See Cecilia Tichi, *High Lonesome: The American Culture of Country Music* (Chapel Hill, NC: University of North Carolina Press, 1994).

26. Rachel Howard, "Constant Sorrow: Traditional Music and Fandom," *Echo* 4, no. 2 (Fall 2002), www.echo.ucla.edu.

27. Anthony Seeger, "Reflections on Anthologized Recordings: The Alan Lomax Collection on Rounder Records and the John A. and Ruby Lomax 1939 Southern States Recording Trip on the Library of Congress American Memory Website," *Echo* 4, no. 2 (Fall 2002). www.echo.ucla.edu.

28. Carter Burwell, "Carter's Notes" on *No Country for Old Men*, Body Inc., accessed June 29, 2011, http://www.thebodyinc.net/projects/NCFOM.html.

CHAPTER 6

You've Heard This One Before: Quentin Tarantino's Scoring Practices from *Kill Bill* to *Inglourious Basterds*

KEN GARNER

A wind-up gramophone features in a set-piece, 20-minute scene in Tarantino's *Inglourious Basterds* (2009). We see it twice. It's clearly the source of diegetic music playing in a French basement café where Allied conspirators are meeting in 1944 to discuss "Operation Kino," their plan to blow up members of the Nazi hierarchy as they attend a film premiere at a Paris cinema. There is a fleeting extreme close-up, sideways and at eye level, of the needle and arm riding in the record groove as a song plays. The needle is brought into focus for a moment, so we can locate the period music's source. We see it a second time, but this time in a long shot, as an SS officer appears from a table that was hidden from view, and lifts the stuck needle from the record's center—the spinning, crackling run-out groove underlining the awkward human silence and inertia that have fallen, everyone frozen by the Nazi's shouted inquiry from the wings (figure 6.1).

Having performed its cinematic function, the gramophone is not referred to again. There is no more music in the scene. A chill has descended on the evening, and perhaps no one felt like putting another record on anyway. We never learn who had selected the records either, or why they chose those 78s in particular. Three records are heard in the café scene. Two were big hits from Nazi-era movie musicals: "*Davon geht die Welt nicht unter*" from *Die grosse Liebe* (1942), sung by Zarah Leander; and "*Ich wollt ich wär ein Huhn*" from *Glückskinder* (1936), sung by Lillian Harvey and Willy Fritsch. In between those two, we hear an entirely fake French re-recording of June

Figure 6.1: *Inglourious Basterds*: An SS officer takes control of the gramophone and the action ("The Man with the Big Sombrero").

Havoc's 1943 hit "The Man with the Big Sombrero" from the Hollywood musical comedy *Hi Diddle Diddle*. This is a tune and performance that Tarantino apparently liked so much, he arranged for L.A.-based cabaret singer-songwriter and performer Samantha Shelton to re-record it in French with new instrumentation. Then he combined the new performance with elements of the original and mixed the two to sound like a '40s record, complete with added surface noise for verisimilitude. Tarantino even produced Shelton in a promotional video for the soundtrack CD release, directed by Merit Avis, a spot that more or less exactly sought to replicate June Havoc's performance in her original film. Shelton bizarrely duets with herself here, appearing in the flesh in a restaurant alongside a movie image of herself, in shot, doing her number in a "soundie." No listener on first hearing would spot any historical differences between the original "Man with the Big Sombrero" and Shelton's re-recording. The period effect is absolutely convincing. They sound just like real records of the '30s and '40s that some celebrating off-duty Wehrmacht soldiers might have selected from an accommodating French café owner's collection of recent hits.

To anyone familiar with how music was used in Tarantino's early films, this scene is surprising. In its use of diegetic music, it is unlike any other scene in any other Tarantino movie. What's shocking is its conventionality. The music is selected and produced by the director, and it is located in the diegesis via the on-screen gramophone simply to authenticate the location, period, and nature of the social occasion for the soldiers. In contrast, anything unconventional or distinctive, everything that we had come to expect of the use of diegetic music in Tarantino's films, is missing from this scene. We do not see a human hand selecting a specific record. No individual character speaks, sings, dances, or lip-synchs along to any of them. No characters in the scene talk about or otherwise show us what this music or playing these particular records means to them. The film does not foreground the song's selection. The song is not included or featured in order to tell us anything about any specific character or any relationship between specific characters.

Then there is the sheer production effort that has gone into authenticating less than three minutes of one scene's music, namely the French reworking of "The Man with the Big Sombrero." Quentin Tarantino commissioning new musical recordings for a film? Whoever would have imagined that back in the '90s? It should be mentioned that *Inglourious Basterds* was not the first production in which Tarantino did this. He commissioned hip-hop artist RZA to contribute original sound elements, fragments, and tracks to *Kill Bill, Vol. 1 and Vol. 2* (2003, 2004). But in effect, with the exception of two short rhythm track instrumentals, these turned out to be little more than stings, special effects, tops, and tails of various source existing tracks—included either to audio-animate or set up action scenes, most notably blow and collision effects in the "House of the Blue Leaves" fight sequence between the Bride and Crazy 88.

These somewhat overlooked, fleeting aspects are, it's true, not representative of the scoring practices in *Kill Bill, Vols. 1 and 2, Death Proof,* and *Inglourious Basterds*—Tarantino's films since the millennium. But these aspects are undeniably different from what had gone before. Ten years ago, analyzing Tarantino's use of music in *Reservoir Dogs, Pulp Fiction,* and *Jackie Brown,* I argued that "it is the choice of this-music or that-music in these particular circumstances, its switching on and off—rather than just the music itself—which is made indicative of character and situation." I also concluded that his scoring of his main titles with largely forgotten pop records characterized by distinctive or even unique musical voices (whether vocal or instrumental) was not, when analyzed in detail, "ironic," or "in contrast," or "in counterpoint" with the visual and textual material—as popular critical convention then had it—but in fact was wholly synchronous and in harmony with the total intended message.[1] Robert Miklitsch's persuasive analysis of *Jackie Brown* offers further evidence of the way the racial "gaze" and "audiophilia" in Tarantino's scoring choices serve to "transfigure" actress Pam Grier, authenticating her character in *Jackie Brown* 20 years after she had played the blaxploitation role of Foxy Brown: "[S]he moves not simply to, but with, the music," the music telling us that "she is a woman with her feet planted firmly *on* the ground."[2] In their introduction to the edited collection *Film's Musical Moments,* Estella Tincknell and Ian Conrich cite *Pulp Fiction* as an example of recent films that show signs of the "music video aesthetic" as identified by John Mundy (1999), an aesthetic in which "musical moments not only break narrative continuity, they are also frequently self-consciously non-realist in style, using montage editing and an aesthetic that defies continuity to produce textual disruption."[3] But Tincknell offers a subtle contrast of perspective in her later chapter in the same book, where she analyzes in some detail Vincent Vega and Mia Wallace's dance to Chuck Berry's "You Never Can Tell" in the "Jack Rabbit Slim Twist Contest," and concludes that it is "the only point in the film where narrative and music are fully integrated...where the affective discourse of the music may overturn the disaffective knowingness of the narrative." Tincknell proposes, in other words, that this seeming disruption of the narrative by a musical "performance" is in fact nothing of the kind, but just as much a part of the film's story as any other moment.[4] Thinking along similar lines, Mervyn Cooke is also surely correct to suggest that in *Pulp Fiction*, "music is generally foregrounded in the film's more consciously stylised scenes, and does not interfere with the *verité*-style narrative advancement."[5] The music propels the action throughout, whatever the context, while its precise meaning for the characters remains fluid or at least of lesser interest to the director. As Lisa Coulthard argues in her analysis of Tarantino's influence on "the scoring of cinematic violence," he stresses "an aesthetic of superficial, kinetic energy over affective or intellectual engagement."[6] Claudia Gorbman has gone so far, in her essay "Auteur Music," as to call Tarantino one of those contemporary auteur directors who demonstrate her idea of the *mélomane*, the term taken from the French word for "music lover." "For many filmmakers," Gorbman writes, "music is a platform for the idiosyncratic expression of taste, and thus it conveys not only meaning in terms of plot and theme, but meaning as authorial signature itself."[7]

TARANTINO'S NEW SIGNATURE: SCORING WITH SCORES

This much was evident from Tarantino's first three films. Scrutiny of his music selection and use in his more recent work, however, suggests something has changed in this "authorial signature"—if not in terms of his musical taste, then at least in his desire to display that taste. And what we find, although not necessarily prompting wholesale revision or the outright junking of my own and other scholars' arguments about the earlier work, does demand that we modulate some of our claims and our emphasis on a sustained Tarantino-esque originality in his deployment of musical effects. In 2001, I argued there were three distinct, different roles for music in his films, each of which he deployed to unique effect: (1) music for main themes and scoring; (2) unselected, incidental diegetic music; and (3) diegetic music selected by characters.[8] That simple taxonomy does not quite hold true anymore for all six of his major films (counting *Kill Bill* as one) for three reasons: First, the balance among these roles for music has changed substantially, as has the impact of those roles; and second, the kinds of music selected, their deployment and effect, and Tarantino's evident reasons behind such directorial choices, especially for main themes and scoring, have altered almost beyond recognition. And finally, to that list must be added a new and fourth use for music, seeming at least on the surface to embrace Mundy's declared "music video aesthetic": This is Tarantino's set-piece, non-realist scenes scored with existing music that is at stylistic odds with the rest of the soundtrack. This reevaluation points us to the following new aspects of Tarantino's musical priorities:

- non-foregrounded diegetic music
- foregrounded, character-selected diegetic music
- non-diegetic "scored" music, selected overwhelmingly from existing commercially released sources, including for main titles
- non-diegetic, non-realist scored scenes out of sync with the majority of the soundtrack

In summary, two relatively minor if still revealing changes in Tarantino's directorial approach to music are his non-foregrounded diegetic music use and his commissioning of modest fragments of new musical performance for the sake of aural verisimilitude in specific scenes—this last including the *Inglourious Basterds* café scene, as well as the 5-6-7-8's live performance of surf guitar-style numbers in *Kill Bill, Vol. 1's* "House of Blue Leaves" scene, and RZA's and Robert Rodriguez's riffs and stings in *Kill Bill, Vols. 1* and *2*.

But it is the third and fourth elements of the reprioritized list above that represent the defining, more substantial, and significant changes in Tarantino's scoring trends across his recent films. The most far-reaching of these is his movement away from scoring scenes with relatively obscure preexisting pop records and toward scoring his non-diegetic music almost entirely with themes and fragments from existing composed film scores. When these examples of recycled film scoring accompany main title or non-realist chapter headings or character flashback non-realist scenes, they are furthermore mixed with a self-conscious, deliberate addition of analog vinyl and film sound surface noise, including scratches, jumps, and other sound-effect "accidentals." It is not just that Tarantino is now scoring his movies with old movie soundtrack albums, he also wants you to hear that this is what he's doing. Even when he is not showing the needle dropping into the record groove, he makes sure we hear it.

There are still flashes of the old Tarantino mixed in with these recent, reprioritized examples. The first act of *Death Proof*, for instance, is scored almost entirely with diegetic music apparently selected by people on-screen. (The exceptions are the main titles and two repeats of a brief fragment of

Morricone's "Paranoia Prima" from *Il Gatto a Nove Code,* accompanying Stuntman Mike's mysterious first stalking of the character Arlene, and the "Sally and Jack" theme from *Blow Up* while Julia texts her guy.) In *Death Proof,* this character-selected diegetic music culminates with local radio DJ Jungle Julia phoning in a request for her colleagues at the station to play Dave Dee Dozy Beaky Mick and Tich's "Hold Tight," the song they groove to in the car until the moment Stuntman Mike fatally rams them head-on.

But the character-selected music begins 35 minutes earlier when the women arrive at the Texas Chili Parlor and we see Julia dancing in front of the bar's jukebox to Smith's 1969 hit cover of "Baby It's You." This is the first of six late-'60s-to-early-'70s records that we hear coming from the juke-box—all of them chosen by people in the bar, if not always by named characters. One of the songs, Eddie Floyd's March 1966 debut B-side of Stax 187, "Good Love Bad Love," gets played twice. There are frequent close-ups of the workings of the jukebox, with the records spinning and the needle in the groove. Jungle Julia clearly has chosen "Baby It's You," and Arlene chooses "The Love You Save" by Joe Tex and then the Coasters' "Down in Mexico" for her lap dance for Stuntman Mike. In between, unknown persons pick T Rex's "Jeepster," Pacific Gas & Electric's "Staggolee," and the Eddie Floyd B-side twice.

The lyrics to all these songs are about desire and desire gone wrong, and the music is generally in a soul style combining commercial funkiness with a seemingly authentic black witness to the time of its making. In particular, Brian Ward has commented on how the Joe Tex song that we hear in the Texas Chili Parlor scene "described how racism and its psychological and economic consequences still accounted for much of the domestic instability in black America, and thereby inspired black unity and progress." Ward notes with admiration how Tex artfully "placed his own travails and observations at the centre of a song which evoked all too common experiences in black America"—it's a cautionary tale of personal violence, in other words, yet sung in the language of social and political abuse.[9] But in Tarantino's Texas Chili Parlor scene, these records serve merely to underscore the drunken abandon of our barely dressed, long-legged heroines as they apparently set out on a quest for an imagined authentic black cultural experience. They do this while on a girls' night out on a hot and sticky evening down near the border with Mexico, whose exotic bars, social transgressions, and provocative dancing are celebrated in the Coasters' hit, capping the sense of looming if unspecified danger lurking behind the sensuous promise of the songs in this scene. On one level, then, music would seem to serve the same function in the Texas Chili Parlor scene that it does in Tarantino's earlier films, "foregrounding the central female characters' music selection and control of the aural environment," and helping the characters show themselves to be "in control enough to choose, yet choosing music which just might drive [them] out of control."[10]

But on further examination, there is another, somewhat more detached way to listen to this sequence. The AMI Continental 2 jukebox that we see in the Texas Chili Parlor scene is actually Tarantino's, as he has confirmed in an interview: "By the way, in *Death Proof*, the jukebox...that's my jukebox, her name is Amy. They're not just 45s in there, they're all original 45s, they're all the original labels, it's Stax, it's Redbird, there's some European pressings in there."[11] The records in the Texas Chili Parlor jukebox are all his, and the card index of the 45s—shown on-screen in a close-up—is all written in his own hand. The full list he has supplied of the 50 discs on his own machine (see appendix 6.1, *The Quentin Tarantino Archives*, 2011) reveals they are almost all from the mid-1960s to the late '70s, the time of Tarantino's childhood and early teens, and include many single favorites previously used in his soundtracks—"Miserlou," "Little Green Bag," "Natural High"—as well as those played in the Texas Chili Parlor. That is, all of the Chili Parlor songs except one: The Coasters' "Down in Mexico" is missing. This explains why we do not get to see it being selected or spinning in close-up. There's a simple reason why it's not on Tarantino's jukebox: The version used in *Death Proof* was never released as a 45 rpm single, and Tarantino only has it on LP. The song is a re-recording made in the mid-'70s for the group's *16 Greatest Hits* LP released on Trip Records in 1975. Tarantino has said that of all the records used in his films, this is "hands-down, no competition, the rarest" because it was "newly recorded...the classics redone."[12] A long discussion and investigation of Coasters discographies by vinyl collectors has confirmed that "Down in Mexico" cannot be traced as a 45.[13]

LISTEN TO MY SCRATCHED SOUNDTRACK LPS

This somewhat paradoxical and self-indulgent deployment of Tarantino's musical sources here is of a piece with his use of location. The real Texas Chili Parlor on Lavaca Street in downtown Austin, Texas, a favorite of Tarantino's and the place where he shot the interiors and one establishing shot at the front, does not have a back porch or parking lot out in back, and no nacho grande platter, no virgin piña colada, and of course no AMI Continental 2 jukebox full of R&B oldies.[14] In the film, the owner of the bar is named Warren and is played by Tarantino, and Warren's musical taste, menu, and drinks are celebrated in the dialogue, which Tarantino wrote himself. While Stuntman Mike's recounting of his career in '60s and '70s TV shows such as *The High Chaparral* and *The Virginian* is mocked by the script and characters, this is not the case with the music that Warren's jukebox offers.

Figure 6.2: *Death Proof:* Arlene lap dances to Tarantino's records on Tarantino's jukebox for Tarantino's camera ("Down in Mexico").

The characters' selection and enjoyment of his old 45s display no irony or distance. Jungle Julia and Arlene are lap dancing for Quentin Tarantino's directorial pleasure, celebrating his musical taste rather than making their own record selection (figure 6.2). The director is clearly not aiming for realism: What Texas restaurant today would have a vinyl jukebox, much less one with 45s? By choosing instead to ground the scene in multiple known, documented details of his own taste, yet at the same time manipulating them sonically to make sure they are perceived as realistic, Tarantino only draws the filmgoer's attention to his layers of authorial artifice.

It is instructive to hear what happens on the soundtrack when Julia sends her text message. To begin with, it's a visual jolt to see a mobile phone close-up, in a film that so far has been edited, art directed, scored, and post-produced to look like a cheap, early '70s "grindhouse" production. But the diegetic sound and music in the restaurant disappear altogether during her actual texting, with any contemporary phone sounds also removed until the very end, wholly replaced by "Sally and Jack" from *Blow Up.* Instead, we hear, quite loudly, the record scratches and surface noise from the soundtrack LP. Tarantino's touchstone for the authenticity he seeks to recreate in the Texas Chili Parlor scene is simply the vinyl pedigree of his own much-played record collection.

Tarantino's explicit celebration of the vinyl provenance of his non-diegetic sources is a relatively recent characteristic of his soundtracks. It's clearly a step beyond the main titles of *Reservoir Dogs* and *Pulp Fiction,* where a DJ's voice or radio retuning filled the cinema upfront with the sounds of the characters' chosen musical consumption, and the intensity of that consumption precluded any vinyl surface noise, scratches, or distortion. But in his later films, it is precisely in the main titles where these sounds of provenance have become most obvious. Morricone's "A Silhouette of Doom" from his score for *Navajo Joe* (1966), in an edited form, pounds and scrapes menacingly at the opening of *Kill Bill, Vol. 2*: behind the titles, the reprise of Bill's shooting of the Bride and her backstory of *Vol. 1* while driving to the denouement. Surface noise and crackles are clearly audible in the opening bars over the studio and producer credits. *Death Proof* and *Inglourious Basterds* go one step further in selecting for their main titles the title theme itself from another film. Songwriter and film composer Jack Nitzsche's guitar instrumental "The Last Race" was originally the theme for the 1965 teen sci-fi comedy *Village of the Giants*, although the tune had been released by Reprise Records as a Nitzsche 45 rpm B-side the year before. In the main titles of *Death Proof*, the track is subject to crackles and scratches as part of the deliberately "cheap" continuity and editing lapses that Tarantino wanted for his *Grindhouse* double-feature project. For *Inglourious Basterds*, he uses "The Green Leaves of Summer," the famous title theme from 1960's *The Alamo*—though not the song from Dmitri Tiomkin's original *Alamo* soundtrack, but an instrumental version performed by accordionist/arranger Nick Perito and his Orchestra and Chorus that was released in the U.S. and U.K. both as a 45 rpm single and on a compilation album, *Original Soundtracks and Hit Music from the Great Motion Picture Themes*. Once again, this vinyl provenance of the source is foregrounded in the final soundtrack mix, with scratches, surface noise, and some distortion in the strings at high volume.

The exception to these recent scoring practices with Tarantino's main titles is his use of Nancy Sinatra's 1966 cover version of Cher's hit "Bang Bang (My Baby Shot Me Down)" for *Kill Bill, Vol. 1*. We hear the song just after seeing the Bride shot by an off-screen Bill in the pre-credit sequence (figure 6.3). On one level, "Bang Bang (My Baby Shot Me Down)" fits very well as a theme song, although Tarantino takes a song in which a children's game serves a woman as metaphor for her husband's abandoning her, and reduces that game ("Bang Bang") to a mundane literalism; in *Kill Bill*, the Bride's "baby" really did shoot her down. "Bang Bang (My Baby Shot Me

Figure 6.3: *Kill Bill, Vol. 1*: "Bang Bang"—Billy Strange's tremolo electric guitar is Tarantino's first statement of how he is going to direct *Kill Bill, Vol. 1* ("Bang Bang [My Baby Shot Me Down]").

Down)" is an exception for Tarantino in that he neither sources it from an existing film soundtrack nor presents it to our ears with vinyl faults. The song benefits from a stylishly stripped-down performance, Sinatra's reverberating vocal in one channel balanced and accompanied only by the tremolo electric guitar of Billy Strange in the other. In this sense it could be said to offer the start of the story *two* distinct musical voices as our emotional guides, in a comparably confident way as a solo performer, an "unmistakenly expressive…singular musical personality,"[15] did in *Pulp Fiction* (Dick Dale's surf guitar), or *Jackie Brown* (Bobby Womack's voice). Given the relation between the lyrics and on-screen action, it is not fanciful to hear Nancy Sinatra's voice as that of the Bride, conveying the film subject's emotions, while Strange's solo guitar is heard as a textural commentary—electrically and acousmatically treated—on this character's experience.

Strange's guitar would thus stand for Tarantino's direction itself, telling us in advance something about how he will present the Bride's story. Unfortunately, this apparent clarity of scoring purpose does not continue. Although Dale's guitar sound in *Pulp Fiction* sets an extreme intensity of musical expression that the rest of the non-diegetic score of surf instrumentals seeks to follow stylistically, and *Jackie Brown* grounds the title character's past and mature development-through-action in '70s soul, the specific sound environment of Sinatra's record does not recur in *Kill Bill, Vol. 1*. Indeed, this plays out as the most musically and stylistically diverse of all Tarantino's soundtracks—whether or not to the film's benefit is a topic for later discussion.

There is perhaps a vague hint that this main title song, taken from the second LP released by a cult '60s act, may have a place in the on-screen Bride's own musical world. In the opening scene of *Kill Bill, Vol. 2*, she tells Bill that her fiancé Tommy owns "a used record store here in El Paso," and that she now works in the store: "I get to listen to music all day long, talk about music all day long, it's cool." The Bride is an assassin, and this sounds as implausible a career change to us as it evidently does to Bill. But if Tarantino had wanted to give any suggestion of her new job on the *Kill Bill* soundtrack, it would indeed have been more appropriate here than in any of his other films to let us hear—for instance, during the many times the Bride is shown driving—the scratches on records associated with her musical taste, listening choices, or new occupation. But there is no scratchy or diegetic music in either *Kill Bill* movie that was expressly chosen by the Bride.

With that exception, then, what might this vinyl-centricity of Tarantino's recent films' main title music signify? The audience hears an old record being played. For most, that will be the only obvious and immediate knowledge about this audio they have, that it is from an old record. A minority might think that it sounds like an old movie soundtrack. Just a few cognoscenti might recognize the specific soundtrack appropriated. As the journalist Steve Kandell put it to the director himself, "[A] lot of the pieces you play are not pieces that people really know."[16] These perceptions might entice us into a postmodern analysis of Tarantino's methods and intentions. In such an analysis, the opening theme's audio glitches, vinyl scratches, and surface noise are signs of each film's intertextuality, its invitation to the audience to be conscious above all else that this film is a construct formed of various media and ways of telling. In this sense, audiences may not distinguish between scratches on a vinyl LP (or 78 rpm surface noise, as in *Inglourious Basterds*) and soundtrack wear and tear on the film reel itself (as in *Death Proof*). In a matter of seconds, the audience may thus form two perceptions of the film's deliberate playfulness in establishing its audio environment: that this movie is going to sound a bit like old movies, and someone in this movie is playing us some old records. That someone is clearly the director Tarantino himself, whether the audience consciously resolves this personification fully or not. What remains to be seen is whether the soundtrack source selections develop as the film proceeds into an integrated, consistent sound, one in which the various musics are persuasive enough in their total emotional effect—are sufficiently grounded in plot and character—to hold our awareness of the director's egotistic musical auteurism in check.

KILL BILL, VOLS. 1 AND 2: ALLUSION, INCONSISTENCY, AND ARPEGGIOS

But the soundtracks of *Kill Bill, Vols.* 1 and 2 appear on the surface to demonstrate little consistency of musical selection, scoring, or effect. The effective main theme of *Vol. 1*—Nancy Sinatra's "Bang Bang (My Baby Shot Me Down)"—is neither substantively repeated nor, at least until the end titles, has its musical style echoed in any other selections. (Strange's four-bar solo guitar intro is heard again briefly just once when the Bride arrives at Hanzo's noodle bar on Okinawa.) The only connection it has with the music heard during the main action—a tenuous connection, it must be said—is with Gheorghe Zamfir's "The Lonely Shepherd," heard repeatedly later. "Bang Bang (My Baby Shot Me Down)" and "The Lonely Shepherd" are both cult vinyl classics, whether as an LP track (Sinatra) or a 45 rpm single (Zamfir). Each has a clear mood of lament—at least in a conventionally musicological, western sense—with a slow solo melodic "voice" in the minor key, whether vocal or instrumental, and the opening accompaniment centered on an arpeggiated figure on guitar. Zamfir is accompanied by the James Last Orchestra, whose trademark precision trumpet section arrangements feature prominently as the song builds. Both songs stand for the Bride, the plaintive solo lead voice/instrument accompanying her story at key moments to emphasize her isolation and lonely quest, be it her would-be execution, her acquisition of the Hanza sword, or her updating the execution list on her flight home at the end, and over the end titles.

But a further, subtle musical connection might link Tarantino's deployment of these two records with his use of two famous Japanese vocal film themes, both sung by the actress Meiko Kaji, over the film's conclusion. Playing over the final defeat and death of Ishii at the Bride's hands in the snow-covered roof garden is *"Shura No Hana"* or *"The Flower of Carnage,"* the theme song from the 1973 female revenge thriller *Lady Snowblood*—the plot of which clearly inspired the Manga backstory for Tarantino's Oren Ishii character. And then we hear *"Urami-Bushi,"* the theme song from the *Sasori* women's prison films from 1972–73, following the reprise of Zamfir over the end credits. Both songs are again ballads in the minor key, here in 6/8 rhythm, with the solo female voice accompanied prominently by an arpeggiated figure played on acoustic guitar with orchestra and counterpointed with melodic lines played either on the panpipes (*"Shura No Hana"*) or trumpet (*"Urami-Bushi"*). The latter also features prominently in an accompanying reverberated electric guitar part. In short, these two songs have much in common with the Sinatra and Zamfir tracks in terms of harmony, vocal treatment, arrangement, and instrumentation. To get the musical message, no one in the cinema needs to know that these songs come from Tarantino's filmic models for *Kill Bill*, or that the lyrics tell of a woman's journey of suffering and falling to the ground (*"Shura No Hana"*)[17] and the endless blues that men cause women (*"Urami-Bushi"*). Through their association with each other and with the on-screen action, all these voices tell of a woman alone on a journey and beset by troubles.

The movement in sequence between these pieces—from Sinatra to Kaji via Zamfir, and from America to Japan via panpipes—matches the Bride's journey and the action's location. At first, it's possible that to a present-day American audience, the Kaji tracks, being Japanese, speak for the death of Oren Ishii. But surely that conception cannot last for long. Their appearance is a testament to Tarantino's boldness in appropriating these Japanese film themes, and he has us effortlessly transfer their mood and emotion to the Bride's sufferings and journey. The musical assortment within this film is also emblematic of Tarantino's movement away from using artist record releases and toward the use of soundtrack albums. We can find a demonstration of his move away from artists' releases at the opening of the final battle, where he gives us just two minutes of the rhythmic instrumental break from Santa Esmeralda's 1977 Latin-disco version of "Don't Let Me

Be Misunderstood"—the handclaps, drums, bongos, and acoustic guitar figures heard from 3 min./55 sec. to 5 min./55 sec. on the soundtrack CD's 10-minute version—before, more importantly, Oren Ishii dies to the sound of old film songs, which are heard in full.

The soundtracks he has chosen from here, excluding the two Kaji '70s themes, are diverse. They vary from Japanese yakuza films through spaghetti westerns and Italian cop movies, to mainstream Hollywood thrillers and TV detective and superhero series. They deploy themes from composers and songwriters, including Bernard Herrmann, Ennio Morricone, Elmer Bernstein, Luis Bacalov, Al Hirt, Isaac Hayes, and Quincy Jones. But most of these are used in fragmentary form, only a few seconds of a strong musical figure or percussive rhythm (often electronic, blaring, or distorted, with strong bass), and are combined with RZA's original loops, stings, and crashes to audio-animate or trigger the many fight sequences. The only thing that unites the appropriated soundtracks, apart from this characteristic violent deployment of extreme or percussive repeated figures, is that they are all drawn from the years 1967 to 1974. Finally there are the more recent Japanese film score tracks that Tarantino selects for *Kill Bill*, most notably Tomoyasu Hotei's funky re-recording of his theme from the 2000 film *Another Battle/ Shin Jingi Naki Tatakai*, "Battle without Honour and Humanity"; this is itself a tribute to an earlier series of Japanese yakuza films and features prominently at the appearance of Oren Ishii and in the *Kill Bill* trailers. Amid this audio diversity, and in contradiction to my argument about the Bride's and Tarantino's journey from songs to scores and from the U.S. to Japan, it is probably "Battle without Honour and Humanity" that most people recall as the defining contemporary, funky, and violent "theme" of *Kill Bill, Vol. 1*.

Then, in *Kill Bill, Vol. 2*, we are surprised to find that Tarantino has wholly abandoned the Japanese yakuza, kung fu, and TV theme influences; he scores most of the action with film soundtrack themes, this time mostly from Morricone's scores for *Il Mercenario, A Fistful of Dollars*, and *Navajo Joe*.[18] These are interspersed with brief original guitar-based themes by Robert Rodriguez that aspire to these models' spaghetti-western style and arrangements, without matching their intensity, originality, or memorability. And then, suddenly, there's a turn back; in the final chapter and end titles, these soundtracks and snippets are largely replaced by original artist records—music by Lole y Manuel, Malcolm Maclaren, Chingon (Rodriguez's own band), and Shivaree—songs that aspire to create what might be a contemporary spaghetti western, or rather a Tex-Mex sound palette, as the action goes south of the border for the Bride's showdown with Bill. Here the music increases in pace and percussive Latin effects, characterized across several tracks by handclaps, flamenco guitars, wailing female vocals, and, once again, tremolo and arpeggiated electric guitar figures.

More than anything, it is this musical style that holds the frankly disappointing final chapter together, shifting the movie from past genres into an imagined dangerous and contemporary exoticism, a possible present tense. But it comes too late to save the soundtrack. Just as Tarantino used up all his best set-piece scenes in *Vol. 1*, so he seems to have run out of scoring ideas in *Vol. 2*. Little of the music chosen is especially memorable or has meaning recast by its narrative deployment, as is true of the Nancy Sinatra and Gheorghe Zamfir tracks in *Vol. 1*. Above all, the interaction between Morricone's and Rodriguez's themes is self-defeating; the latter fail to bring that characteristic sense of impetus, shock, and "musical moment"—to use Conrich and Tincknell's term[19]—that drives Tarantino's better soundtracks. And perhaps it's the need to maintain audio consistency with the new Rodriguez recordings that has discouraged any reflective display of vinyl or film-track glitches in the Morricone tracks after the main titles. The film finally gives the impression that it cannot decide if it wants to remind you what a spaghetti western sounded like, or if it wants instead to define an all-new Tex-Mex yakuza genre through audio means.

DEATH PROOF: TWO-ACT MOVIE, TWO-ACT SCORE

In contrast, the soundtrack to *Death Proof* does on its own limited terms have a basic formal symmetry mirroring the film's two-act, crime-revenge structure. Setting aside the main titles, and the usual brief snippets of non-diegetic creepiness from Morricone and other scores as required, the first half is dominated by the R&B classic oldies that the girls choose from the jukebox in the Texas Chili Parlor. The second act, however, is scored mainly non-diegetically by hard-driving rock guitar and funk tunes and themes from Italian cop movie soundtracks of the '70s—sounds that really rev up in the "ship's mast" car chase conclusion. These uptempo driving tracks are clearly linked in style to Jack Nitzsche's guitar instrumental main title theme—quite apart from its being repeated, once only, at the very moment when the female stunt actresses decide to "get the bastard." Nitzsche also produced the soundtrack album for Brian De Palma's gay serial killer thriller *Cruising* (1980), featuring four tracks by Willy DeVille including "It's So Easy." The same cut features briefly in the *Death Proof* diegesis: Playing very forward in the mix and seemingly non-diegetically, the song is unexpectedly silenced when Stuntman Mike pulls up at the convenience store in Lebanon, Tennessee, alongside our new heroines, and turns off his in-car audio. Similarly, Lee is seen in the same scene singing along in the girls' car to Smith's version (presumably) of "Baby It's You," the song previously heard on the Texas Chili Parlor jukebox and now playing on Lee's iPod.

As in several Tarantino films, women seem to take over for themselves the emotion of the score. The women in *Death Proof* don't do this the way the women in *Pulp Fiction* or *Jackie Brown* do, by having us see them choosing the records themselves; here, rather, in becoming the avenging instigators of the final chase in the second act, the women acquire the drive and excitement of the instrumental guitar rock tracks and Italian thriller themes as an agent or aid to their motivation, and we inevitably come to associate this power with them. Up to this point, these themes and loud guitars had been explicitly connected with the original pursuer, Stuntman Mike, and not just by the diegetic moment indicated above; in the main titles and under Nitzsche's theme, we see several shots through his windshield of the roads and countryside where his second crime attempt will take place. In crude gender-positioning terms, we can say the film sets up a rather simple opposition, equating on the one hand R&B soul hits on the jukebox as providing the first-act girls with an alluring female sexual identity of consumption, but a kind of pleasure whose side effects they cannot control; and on the other hand, driving rock guitar soundtracks with the kind of machismo speed, pursuit, and violence that threaten death, but which our stunt-girl heroines in the second act are nevertheless able to master and claim as their own. The end titles juxtapose April March's kitsch-retro cover of Serge Gainsbourg's "Chick Habit"—a song combining '60s girl group arrangements, driving reverb guitar, edited-to-the-beat triple blasts of trumpet choruses, and female backing vocals—with still images of both '60s girls and our heroines from the film in smiling out-takes. In doing so, the titles offer some recuperation in their amusing silliness and finger-wagging lecturing of predatory men. But Tarantino's music, like his plot, leaves you wondering at an aesthetic that can casually assign gender-specific uses to entire music genres, even if one of those assignments gets flipped in the end. Given these simplistic aspects, *Death Proof* seems a long way from *Jackie Brown* and Tarantino's nuanced use there of the Delfonics, Randy Crawford, and Bobby Womack.

INGLOURIOUS BASTERDS: A NEW UNITY OF SCORING PRACTICE

If, as suggested, Tarantino has moved away from both character-based music selection in the diegesis and the use of artist releases, and turned to non-diegetic scoring using old film scores, that new musical-filmic style reaches its apotheosis with *Inglourious Basterds*—a movie with 29 musical cues, all of them drawn from previous soundtracks. There is one fleeting exception: a brief percussive rhythm break from the middle of Rare Earth's 1971 long recording of "What'd I Say," which accompanies two of the "basterds" in the final cinema showdown when they reconnoiter the corridor leading to the box where Hitler and Goebbels are watching *Stolz der Nation*. Even the original '30s and '40s 78s played in the café scene are from movies or, in the case described at the beginning of this chapter, reconstituted as a facsimile recreation of such. Overall, then, Tarantino chose all but one of the musical selections from just 22 years of popular film history: most of them from 1966–1973, as in *Kill Bill* and *Death Proof*, the earliest being the main title theme from *The Alamo* (1960) and the latest being David Bowie's "Cat People (Putting Out Fire)" from the end credits of *Cat People* (1982).[20]

Tarantino utilizes almost all these soundtracks non-diegetically in three main ways, for three different functions—irrespective of the music's provenance, genre, or composer; whether American or European; spaghetti western, thriller, war movie, teen, or blaxploitation; by Morricone, Giani Ferrio, Charles or Elmer Bernstein, Jacques Loussier, Billy Preston, Lalo Schifrin, or Davie Allan and the Arrows. The most common scoring purpose is for Tarantino to select brief, atmospheric fragments to accompany scenes of tension building, anticipating future violence or occasionally recalling violent moments. These borrowings are mostly slow or middle tempo, featuring a melodic figure from harmonica, whistling, or guitar, or with strong rhythmic figures doubled by piano, bass, guitar, or brass with percussion. The earliest example of this is the sequencing of Bernstein's main title theme from *White Lightning* into Morricone's theme from *Il Mercenario*, to introduce us to the aftermath of a basterds ambush as seen through the eyes of a surviving but soon to be disfigured German; *White Lightning* is reprised at the end of the scene and then links to Shosanna changing the billing outside her cinema in the next chapter. Moments of actual violence themselves, in contrast, tend either not to be scored at all or scored by different sounds—discordant brass and strings, or fuzz-distorted electric guitar over fast rock or funk rhythms. For instance, Morricone's "L'incontro Con La Figlia" accompanies the execution of the Dreyfus family hiding under Monsieur LaPadite's farmhouse floorboards; and Billy Preston's "Slaughter" underscores the flashback of Hugo Stiglitz's killings of Gestapo officers.

Then there are three memorable uses of slow, more lyrical orchestral pieces, which collectively connect with the theme of Shosanna's story. Both the *Alamo* main title theme by Tiomkin, and Ferrio's main theme from *Un Dollaro Bucato*, which accompanies Shosanna's second meeting with Zoller, are from westerns, in a minor key, and with the melody played on accordion accompanied by strings. As Mark Brownrigg explained, the "accordion crops up in westerns constantly," along with the Jew's harp, banjo, and harmonica,[21] and as a portable instrument, is often associated with stories of solitary quest or isolation amid the wide-open Wild West. Phil Powrie has written that the accordion, once a straightforward indicator of folk community, has in contemporary French cinema become "a postmodern marker which combines utopia and an ironic and self-aware nostalgia."[22] Tarantino's heroine is indeed French and the setting is France, but perhaps only the postmodern nostalgia of that context survives here, and our familiarity with the accordion from the filmic genre of the western offers a more powerful association, as Tarantino intends: "In the first half of the movie, the first two chapters, that's the spaghetti western vibe of the film...so I use a lot of Morricone."[23] Supporting this, both the Tiomkin and Ferrio themes are in 6/8, the western time signature that most closely replicates the rhythm and tempo of a jog or slow trot on horseback, the equine pace that horses can comfortably maintain for hours on end and therefore very common for cowboys to choose—and for film composers to adopt for western themes. Few filmgoers today might spot the *Alamo* or *One Silver Dollar* themes, but this minor-key solo lament, instrumentation, and cultural and film context means many would get the message that the character at the heart of our story is on a lonely and tragic journey, and that—as she herself ends up saying on film to the cinema audience after her own demise—everyone is "going to die." This association of meaning carries right through into the use of Morricone's "*Un Amico*" for the dying Zoller's shooting of Shosanna. It hardly matters any more that this piece of music is from a thriller, in 4/4, and with the sweeping minor-key melody played on the strings and not the accordion: The mood of lament is overwhelmingly powerful.

By carefully selecting these stylistically related soundtrack extracts, Tarantino largely manages to avoid the fragmenting effect of such a practice. The intention behind his music selections has always been, as he says, to "never just throw stuff over it, it's supposed to be exciting, it's supposed to rev you up. It's supposed to get you going."[24] The danger in scoring with 29 eventful and arresting "musical moment" cues from multiple composed soundtracks is that the emotion of the film could seem to restart from scratch 28 times. When working without thematic or stylistic continuity— as he does most notably in *Kill Bill, Vol. 2*—Tarantino can fall into this trap. But with *Inglourious Basterds*, many cues do relate stylistically as he deploys them for particular kinds of action. Moreover, it is ironic how he scores the two most musically out-of-style scenes that confirm what actually unites the score's purpose: Shosanna's preparations for the premiere to the sound of David Bowie's "Cat People (Putting Out Fire)," and to a lesser extent, the Hugo Stiglitz backstory.

Figure 6.4: *Inglourious Basterds*: Shosanna prepares to put out fire with fire in a micro-narrative music video to David Bowie ("Cat People [Putting Out Fire]").

The shock of hearing crashing synths, synthesized percussion, and Bowie's voice over the image of Shosanna leaning against an upstairs window of her movie theatre at the start of the scene does not diminish with repeated viewings (figure 6.4). It's true that "Cat People" appeared only a couple of years after Elmer Bernstein's "Zulus" from *Zulu Dawn* (itself heard a few minutes later in the film), but in performative and electronic style, it is from a different aesthetic altogether. The shock value lies in its distance from the sound world of the rest of the soundtrack, not in its distance from the period of the mise en scène. It is certainly the kind of eventful musical moment Tarantino strives for. He's said he was always amazed that *Cat People* director Paul Schrader and composer Giorgio Moroder threw the track away on the end credits, and thought it would be great to use it for a set-piece scene.[25] On one obvious level, the song title and chorus fit the "fire" that Tarantino is about to give us, but once again, this is a literal reduction of lyrics that are in fact metaphorical, referring to the obsessive and perverse desire that pervades Schrader's plot.

More important is what Tarantino has us see while we hear "Cat People (Putting Out Fire)," all of it shot and cut to the beat of the song: Shosanna dressing up and putting on makeup for the intended nitrate film stock fireball massacre, intercut with a micro-narrative backstory of how she and her lover Marcel made the film they would burn. The scene is thus a perfect example of John Mundy's "music video aesthetic," being "self-consciously non-realist in style, using montage editing and an aesthetic that defies continuity to produce textual disruption"—and continuing in that style right through to the concluding overhead crane shot that follows Shosanna out of the projection room door and down onto the balcony overlooking the "party" for which she has prepared. More specifically, the scene is typical of a common type of micro-narrative pop music video, one "devoted to completing a single process" such as "getting everyone to the party on time."[26] In celebrating this typical kind of pop video, Vernallis argues that its repetition of simple tasks for the players "create[s] qualities of volition and determination befitting musical materials that function similarly." In other words, the simple actions cut to the beat acquire the irresistible drive of the musical structure, forcing the listener onward to the "hook" or chorus; Very soon, in just a few seconds' time, we're all going to put out fire with gasoline. All that the "textual disruption" manages to upset here is the normative expectations of classical narrative cinema: Within itself, this scene or micro-narrative is a wholly coherent example of a music video. Audiences are clearly meant to enjoy its transfusion of anticipatory energy in this spirit, as any quick scan of the fan comments appended to the YouTube postings of this scene can attest. What's wrong with having a video within a movie? Likewise, why not stick in a spoof of 1970s film trailers as a way of showing us Stiglitz's backstory? They too are a film form with which we are all familiar.

I've described Tarantino's unity of scoring practice in *Inglourious Basterds* and presented this score as an effective summing-up of the approach he's developed through his post-millennium productions—portrayed it, therefore, as a summary of the overall tendency of effect in his soundtracks. His music is now all about recalling the audio experience of viewing—whether of '60s and '70s movies, pop videos, or movie trailers. The range of visual media forms that Tarantino celebrates, while signifying them through his particular reuses of earlier soundtracks, therefore embraces multiple generations of cinemagoers. But the key consistency comes from scoring with music sourced overwhelmingly from film soundtracks dating between 1960 and 1979. The cues' shared historical provenance is in fact their strongest association. With his movies from after the millennium, Tarantino tries to remind us of what it feels like to listen to 40-year-old spaghetti westerns, war movies, and teen exploitation films. Including vinyl surface noise, scratches, and soundtrack wear and tear on the main titles ensures that we are conscious of the authentic physicality of the sound sources, and it underlines the historical audio experience that we are going to get. The director's periodism is confirmed by the fact that although he is using fewer and fewer artist releases, they too are drawn from these decades. In removing music selection from his characters' control in the diegesis, and instead using audible (scratches) and visual (his jukebox) signs to show his own pre-selection and ownership of the music, Tarantino underlines this periodism as his, and his alone.

Each film's heroine will get at least one scene scored by a theme song in a minor key in 6/8 time from a '60s or '70s movie, with the melody sung or played on accordion, panpipes, or trumpet accompanied by arpeggiated guitar and string orchestra. Each film will have some of its scenes of violence scored by a rock or funk fuzz guitar instrumental from a blaxploitation or '60s teen movie. Each film will have some scenes of tension scored by bits of Morricone from his Italian-productions period. The keen-eared can spot Tarantino's favorites being spun again and again in multiple films: cues from Bernstein's *White Lightning*, Herrmann's *Twisted Nerve*, Morricone's *Il Mercenario*. But this repetition does not concern him, as long as each individual cue from his collection is consistent with the (vague) genre memory and period emotion memory that he wishes to strike up in each individual scene. In this way, Tarantino's practice could be described as "scoring to picture," creating up to 30 potentially unrelated "musical moments" in each film. The British film and TV composer Howard Davidson has recently derided such scoring to picture, or "conformance," instead advocating scoring to the "idea" of the program, series, or film.[27] But what ultimately is the idea behind any Tarantino film? Given his increasingly programmatic and formulaic music selections, it's clear that Tarantino is neither simply scoring to the picture nor scoring to the idea behind the plot or characters. He scores to musical period and film genre; and we are locked in the sound-editing booth with him.

APPENDIX 6.1

The complete list of fifty 45 rpm original discs on Tarantino's 1962 AMI Continental 2 jukebox, as featured in *Death Proof*.

01. Isaac Hayes—Theme from Shaft / Ellie's Love Theme
02. Barry White—You're the First, My Last, My Everything / Can't Get Enough
03. Bob Dylan—George Jackson (Acoustic) / George Jackson (Big Band Version)
04. Stevie Wonder—Lately / If It's Magic
05. The Chi-Lites—Have You Seen Her / Oh Girl
06. The THP Orchestra—Theme from S.W.A.T., Pt. 1 / Pt. 2
07. Stevie Wonder—I Ain't Gonna Stand for It / Knocks Me off My Feet
08. Bloodstone—Natural High / This Thing is Heavy
09. Don McLean—American Pie, Pt. 1 / Pt. 2
10. The Sweet—Little Willy / Man from Mecca
11. The Isley Brothers—Take Me to the Next Phase, Pt. 1 / Pt. 2
12. The Miracles—Love Machine, Pt. 1 / Pt. 2
13. Bob Dylan—Subterranean Homesick Blues / She Belongs to Me
14. Honey Cone—Stick Up / V.I.P.
15. Earth, Wind and Fire—Shining Star / Yearnin' Learnin'

16. Amii Stewart—Knock on Wood / When You Are Beautiful
17. Honey Cone—Want Ads / We Belong Together
18. Kool & the Gang—Hollywood Swinging / Jungle Boogie
19. Bob Dylan—Band of the Hand / Theme from Joe's Death
20. The Sweet—Wig-Wam-Bam / New York Connection
21. The Friends of Distinction—Grazing in the Grass / I Really Hope You Do
22. Marvin Gaye—Trouble Man / Don't Mess With Mr. T
23. Bob Dylan—Stuck Inside of Mobile with the Memphis Blues Again / Rita May
24. Pacific Gas & Electric—Are You Ready? / Staggolee
25. Donna Summer—Love to Love You Baby / Need-A-Man Blues
26. Michael Zager Band—Let's All Chant / Love Express
27. Santa Esmeralda—Don't Let Me Be Misunderstood / You're My Everything
28. JigSaw—Sky High / Brand New Love Affair
29. George Baker Selection—Little Green Bag / Pretty Little Dreamer
30. The Sweet—Blockbuster / Need a Lot of Lovin'
31. Eddie Floyd—Good Love, Bad Love / Things Get Better
32. Joe Tex—The Love You Save / If Sugar Was as Sweet as You
33. Bob Dylan—Gotta Serve Somebody (Long Version) / Gotta Serve Somebody (Short Version)
34. Dick Dale—Misirlou / Eight 'Till Midnight
35. Lee "Shot" Williams—They Told a Lie / I'm Tore Up
36. William Bell—Formula of Love / You Don't Miss Your Water
37. Dinah Washington—Mad About the Boy / Stormy Weather
38. The Box Tops—Cry Like a Baby / The Door You Closed to Me
39. The Checkmates, Ltd.—Black Pearl / Lazy Susan
40. The Sweet—Fox on the Run / Miss Demeanor
41. The Delfonics—Didn't I / La-La Means I Love You
42. Brothers Johnson—Get the Funk Outta Ma Face / Tomorrow
43. Bob Dylan—Hurricane, Pt. 1 / Pt. 2
44. ABBA—Waterloo / Watch Out
45. T. Rex—Jeepster / Life's a Gas
46. Melanie—Ruby Tuesday / What Have They Done to My Song, Ma?
47. Commander Cody—Hot Rod Lincoln / Beat Me Daddy, Eight to the Bar
48. Robert Mitchum—Thunder Road / The Tip of My Fingers
49. Dean Martin—Rio Bravo / My Rifle, My Pony, and Me
50. Dave Dee, Dozy, Beaky, Mick & Tich—Hold Tight! / You Know What I Want

[http://www.tarantino.info/wiki/index.php/Death_Proof_movie_references_guide/AMI_Jukebox]

NOTES

1. Garner, "Would You Like to Hear Some Music?: In-and-Out-of-Control in the Films of Quentin Tarantino," in *Film Music: Critical Approaches*, ed. Kevin J. Donnelly (New York: Continuum, 2001), 189, 191–197.
2. Miklitsch, "Audiophilia: Audiovisual Pleasure and Narrative Cinema in *Jackie Brown*," *Screen*, vol. 45, no. 4 (Winter 2004), 287–304.
3. Tincknell and Concrich, eds., *Film's Musical Moments* (Edinburgh, UK: Edinburgh University Press, 2006), 5.
4. Tincknell, "The Soundtrack Movie, Nostalgia and Consumption," in *Film's Musical Moments*, 136–138.
5. Cooke, *A History of Film Music* (Cambridge, UK: Cambridge University Press, 2008), 486.
6. Coulthard, "Torture Tunes: Tarantino, Popular Music, and New Hollywood Ultraviolence," in *Music and the Moving Image*, vol. 2, no. 2 (Summer 2009).
7. Gorbman, "Auteur Music," in *Beyond the Soundtrack: Representing Music in Cinema*, eds. Daniel Goldmark, Lawrence Kramer, and Richard Leppert (Berkeley, CA: University of California Press, 2007).
8. Garner, "Would You Like to Hear Some Music?" 190–191.
9. Ward, *Just My Soul Responding: Rhythm and Blues, Black Consciousness, and Race Relations* (London: University College London Press, 1998), 300.
10. Garner, "Would You Like to Hear Some Music?" 200, 203.
11. *The Culture Show*, "Quentin Tarantino talks to Lauren Leverne about the secret of creating a great movie soundtrack," BBC 2 TV, UK, October 13, 2007; also at http://www.youtube.com/watch?v=gTF5XvwcYZI, last accessed July 11, 2011.
12. Ibid.
13. "Discographies, discoveries, discussions: an online archive dedicated to the magic of the vinyl seven inch single," http://www.45cat.com/record/os13004, last accessed July 11, 2011.
14. Texas Chili Parlor, http://www.txchiliparlor.com/webdev/, last accessed July 12, 2011; *Urbanspoon.com*, "Home > Austin > Downtown > Texas Chilli Parlor, If you love Death Proof, you gotta check this place out!" http://www.urbanspoon.com/r/11/142346/restaurant/Downtown/Texas-Chili-Parlor-Austin, last accessed July 12, 2011.
15. Garner, "Would You Like to Hear Some Music?" 192.
16. Kandell, "Quentin Tarantino Talks *Inglourious Basterds* Soundtrack," *Spin*, 2009.
17. Peter A. Romanov, "Soundtrack: the Significance of Music in the Films Written and Directed by Quentin Tarantino" (unpublished M.A. thesis, Wake Forest University, 2006), 41.
18. Romanov, "Soundtrack," 49–57.
19. Conrich, Ian, and Estrella Tincknell, eds. *Film's Musical Moments*, Edinburgh, UK: Edinburgh University Press, 2006.
20. The sole outlier to that period is four seconds of screen time (two measures only) of a solo electric guitar single-note gallop rhythm, extracted from Sherman Chow Gam-Cheung's score for the 1987 Hong Kong kung fu/Vietnam war movie *Eastern Condors*, as one of the "basterds" runs in slow motion to kill the second guard outside Hitler's box.
21. Mark Brownrigg, "Film Music and Film Genre" (unpublished Ph.D. thesis, University of Stirling, 2003), 74.
22. Phil Powrie, "The Fabulous Destiny of the Accordion in French Cinema," in *Changing Tunes: The Use of Pre-Existing Music in Film*, eds. Powrie and Robynn Stilwell (Aldershot, UK: Ashgate, 2006), 150.
23. Steve Kandell, "Quentin Tarantino Talks *Inglourious Basterds* Soundtrack," *Spin*, 2009.
24. Ibid.

25. *The Culture Show*, "Quentin Tarantino Talks to Lauren Leverne about the Secret of Creating a Great Movie Soundtrack," BBC 2 TV, UK, October 13, 2007.
26. Carol Vernallis, *Experiencing Music Video: Aesthetics and Cultural Context* (New York: Columbia University Press, 2004), 20.
27. Howard Davidson, "Soundtracks with Street Credibility" (letter to the editor), *Guardian*, 6 August 2011, 37. For more on the idea of "conformance," see Nicholas Cook, *Analysing Musical Multimedia* (Oxford, UK: Clarendon, 1998); and Pwyll ap Sion and Tristian Evans, "Parallel Symmetries? Exploring Relationships Between Minimalist Music and Multimedia Forms" (paper delivered at the First International Conference on Music and Minimalism, Bangor University, August 31–September 2, 2007).

CHAPTER 7

Wes Anderson, Ironist and Auteur

ARVED ASHBY

Auteurism, like irony, can be defined as a form of "dissimulation and pretense."[1] As a type of irony, or at least a blood relative, auteurism also counts as a form of digression. "Irony tends to occasion interruption, deflection, and digression," as literary scholar Kevin Newmark puts it, adding that irony can even be defined as an active manner of "digressive force."[2] Digression might seem antithetical to the auteur's work and all its "writtenness," but it is in fact a basic part of conscious authorship: As described by literary scholar Philip Lopate, digression implies not only a first-person author, but more specifically, a self-conscious first-person author. "The digression must wander off the point only to fulfill it. A kind of elaboration, it scoops up subordinate themes in passing." In other words, before one can digress, one must have a basic authored text to digress *from*, which is another way of saying that life has no digressions, but authored lives do. A digression outside the context of a clear authorial manner is just another sentence, paragraph, or page; whereas a digression in the presence of distinctive style becomes a basic tool in auteurist irony. Lopate speaks of irony as "a technique of the personal essay that serves both structural and comic functions," and informs us that "the essayist's comic irony derives from a self-consciousness about digression."[3]

Irony is clearly not just a kind of humor, but a complex and multifaceted matter of outlook. Orson Welles and Stanley Kubrick can seem as dead serious as Luis Buñuel and Terry Gilliam are playful, but that is because the first two appeal to the dictionary definition of irony as "a contradictory outcome of events as if in mockery of the promise and fitness of things."[4] The serious Welles can be called an ironist and grouped with the humorous Gilliam insofar as both directors dissimulate, saying one thing and meaning another. Demonstrably stylized, a film by any of these four director-auteurs must be read on multiple levels. Is it meant to be funny or serious, funnily serious or seriously funny? Does the director in question offer a public or a private message, perhaps even an indulgent filmic discourse on her own style? Is her recognizably different way of doing things, her artistry, suited to film as a communal and shot-and-projected medium, or does it operate in spite of it? These questions mirror the old debate of whether irony is a public or private affair, an objective or subjective practice, a speech act meant to reveal or to obscure.[5]

The auteur's irony and digression are not just authorial idiosyncrasies, but transform her cinematic storytelling. She doesn't tell stories so much as she masters a particular manner of narration: namely, the auteurist's narrative art of narrating the narrative self away.[6] Paradoxically enough, the auteur tends to disappear in the heavy details of style and dual meanings, using the ink of her profligate invention to write herself out of her own work. Laurence Sterne's novel *Tristram Shandy* (1759–67), one of the great comically digressive texts, is written in such a self-occupied manner of the first person that we go in an instant from the droll to the imponderable to the fantastic. Protagonist Tristram is so intensely self-occupied that autobiographical digressions keep delaying him from any account of his own birth, and even when he does arrive at that event, he quickly parenthesizes and hyphenates his way to his opinions on the solar system:

> On the fifth day of November, 1718, which to the aera fixed on, was as near nine kalendar months as any husband could in reason have expected,—was I Tristram Shandy, Gentleman, brought forth into this scurvy and disastrous world of ours.—I wish I had been born in the Moon, or in any of the planets (except Jupiter or Saturn, because I never could bear cold weather) for it could not well have fared worse with me in any of them (though I will not answer for Venus)....

The auteurist filmmaker uses cinematic detail in much the same way that the ironic and digressive writer uses parentheses and hyphens: as a sign of authorship, but also as a distraction away from authorship. Film theorists speak of auteurist "self-reflexive" styles, for instance, when talking about Federico Fellini. That filmmaker titled his film 8 ½ (1963) after a meticulous counting of the films he had previously made, but didn't offer the title as a point of access to the movie itself. Similarly, the amplified colors and smooth, glossy surfaces in Pedro Almodovar's *Mujeres al borde de un ataque de nervios* (1988) and *Mala educación* (2004) do nothing to further their stories qua stories. In *Sleepy Hollow* (1999), Tim Burton gives Ichabod Crane an array of period forensic equipment so creaky-intricate and almost surreal that it nearly steals the film. Intriguing and delightful, all these kinds of detail don't help drive the diegeses of these movies; they become part of the auteur's own style as *metteur en scène*. They aren't party to narration; they are distractions that define their own manner of narrative.

In addition to redefining cinematic detail and the purposes thereof, the auteurist filmmaker is like Tristram Shandy in that she plays with our sense of what is real and what is not. Jean-Luc Godard's *Weekend* (1967) has Tristramesque moments, starting with a self-regarding intertitle that describes the movie as "a film found on a scrap heap." The characters Roland and Corinne undertake a picaresque journey into the French countryside, and their passage into self-conscious filmdom is punctuated with hippie cannibals, apocalyptic car wrecks, and statements like "This isn't a novel, this is a film. A film is life." But Godard leaves the question of film's reality open, and says at one point in *Weekend* that movies are more truthful than reality, that they are real in a way that suggests Tristram's paradoxical reality-through-invention:

Woman in Car: Are you in a film or in reality?
Joseph Balsam: In a film.
Man in Car: In a film? You lie too much.

Given the auteur's digressions and articulations, both invoking and effacing authorship, her texts waver between reportage and self-reflection, between objectivity and subjectivity. She creates a feeling of realism at the same time she dissipates it—making it difficult for the reader to tell whether he is reading fiction or nonfiction. Life is stranger than fiction, as the saying goes, and the auteurist corollary follows that fiction, when it becomes unusually strange, stops sounding like fiction and starts sounding like real life. When we make the surprising discovery in *Dr. Strangelove* that a deluxe buffet has been laid out in the War Room, Kubrick would seem to be telling us something factual about a real place.[7] The same goes for Hank Quinlan's stomach problems and weakness for fortuneteller Tana in Orson Welles's *Touch of Evil* (1958), Jacques Tati's hissing seat cushions in *Play Time* (1967), and the mannerist, even distracting allusions to interwar French culture in Martin Scorsese's *Hugo* (2011). Each of these films has a preponderance of detail that appears extraneous but which the filmmaker has gone to some pains to point out. Such detailed-ness creates an almost desperate verisimilitude: The auteur-ironist ceases to be author and becomes documenter.

Songs can play an essential role in auteurist irony and digression, and that array of dissimulational possibilities has increased over the past 20 years. An auteur can increase the "digressive force" of a scene by using music that predates the film in question, music that by virtue of its preexistence—its paratextual life before and outside the filmic text, its status as cultural artifact—evades any non-diegetic mediation between filmmaker and moviegoer. If irony sits within a disjunction between intention and perception—asking "Nice weather, isn't it?" when it's raining cats and dogs, for example—in a film, it is increased by music that was created independently of the film, and music that does nothing to bridge the distance between filmmaker and viewer. Even in a film where such preexisting songs help establish a particular time and place, they can also appear as arbitrary detail, allusion, digression, and inside joke. Certainly after the MTV revolution of the early 1980s, filmmakers had greater freedom to play with, to tease out, the relevance/irrelevance of any preexisting songs they used. Demotion of the screenplay's importance vis-à-vis the music allowed songs to do the opposite of what they did in classical Hollywood musicals. Whereas they once served to focus emotions and make them more tangible, giving voice, say, to character X's love for character Y, now they fragmented, obscured, and deflected their actions. Indeed, while a film's songs used to "belong" to the script and to the characters themselves, the question opened up in the 1990s of who the songs now answered to, if anyone in particular. They helped filmmakers open a new gap between the script and the cinematic experience, a gap that allowed for all sorts of new filmic meanings.

WES ANDERSON

Wes Anderson, a prime example of the early 21st-century ironist-auteur, effects a cluttered and digressive auteurism in his big-budget features *The Royal Tenenbaums* (2001), *The Life Aquatic with Steve Zissou* (2004), *The Fantastic Mr. Fox* (2009), and perhaps less so in *The Darjeeling Limited* (2007). Jonathan Romney aptly describes Anderson's style as a "cinema of saturation."[8] Though his storylines do unfold in Aristotelian terms—through beginning, middle, and end—such trajectories are all but buried under torrents of detail. Just about any moment in an Anderson movie bursts with superfluities and distractions. To choose just two of many *Royal Tenenbaums* examples, the voiceover tells us near the start of the film that Royal "bought the house on Archer Avenue in the winter of his 35th year" and that he "was a prominent litigator until the mid-'80s, when he was disbarred and briefly imprisoned." Such details are digressions. The facts that Royal bought the house in winter rather than spring, and at the age of 35 rather than 36, and that he was incarcerated "briefly" rather than just incarcerated don't count as plot mechanisms or narrative themes. Their incidental quality isn't the kind of incidental quality attending Chekov's gun above the mantelpiece, whereby an incidental but visible element eventually becomes a real plot mechanism. The gun above the mantelpiece in Act

1, or so the dramatic truism goes, is there for a reason: It will be fired before the end of Act 3. Anderson's terminal, non-metonymic details, on the other hand, don't help guide his narratives to their consummations, but hint at later plot tie-ups involving jail terms and real-estate buying patterns.

Laden with this kind of detail, a "saturated" Anderson film vacillates between stark reality and ravingly innocent unreality, between documentary and absurdist romp. Writing specifically about *The Royal Tenenbaums*, Romney finds that Anderson skews any conventional dichotomy of fictional and real by "furnish[ing] his characters' world to the point of saturation, making them seem not more realistic but more fictional—or rather, making us wonder if we can tell the difference."[9] By the filmmaker's own admission, *Royal Tenenbaums* "contains more perhaps unnecessary visual detail than both of my previous films combined."[10] His thick-grown details are at the same time ironies, parentheses, and faits accomplis. Why is there a partly visible goat's head on the Tenenbaums' wall? Why does Royal hire as his long-term assistant a man who routinely stabs him with a knife? Why is it necessary to the plot for Margot to have her finger cut off with an ax in Indiana? Such details are of course important to Anderson's whimsical mises en scènes—the clicking of Margot's artificial finger appears in more than one scene of the film. But they go beyond that; the filmmaker seems to force details on us as faits accomplis, as documents of their own meaningfulness, but then somehow forgets to give us those meanings.[11]

In Mark Browning's estimation, Anderson "does not shy away from...bury[ing] the audience with an avalanche of information."[12] He is in fact obsessed with digressive minutiae, but he doesn't go in the direction of Robert Altman's piquant character studies or the fragmentations of cinema verité. Rather, Anderson's details recall some of his cinematic influences: Richard Lester's cinematic free-for-alls with the Beatles (*A Hard Day's Night*, 1964, and *Help!*, 1965), Mike Nichols's claustrophobic satire of postwar generation gaps in suburban America (*The Graduate*, 1968), and Bill Melendez's animated Peanuts TV specials (including "A Charlie Brown Christmas," 1965; "It's the Great Pumpkin, Charlie Brown," 1966; and "A Charlie Brown Thanksgiving," 1973). Lester's and Nichols's detailings were improvisatory and absurdist even before they started making movies: Nichols doing brilliant comedy improvisation with Elaine May before he turned to film, and Lester developing an absurdist streak in his early work on "The Goon Show." In *The Graduate*, the Ben character acts out an Andersonesque digression when he dons a full wetsuit with oxygen tanks and jumps into the swimming pool; the act is extraneous to the narrative, an unexplained suburban jeu d'esprit concocted by his maladjusted parents, and its more superfluous details—Ben holds onto a harpoon for dear life through the entire scene—give it a surreal touch.

Preexisting songs, heard as paratextual references and as objets trouvées, facilitate Anderson's auteurist digressions. Well before Anderson, Quentin Tarantino was using preexisting songs as a way of opening up all sorts of ambiguous, unsettling, and darkly comic paratextual spaces. An infamous example is the scene in *Reservoir Dogs* (1992), where Mr. Blonde sings and dances to Stealers Wheel's "Stuck in the Middle with You" as he tortures Marvin the cop and cuts off his ear. Martin Scorsese ends *Goodfellas* (1990) just as ironically with Sid Vicious's rendition of "My Way," taking an abrasive punk cover of an iconic Sinatra song about standing up to life and using it to accompany an ex-mobster in the Witness Protection Program as he steps out the door in his bathrobe to pick up his morning paper. These scenes startled moviegoers when the films first came out, Tarantino's especially, not only because they were complete affective non sequiturs and seemed to digress from the narrative at hand, but also because their musical-visual combinations were so "out there"—they seem less so today—that filmic authorship was both underlined and called into question.

So "Stuck in the Middle with You" and "My Way" function much like Tristram Shandy's parentheses and hyphens. They seem to deflect us away from the characters themselves and point us instead to alternate threads of thinking—into the deepest and most de-centered recesses of the auteur's sensibility, for example, where there seem to be no limits and few strictures. With the main argument deflected by heavy punctuation in Tristram's case, or by startling song choices in Tarantino's case, we are forced to see the world through the eyes of some weird authorial agency and find the experience both funny and terrifying. Although punctuation and film music usually share the basic purpose of aiding cogency and understanding in a text or a movie, when they veer toward the arbitrary, they call into question the actual integrity of the work: If the author is so self-occupied that he can't describe his own birth without distraction, or if the filmmaker chooses a song that undermines the reality of what she is showing us, the very rationale of the opus is called into question.

When the preexisting song is set against the film scene it accompanies, it can qualify the auteurist presence by severing a basic intimacy and long-standing cinematic trust between filmmaker and viewer. Instead of the "sincere" non-diegetic function of underscoring or commissioned theme song (music that in Claudia Gorbman's words creates a "bath of affect" for the moviegoer), the preexisting song wedges the creative and signifying presences of lyricist, songwriter, and singer—not to mention the age of the song itself—between filmmaker and moviegoer. The preexisting song wrenches apart the time-tested intimacy of these two subjectivities, and alienation replaces confidence. When Judy Garland sings the "Trolley Song" in *Meet Me in St. Louis* (1944), she confides her new love to the filmgoer and her fellow characters, and the song, as it starts, seals the empathy pact she has created with them. When Ben lip-synchs Roy Orbison's song "In Dreams" to Frank Booth in *Blue Velvet* (1986), singing into a mechanic's drop lamp as a microphone stand-in, song and listener are violated. The song's iconic emotional innocence collides with the unlikelihood that "a candy-colored clown they call the sandman" will be able to make "everything alright" in Frank's sadomasochist kidnapper's safe house; here Roy Orbison's top-ten hit invokes a vague, aching, and darkly funny vein of horror-sublime that is the opposite of empathy.

Though he has commissioned music by Mark Mothersbaugh, Anderson relies more on preexisting popular songs than on original underscoring; there are examples in *Life Aquatic with Steve Zissou* that fulfill parenthetical and digressive functions. The film includes 12 David Bowie songs from the early '70s, which would be digression enough in a movie that, though it holds some campy and Bowie-esque imagery, has nothing in common with that rocker's themes of persona, image-making, and space travel. To make them doubly digressive, the Bowie songs are sung in Portuguese by Brazilian pop samba singer Seu Jorge. What could be more digressive in an oceanographic docudrama than songs about a fictitious punk rocker who is not only "*de Marte*" ("from Mars"), and therefore from the heavens rather than the deep, but is also described in an offbeat language? The juxtaposition seems especially bizarre when we see Jorge singing them while on Zissou's boat, the Calypso, and even more so in the scene where pirates board the ship and Jorge is so occupied with the music that he fails to notice them; this is an example of a song literally distracting from the narrative. Bowie's song itself presents all sorts of arcane details about Ziggy the Martian rock god. But when we hear that Ziggy "*poderia deixá-los*" and was "*bem pendurado e* snow white tan," the points of his mythical left-handedness, penile endowment, and unnatural skin color seem even more abstruse and extraterrestrial. Jorge's adaptations are both too literal and too free to count as covers, and therefore make them doubly digressive. That translation into another language and the exchange of Mick Ronson's original electric guitar for Jorge's acoustic diffract the meanings that Bowie's original songs had accrued before Anderson's film.

INDIE IRONY

Critics have discerned two general types of ironic mindset. First, there is the earlier structuralist notion that the ironist has a specific message in mind when she dissimulates—that when the author says something different than what she intends, there is still an intended message, a specific "net meaning." As D. C. Muecke describes this system of roles and message in irony, a "transliteral" or "real message" is presented above and beyond the narrowly ironic text. "The ironist conveys his real message to his audience," Muecke writes, "only in the sense that he provides them with the means for arriving at it."[13] In one of his examples, Jonathan Swift writes vis-à-vis English Protestant landlords confronting Dublin poverty, that "I rather recommend buying the children alive, and dressing them hot from the Knife, as we do roasting Pigs."[14] Swift's real message is clear, and it does not involve cooking little Catholics.

Anderson's films inhabit a different manner of irony, poststructuralist or postmodern in that it is an all-enveloping irony suited to a time when truths are relative and conflicting.[15] Steve Zissou is a good example, setting out in search of the fabled "jaguar shark"—this odd oceanographer sets out to bag a rare sea creature just for revenge. His strange lack of eloquence or even clarity of thought, unusual for a scientist and self-styled media figure, makes his voyage of vengeance especially banal: "Now I'm gonna go hunt down that shark, or whatever it is ... and hopefully kill it. I don't know how yet. Maybe dynamite." Zissou's irony has been an irony of inactivity until this moment, when in taking up violence against some creature or other, he happily throws any naturalist-liberal credentials out the window. Another example of Anderson's poststructuralist, "undirected," or perhaps inter-textual irony is Zissou's single-handed and implausible attack against the pirates who have taken over his ship (figure 7.1). The scene reveals Zissou as an icon of cinematic bravery, blasting his way past all armed opposition as if he were a Rambo or Dirty Harry giving payback for some injustice—the film almost seems to change genre at this point, morphing from whimsical satire into a spaghetti western like *The Good, the Bad, and the Ugly* or a 1980s action flick like *Die Hard*. But Zissou's sudden change from bungler to lone gun hero seems precipitated more by Iggy and the Stooges' song "Search

Figure 7.1: *The Life Aquatic*: Steve Zissou becomes Dirty Harry ("Search and Destroy").

and Destroy" on the soundtrack ("I'm a street walking cheetah with a heart full of napalm") than by circumstances of the story. Anderson's "Search and Destroy" scene is a study in undirected irony in that it offers no particular message and ridicules nothing in particular. The scene thereby reflects the paradoxical song itself, which is sung by an Ann Arbor native who was voted most likely to succeed in high school, but went on to roll onstage in crushed glass, score lots of heroin, and—some would say—invent punk music. It's hard to hear the song "Search and Destroy" as something the self-loathing Zissou himself might have cued up to instigate and celebrate his own heroism. Rather, the scene might show the film itself mocking Zissou's ineffectual nature—the scene could be a send-up of Anderson himself and the whimsical aimlessness of his own style.

Though he is quirky and avoids character-driven formulas, Anderson doesn't practice the kind of post-MTV irony we see in the indie film market and its paradoxical mass-marketing of niche sensibilities. He is not a centrist, but he doesn't go in the other direction of embracing the fragmented and self-conscious sensibilities of alternative cultural production and "prosumer" economics. The prosumer is the consumer who is lured to commodities by the promise of a creative role, by the possibility of becoming both *producer* and *consumer*. Because of their malleable aesthetics and longstanding connections with image-making, music and fashion are probably the foremost instruments of prosumer culture—examples would be the new tailorability and interactiveness of music software and the DIY thrift-store appearance of recent clothing trends.

Both indie film and prosumer marketing are big millennial trends that preach sensitivity to the individual, the momentary, and the local. These are also the surface aspirations of faux-indie filmmaking—sometimes called "Hollywood indie"—referring to a movie that shows an alternative sensibility but is funded or distributed by a major studio.[16] The song playlist is an icon of this filmic style, as it is of prosumer culture more generally: music arranged not in a historicist, stylistic, or obviously predetermined order, but by the consumer herself according to individual wishes and personal experience. The faux-indie film, typically a quirky romantic comedy, is structured the way a playlist is, less to conventional, linear plotlines than to the string of various emotional states suggested by the songs; examples would include Cameron Crowe's *Almost Famous* (2000) and *Vanilla Sky* (2001), Zach Braff's *Garden State* (2004), Jason Reitman's *Juno* (2007), and Peter Sollett's *Nick and Norah's Infinite Playlist* (2008).[17] In the eyes and ears of some, this playlist sensibility is one more way indie filmmaking can devolve from rejection of the big-studio approach to outright affectation: Owen Gleiberman of *Entertainment Weekly* referred to *Vanilla Sky* in playlist-driven terms as "…a cracked hall of mirrors taped together by a preposterous what-is-reality? cryogenics plot and scored to Cameron Crowe's record collection."[18]

Faux-indie filmmaking tailors its digressiveness to the market and differs from ironic discursiveness in being more self-conscious. The typical faux-indie romantic comedy will have neurosis, arbitrary detail, and a certain amount of soul-searching. In *Garden State*, protagonist Andrew is caught up in low-grade existential and familial crises, and against these there is not much narrative import in the death of Sam's hamster, Jesse's invention of silent Velcro, or Albert's residence in a Newark quarry. These extraneous details thereby sound like Anderson's work. Going beneath the surface, though, one finds greater differences: Braff's minutiae have none of the manic garrulousness or whimsical obsessiveness that makes up Wes Anderson's pervasive irony. And although digressive detail of the typical faux-indie romantic comedy serves to buoy up the seriousness of its themes and issues—coming of age, the meaning of life, the power of the iconic woman, the complexity of adolescent love—it's questionable if an Anderson film delivers any morals or themes at all. Indeed, Anderson often seems to satirize films that do moralize. His themes don't seem to invite audience participation.

Like faux-indie filmmakers, Anderson uses soundtracks that sound like playlists. The score for *Rushmore* (1998), for example, includes songs by the Kinks, Paul Desmond, Cat Stevens, Donovan, The Who, Yves Montand, John Lennon, and the Faces. Unlike faux-indie films, however, Anderson's songs aren't pleas to action, and taken as a group, they skirt hesitantly around the periphery of the top 40. He also usually avoids songs that are "big" or message-driven or function as obvious "feeling states" within the film; the song's purpose is not to cue emotional responses to particular scenes. One exception to this Andersonian rule is Paul Simon's "Me and Julio Down by the Schoolyard," used in *Royal Tenenbaums* as an empathy vehicle for the montage of Royal's jolly misadventures with his overprotected grandsons. He bonds with them while racing go-carts, hitching rides on garbage trucks, throwing water balloons at taxis, doing cannonballs in public pools (after racing the kids in full view of "no running" signs), and engaging in other joyfully reckless behavior. Simon's paean to delinquency would have us cheer Royal and his kin on, all the more when we hear the lyrics: "The papa said 'Oy, if I get that boy, I'm gonna stick him in the House of detention.'"

Rousing, yes, but "Me and Julio Down by the Schoolyard" is an unusually conventional choice for Anderson. He more often turns a hit song into a critique of itself, as in a more typical *Royal Tenenbaums* scene, where he raids 30-year-old pop charts for a shot of Eli doing drugs with some friends of apparently Middle Eastern origin. We hear the Clash in "Rock the

Casbah" while Eli and his pals unexcitedly score cocaine together and argue disinterestedly over the pronunciation of Tutankhamen's name, which Eli seems in ignorance of and his friends seem well versed in. "I believe it was Tootinkamen." "Tutankhamen." "Tutankhamen?" "Yes, Tutankhamen." The cocaine/Tutankhamen scene doesn't use the song to exhort, but to perpetrate or ridicule cultural insensitivity. "Rock the Casbah" made the top ten, the only Clash song to do so, but Anderson uses the song neither as an anthem nor an expression of empathy and community. It is one thing for a song to invoke such picturesque ethnic divides in 1982—not long after the Iran hostage crisis announced the rise of Islamic fundamentalism to the West—and quite another to score a movie with it in 2001. The lyrics are now embarrassing ("Degenerate the faithful, With that crazy Casbah sound"), but that must be part of Anderson's point: that the Tenenbaum kin are so inarticulate and dysfunctional ("So you're on mescaline," Richie offers Eli, as only so much small talk) that outside beliefs and lifestyles don't even get a look in.

WORDY AUTEURISM

Digressive and ironic, Sterne's *Tristam Shandy* and Godard's *Weekend* concern themselves more with the telling than with the things told. They are, in short, more about words than story. Sterne's text often interrupts itself with such navel-gazing exclamatory bombast as "then, let me tell you, Sir," "bear with me," "let me go on, and tell my story my own way," and "there is no disputing against Hobby-Horses...." Godard pauses over weighty locutions like "I am here to inform these modern times of the grammatical era's end and the beginning of flamboyance especially in cinema." Wes Anderson is as word-obsessed as Sterne and Godard, and this makes his digressive details all the more first-person authorial and funny. His digressive auteurism is not only narrated, but heavily involved with the printed word. Words invade Anderson's films most literally in the form of intertitles and subtitles, almost always in Futura type and often of minimal importance in the actual storytelling ("Margot's Room, 3rd floor"; "Age 12—Starts Smoking"; "Mr. Fox Has a Plan"; "Lacrosse Team Manager"). Anderson takes this wordiness to an extreme in *Royal Tenenbaums*, where each scene opens with a shot of the printed screenplay, so that the family's story materializes not as the usual realistic slice-of-life scenario, but as a kind of script enactment. He is disinterested in the usual setup where the film gives the illusion of doing what it does with no mediation from a script or any other form of the written word, and so ends up giving the start of each scene twice.

How does Anderson's fixation with the written word relate to his fixation with visual detail? Mark Browning refers to Anderson's penchant for "microscopic stylization" and tells us that his detail has more of a visual purpose than it serves to drive performance—as it does with period-authenticity obsessives like David Fincher and Terry Gilliam.[19] One can certainly see Anderson's visual fixation in the production sketches for *Royal Tenenbaums*, executed by Eric Anderson under brother Wes's direction to "suggest the overall look and feeling" of the movie to the crew. But even here the sketches can seem mere excuses for their own written indications, which tell us about the myriad house details of "white floor tile with grey flecks," "clump of Spanish moss," "mouse ladder for vertical tube access," "goat's skull (partly visible)," "bright pink textured damask wallpaper," nightlights colored "a little on the pink side," "javelina boar's head with black eyes," and gold-painted radiators ("except silver in the bathroom").[20]

Fantastic Mr. Fox is a special case of accentuating the telling over the story told, and Anderson uses music in this film to articulate the different levels of presentation, wordiness, and digression. The script often relies on a word or set of words to set the situation in high relief and precipitate the action—as if the story just needs the right word for it to move forward. Or maybe these strategic words just serve Anderson's taste for pedantry. Mrs. Fox, for example, won't join her husband in raiding the squab farm until the plunder is defined: On seeing the sign BERK'S SQUAB FARM, MRS. Fox asks: "What *is* a squab?" Fox: "You know what a squab is. It's like a pigeon, I suppose. Anyway, it's a type of bird we can eat." Fox himself has a strange obsession with animals' Latin genera and species names, and he empowers his companions for their last mission by methodically calling these out along with the abilities they will bring to the final campaign, "Mole! *Talpa Europea!*" "Rabbit! *Oryctolagus Cuniculus!*" "Beaver! *Castor Fiber!*" "Badger! *Meles Meles!*" "Weasel! *Mustela Nivalis!*" The Field Mouse is held back because his genus characteristics aren't in order. Fox: "*Microtus Pennsylvanicus!* Do you do that, in fact? Are field mice violent?" FIELD MOUSE: "Not particularly." Actual printed titles often appear on- screen at iconic moments or at spaghetti-western or blast-'em-up clichés. "My Suicide Mission's been canceled," Fox informs the party in the sewer after learning of nephew Kristofferson's whereabouts. "We're replacing it with a Go-For-Broke Rescue Mission." The next shot, showing the whole animal group schematically from overhead, echoes him with the wry surtitle: "A Go-For-Broke Rescue Mission."

As part of this whimsical narrative self-awareness, Anderson creates a different kind of musical hierarchy in *Fantastic Mr. Fox*. First, the songs are both vaguely and literally relevant: vaguely appropriate by musical style and rhythmic energy to the scenes in question, and textually connected by just one or two salient words in the lyrics. The very first song is a good example. In the opening scene, we see Fox doing his morning exercises next to a young tree on a hilltop, to the accompaniment of the Wellingtons singing "The Ballad of Davy Crockett." The only real connections here between song and scene are—yet again—word-based and superficial in that verbal sense. Fox is himself on a "mountain top" and seems to "know ev'ry tree," including the particular sapling he's stretching against in this scene. The song's refrain, however, is a bit more farfetched. Fox appears very much at home here "in the wild" and was no doubt "raised in the woods." His confident savoir faire also makes him at home in all scenarios, but it's difficult to think of him, nattily dressed in a double-breasted corduroy suit, as "king of the wild frontier." Usually songs appear in films not for such literal word-based but tenuous reasons, but more for reasons of characterization and empathy—more for general reasons of persuasion and style, or to give aria-like voice to a character's thoughts and feelings.

But that's to leave out one important detail: We hear "The Ballad of Davy Crockett," as we do most of the characterizing diegetic songs in the movie, through the tinny speaker of the little WALK-SONIC player that Fox has fixed to his belt. The miniaturized transistor-radio-like sound of the song— its ironic containment within the diegesis—discourages us from falling in with the film's line of empathy and doing the kind of thing we do in *Meet Me in St. Louis*, which is to agree on the basis of the song "The Boy Next Door" that yes indeed, this is such a wonderful and special love that Esther feels for John. In contrast, the small mediated sound of "The Ballad of Davy Crockett" constantly reminds us that the song has been switched on by Fox himself for reasons of self-persuasion, and that it presents him as he wishes to be presented, that it serves not as our soundtrack but as Fox's soundtrack to his own self-image. His WALK-SONIC repertory is also an extension of his own constant verbal natter, the playlist of someone who talks himself into semantic impasses ("I want to say I hate my job, but that would make it seem more important to me than I want people to think it is") and speaks to wolves in French ("*Pensez-vous que l'hiver sera rude?* I'm asking if he thinks we're in for a hard winter"). A 21st-century Tristram Shandy would surround himself with self-regarding music, as well as self-conscious prose, and one imagines his playlist wouldn't be very different from Fox's.

The songs like "Davy Crockett" that Fox selects and plays through his WALK-SONIC are of the kind we'd expect in movies before the 1980s music video revolution brought about new musically induced subjectivities. And yet they are different sorts of mechanisms than what other auteurs, for instance, Tarantino, have their characters cue up for themselves. Fox's WALK-SONIC songs, though literally diegetic music insofar as he switches them on at strategic moments, are like underscoring in that they deal in good old-fashioned pep talks, audience exhortation, and image-making; in this sense, his music player would more truthfully be called NON-DIEGETIC-CLICHÉ-SONIC. Adding to that effect are the facts that his songs are some four decades old and engage in a certain old-fashioned civic cheerfulness. In addition to "The Ballad of Davy Crockett" in the opening exercise scene—sung with brisk Cold-War gusto by the Wellingtons—we hear Fox switch on the Bobby Fuller Four song "Let Her Dance" at the end while the animals dance in the supermarket aisles.

Of course, the empathetic scoring of *Fantastic Mr. Fox* extends to the "actual" non-diegetic score. This "actual" non-diegetic score centers on two Beach Boys' songs, "I Get Around" and "Heroes and Villains." Even here, however, the songs are linked in a way that recalls the garrulous and word-based stream of consciousness of Godard's *Weekend* or Sterne's *Tristram Shandy*. At one point, Tristram goes off on a digression about a parson named Yorick, but all he really manages to say about the man is that, yes, he had the same name as the exhumed man from *Hamlet*:

> That the family was originally of Danish extraction, and had been transplanted into England as early as in the reign of Horwendillus, king of Denmark, in whose court, it seems, an ancestor of this Mr. Yorick's, and from whom he was lineally descended, held a considerable post to the day of his death.... It has often come into my head, that this post could be no other than that of the king's chief Jester;—and that Hamlet's Yorick, in our Shakespeare, many of whose plays, you know, are founded upon authenticated facts, was certainly the very man.

Just as the Yorick garrulously discussed by Tristram is less a character than a verbal-textual allusion, a passing reference to a set of words outside and beyond the present text, Anderson's use of the two Beach Boys' songs sounds more like a verbal-musical tic than a sincere and meaningful exhortation through preexisting music. Yes, Mr. and Mrs. Fox do play "heroes and villains" when they go on their squab-hunting adventure, but pretty much all the 40-year-old paratextual "life" of the Beach Boys' song is irrelevant to Anderson's movie: He has chosen the song for the opening line of its lyrics, but then ten more recent and more specifically apropos songs could have filled that same function.

One non-diegetic song that appears in *Fantastic Mr. Fox* is the Rolling Stones' "Street Fighting Man," used as a backdrop to the three farmers' all-out assault on Fox's home with a little help from three high-powered excavators. In giving this anthemic ode to rebellion a deeply ironic context, Anderson seems to be turning the tables and satirizing the song itself. "Street Fighting Man" begins with the irrefutable words "Ev'rywhere I hear the sound of marching, charging feet, boy; 'Cause summer's here and the time

Figure 7.2: *The Fantastic Mr. Fox*: Farmers Boggis, Bunce, and Bean boil, crank, and grind their way into Fox's subterranean home ("Street Fighting Man").

is right for fighting in the street, boy," but in the excavation scene, it soon fades to awkward and ineffectual silence. The farmers give up the hunt and the machinery sputters out after they've obliterated the landscape but well before the song can finish, showing just how absurdly over the top both the equipment and the musical cue are—literally over the top, because music and excavators are all pushed "into the red" (figure 7.2). Charlie Watts recalled how the Stones recorded the song on a rudimentary cassette setup with the express purpose of causing overload, and then intensified the buzz by over-miking him on a toy drum kit.[21] But the musical and mechanical mojo is to no avail, and the Stones' call to action doesn't make much difference in either scenario: De Gaulle's government wasn't toppled by the 1968 student riots, and the farmers' boiling-cranking-grinding campaign only drives Fox's family further underground. In short, Anderson exposes "Street Fighting Man" as an exercise in futility.

SONG AND CINEMATIC STYLE

So Anderson doesn't exactly avoid hit songs but, as one might expect of such a digressionist, he generally prefers to use less iconic songs dating from a particular period—specifically, from about four decades ago when pop tastes had fragmented and moved away from the mainstream. Some three decades ago, in 1978, Greil Marcus diagnosed the musical-cultural division that Anderson seems most interested in: a kind of post-rock state, where "people have staked out their territory in rock and roll, but they don't feel much like members of anything big enough to take over the world—which…is what rock and roll is supposed to do." This was post-Elvis, after the Beatles, and subsequent to the British-Invasion Stones, a time when any central, post-'60s sense of belonging was gone and "rock and roll, as culture, [had] lost much of its shape."[22] Writing again some seven years after that, Marcus described a different climate where that sense of belonging had been replaced by interchangeable celebrity, a state where "the shapeless mainstreaming of pop music has produced a perfect, balancing compensation: the process by which the pop milieu, now merely the milieu of everyday diversion, is continually reorganized around a single replaceable figure."[23] He was speaking here of the pop-superstar revolving door where Michael Jackson was replaced by Bruce Springsteen, who was replaced by Madonna, who was in turn replaced by Prince, and so on.

So Anderson turns mostly to the post-rock, pre-celebrity interregnum that Marcus describes, meaning that he avoids anthemic songs and avoids songs that continue—these decades past—to speak loudly through pop superstar voices. In *Royal Tenenbaums*, we hear the Velvet Underground song "Stephanie Says" when the hawk Mordecai flies back to Richie while he is talking with Royal on the roof of the Lindbergh Hotel. The scene could almost be a satire of Hollywood cliché: The proud animal, set free at a moment of crisis, soars back to his owner at a moment of renewal and rec-onciliation. But the music is again an unusual and unexpected choice, not at all the uplifting and anthemic example one might expect from a more pre-dictable filmmaker. Lou Reed's voice is immediately recognizable, as is the sound of the band. But "Stephanie Says" is fairly obscure as a Velvet offer-ing—it was recorded in 1968 but not released until 1985—and equally obscure in its possible connection with the hawk's homecoming, unless the connection relates to crossing big communicational divides ("What coun-try shall I say is calling from across the world?") or the hostile environment mentioned in the refrain ("It's such an icy feeling, it's so cold in Alaska").

Anderson makes more strategic use of later 1960s and 1970s "interreg-num" songs in two *Royal Tenenbaums* scenes centering on Margot, scenes where the director exploits and connects with the musical styles in ques-tion. My first example is the exposé of Margot's sordid past as accompa-nied by the Ramones' "Judy Is a Punk." We hear the song while the private investigator hired by Margot's husband presents the details of her hidden life, from her first cigarettes at the age of 12 to her torrid affairs in the wilds of New Guinea and the cross-town subway (see figure 7.3). The lyrics are relevant—Margot herself, one-time child genius of the theater, is revealed as a promiscuous sociopath—and they must have been the main reason that Anderson chose this song.

There are other Anderson songs that connect lyrically with the subject matter of a scene. But this scene also presents instructive parallels between

Figure 7.3: *The Royal Tenenbaums:* Margot's intercontinental debauchery is revealed ("Judy Is a Punk").

Anderson's visual production and the Ramones' style. Anderson is a digressionist but he, perhaps as compensation for that uncontrolled-ness, tends to make highly "composed" use of the frame. This self-conscious cinematography resonates with the retro-stylism of the Ramones' bubblegum pop. Visuals and music are both constrained as a basic matter of their style, but newly composed music wouldn't have allowed the irony of these matched constraints. "Judy Is a Punk" arrives as something of a shock, because this frenetic song is paired with some of the most static motion in the film, and because the style of "Judy Is a Punk" is so distinctly of its time that it upends the basic chronological unrootedness of the movie. Both these restraints—visual and musical impositions—are emblematic and schematic. The filmic and musical messages bridle against them and are in fact augmented by that imposition. But that strength and digressiveness finally prove amusing in an ironic and whimsical way: Margot's delinquency isn't dangerous or fearful; it fills out a depressive and hitherto one-sided character, and our seeing it proves salutary.

If the "Judy Is a Punk" scene shows one visual-musical style that became possible in the age of music video, another highly stylized *Royal Tenenbaums* moment demonstrates a different kind. This is the point in the film where Margot exits a bus for her rendezvous with Richie and sees him for the first time in years (figure 7.4). On the soundtrack, we hear Nico singing Jackson Browne's "These Days," in what seems to be a direct expression of Margot's state of mind: "Well I've been out walkin' / I don't do that much talkin' these days." Anderson exercises filmic self-consciousness of a different kind here. While he obsesses over composition within the frame in the "Judy Is a Punk" scene, in the "These Days" scene, he seems to be satirizing music video style—or more specifically the music video's tendency to create, as Ken Dancyger calls it, a "self-reflexive dream-state" that "obliterates time and space."[24] Apart from the opening scene of *Darjeeling Limited* where Peter Whitman barely catches his train to the Kinks' "This

Figure 7.4: *The Royal Tenenbaums*: Margot meets Richie at the bus station ("These Days").

Time Tomorrow," no example comes to mind of Anderson accompanying a pop song with such a film slow-down. The film slows just as the melody for "These Days" begins, the camera practically fetishizing Margot in a reverse tracking shot, followed by intimate 180-degree pans between her and Richie. Richie's image is itself heavily posed, and the items next to him in the shot—a line of suitcases, a cleanly parabolic line of military men—are positioned with self-conscious artistry.

At first glance, Anderson's "These Days" scene would seem to be a music video based on a love ballad. But that impression in itself constitutes a dissimulation and digression because there really is no love to be focusing on here: Richie doesn't express his love for Margot, only mentioning his love in passing to others, and the closest Margot comes to returning his feelings is her enigmatic statement, "I think we're just going to have to be secretly in love with each other and leave it at that, Richie." On closer inspection, Jackson Browne's song isn't about love either: "These Days" explores feelings of withdrawal and regret, not passion but an absence of emotion. On second glance, the scene also comes across as a satire of pop-market image-making. Margot's hair blows gently in the breeze, and Richie is initially poised like a rakish lover, but this too is ironic as we know that both characters are clinically depressed under-groomed has-beens.

ANDERSON AND THE "IRONIST'S CAGE"

Wes Anderson's irony is undirected, suffusive, and ambiguous, coming across less as a humorous practice and more as a contemporary condition or mood. As such, it is especially appropriate to the early 21st century. According to Michael S. Roth, liberalism and social criticism have been severed from political action, and he describes an "ironist's cage" as endemic, indeed inescapable, at such a time. He calls this "the prison of cultural critics who realize they have no position from which to make their criticism."[25] This is not the "relativism of truth" presented by journalistic takes on postmodernism. Rather, the ironist's cage is a state of irony by way of powerlessness and inactivity: In a world where terrorism makes cultural relativism harder and harder to defend against its critics, marauding international corporations follow fair-trade practices, increasing right-wing demagoguery and violence can't be answered in kind, and the first black U.S. president turns out to lean right of center, the intelligentsia can see no clear path of action. Irony dominates as a "mockery of the promise and fitness of things," to return to the OED definition of irony.

This thinking is appropriate to Wes Anderson, whose central characters are so deeply locked in ironist cages that his films become two-hour documents of them rattling their ironist bars. Without the irony dilemma that Roth describes, we would find it hard to explain figures like Max Fischer, Steve Zissou, Royal Tenenbaum, Mr. Fox, and Peter Whitman. I'm not speaking here of specific political beliefs. The characters in question aren't liberals; they may in fact, along with Anderson himself, have no particular political or philosophical interests. But they are certainly involved in a frustrated and digressive kind of irony that suggests a certain political situation. Though intensely self-absorbed and central to their films, Anderson's protagonists are neither heroes nor antiheroes. These characters are not lovable eccentrics. They are not flawed protagonists either, but are driven at least as much by their unsavory characteristics as by any moral sense. They aren't flawed figures who try to do the right thing; they don't necessarily learn from their mistakes; and we aren't asked to like them in spite of their obvious faults. Though they usually aren't interested in making good, they do set themselves some kind of mission—Anderson's films are mostly quest movies in an age that no longer believes in quests, and this gives them both an old-fashioned flavor and an air of disillusionment and futility.

Anderson shows how the music video-influenced style of auteurism belongs to our time of "ironist's cages." Popular music has become an integral part of filmic allusion, and preexisting songs color particular auteurisms with such various telltale directionalities: A filmmaker's musical references can be subliminal, spiraling, sideways, obvious, funny, automatic, surprising, pretentious, script-inspired, or as unnoticed by the moviegoer as they are dear to the director. It's a telling paradox that the more original a new auteurist filmmaker is, the more allusive, and the more variously allusive, she often seems to be. Wes Anderson is original in the way he joins allusiveness with ironist digression. He tends to use multiple, not-so-obvious songs from some point in the past. And his widely varied songs tend to be in disharmony with the characters and situations presented, yet there is a basic distance and ambiguity to their—apparently forceful—critique. As Anderson uses them, popular songs allude and laugh and follow distinct tangents—but at what and for whom?

It is a comment on our era that cinema—like the broader public discourse referenced by this art form—has become so authorship-involved and yet so fragmented. The authorship is now largely a commercial construct, and the fragmentedness a symptom of political division and socio-historical alienation. At such a paradoxical time in history, the would-be critic—as Roth describes her—can only joke her way past and alongside the issues. "Ironic sophistication," Roth says, "marks the distance that some intellectuals have been able to take on political issues outside the academic realm."[26] Sophistication, irony, and "distance" are all important aspects of Anderson's films, just as popular songs have allowed him to develop a kind of cinematic texture that is clearly his own. For all these reasons, not least for the redefined and revivified auteurism that Anderson offers, his work is very much of its time.

ACKNOWLEDGMENT

Thanks to Giorgio Biancorosso for criticisms of an earlier draft, commentary that proved indispensable in both focusing the chapter and presenting my examples. Any polemics, misunderstandings, or misjudgments remain my own.

NOTES

1. "Irony, n.," *OED Online*, Oxford University Press, http://www.oed.com.proxy.lib. ohio-state.edu/view/Entry/99565?rskey=T4EeCX&result=1 (accessed May 4, 2012).
2. Moreover, according to Newmark, irony is constantly changeable, digressing even from the ironist's place and time in history: "[T]o the degree that irony names a deflection of meaning, it also entails a divergence from historical and thematic models of understanding." Kevin Newmark, *Irony on Occasion: From Schlegel and Kierkegaard to Derrida and de Man* (New York: Fordham University Press, 2012), back jacket and 8. I feel compelled to underline the relevance of the literary perspective with which I open my own chapter. François Truffaut, for one, considered himself an auteur in a specifically literary sense: He had originally wanted to write novels and planned to retire from directing to devote himself to writing, and said in fact that before he was influenced by films, it was Emil Zola, Honoré de Balzac, and other novelists who inspired him to become a *metteur en scène*. See John Anzalone, "Heroes and Villains, or Truffaut and the Literary Pre/Text," *The French Review*, vol. 72, no. 1 (October 1998), 48–57.
3. Phillip Lopate, "Introduction," *The Art of the Personal Essay: An Anthology from the Classical Era to the Present* (New York: Anchor, 1995), xi.
4. These several definitions of irony were taken from "irony, n.," *OED Online*.
5. See D. C. Muecke, "Introduction," in *Irony and the Ironic* (London and New York: Methuen, 1982), 1–13.

6. As Paul De Man writes, "[A]ny theory of irony is the undoing, the necessary undoing, of any theory of narrative." De Man, *Aesthetic Ideology*, ed. A. Warminski (Minneapolis: University of Minnesota Press, 1996), 179.

7. As is commonly recounted, Kubrick scripted and filmed a climactic food fight in the War Room but ended up cutting it, leaving behind one or two unexplained glimpses of lavish precooked food at earlier points in the film.

8. Romney, "Family Album," *Sight and Sound*, vol. 12, no. 3 (2002), 15. I should mention here the different assessment offered by Jim Collins, who associates Anderson with a "New Sincerity" trend in filmmaking that "rejects any form of irony" and undertakes a "sanctimonious pursuit of lost purity." The description is puzzling, though it might be explained by its very early date within Anderson's film career: The maker of *Bottle Rocket* (1992, 1996) had not yet become a full-scale digressionist. Collins, *Film Theory Goes to the Movies*, eds. Jim Collins, Hilary Radner, and Ava Preacher Collins (New York and London: Routledge, 1993), 243.

9. Romney, "Family Album," 15.

10. Production sketches reproduced with Criterion Collection DVD issue of *The Royal Tenenbaums*, 2002.

11. Joshua Gooch sees the loss of Margot's finger, accidentally severed by her biological father, as Anderson's declaration of her "lost" paternity. But the scene is so brief and glossed over that it hardly amounts to more than just another detail in the film's welter of information: The moment doesn't articulate narrative importance, but seems in fact to avoid or even satirize such significance. Gooch, Joshua, "Making a Go of It: Paternity and Prohibition in the Films of Wes Anderson," *Cinema Journal*, vol. 47, no. 1 (Fall 2007), 26–28.

12. Browning, *Wes Anderson: Why His Movies Matter* (Santa Barbara, Denver, and Oxford, UK: Praeger, 2011), 41.

13. Muecke, *Irony and the Ironic*.

14. Swift, *A Modest Proposal*, as cited by Muecke in *Irony and the Ironic*, 49.

15. See Umberto Eco, "Postmodernism, Irony, the Enjoyable," in *Modernism/Postmodernism*, ed. Peter Brooker (London: Longman, 1992), 225–228.

16. D. K. Holm writes, "If the studios are often less cookie-cutter-like in their approach to filmmaking than critics claim, the so-called independent film is often less 'independent' than it appears to be. To offer a movie that is wholly financed by the Disney Corporation, as most Miramax movies were from 1995 on, and label it 'independent' is simply ludicrous. In both the past and present, changes in the movie industry have come not from within, but via threats from without...." Holm, *Independent Cinema* (Harpenden, UK: Kamera, 2008), 19.

17. For his input on faux-indie film culture and its connection with prosumer economics, I thank Joe Nebistinsky, participant in a film music seminar I led at Ohio State University in autumn 2008.

18. Gleibermann, "Movie Review: *Vanilla Sky*;" originally posted January 4, 2002, http://www.ew.com/ew/article/0,,252715,00.html.

19. Browning, *Wes Anderson*, 53, 35. Browning also discusses Anderson's fascination with the Futura typeface at 108–109.

20. Included in insert for Criterion Collection DVD issue of *The Royal Tenenbaums*, 2002.

21. *According to the Rolling Stones* (London: Weidenfeld and Nicolson, 2003), 110–111.

22. Marcus, "Introduction," *Stranded: Rock and Roll for a Desert Island*, ed. Greil Marcus, second edition (New York: Da Capo, 2007), xx.

23. Marcus, "Corrupting the Absolute," in *On Record: Rock, Pop, and the Written Word*, eds. Simon Frith and Andrew Goodwin (New York: Pantheon, 1990), 475–476.

24. Dancyger, "The MTV Influence on Editing I," in *The Technique of Film and Video Editing*, fourth edition (Amsterdam and Boston: Focal, 2007), 190.

25. Roth, *The Ironist's Cage: Memory, Trauma, and the Construction of History* (New York: Columbia University Press, 1995), 8. Writing before the turn of the century and the regimes of George W. Bush and Tony Blair, Roth was describing a post-Cold War world. The "ironist's cage" construct seems even more apropos to the present, however. After the infamous 2010 Supreme Court decision in *Citizens United v. Federal Election Commission*, one can hardly doubt the broader truth of Roth's statement that "historical knowing seems to be little more than a form of self-congratulation, the winners getting to construct their histories so as to validate their victories" (6).

26. Roth, *The Ironist's Cage*, 3.

BIBLIOGRAPHY

Altman, Rick. *The American Film Musical* (Bloomington, IN: Indiana University Press, 1987).

Anderson, Tim. "As If History Was Merely a Record: The Pathology of Nostalgia and the Figure of the Recording in Contemporary Popular Cinema," *Music, Sound, and the Moving Image* 2, no. 1 (2008).

Anon. "Kevin's Bloody Great!: Sofia Coppola raves about the cult star's BAFTA-nominated contribution to the soundtrack...." *New Musical Express*, January 20, 2004. http://www.nme.com/news/my-bloody-valentine/15950.

Anon. *Lost In Translation*. Focus Features, http://www.lost-in-translation.com/qaPopup.html.

Anzalone, John. "Heroes and Villains, or Truffaut and the Literary Pre/Text," *French Review*, vol. 72, no. 1 (October 1998).

Armstrong, Liz. "The Haves: Of jet-setters and 18th-century teenage queens," *Chicago Reader*, October 26, 2006, http://www.chicagoreader.com/chicago/the-haves/Content?oid=923459.

Ashby, Arved. "Modernism Goes to the Movies," in *The Pleasure of Modernist Music: Listening, Meaning, Intention, Ideology*, ed. Ashby (Rochester and New York: University of Rochester Press, 2004).

Barthes, Roland. *The Eiffel Tower and Other Mythologies* (New York: Noonday, 1979).

Bayton, Mavis. "How Women Become Musicians," in *On Record: Rock, Pop, and the Written Word*, eds. Simon Frith and Andrew Goodwin (London: Routledge, 1988).

Bayton, Mavis. "Women and the Electric Guitar," in *Sexing the Groove: Popular Music and Gender*, ed. Sheila Whitely (London: Routledge, 1997).

Beebe, Roger. "Paradoxes of Pastiche: Spike Jonze, Hype Williams, and the Race of the Postmodern Auteur," in *Medium Cool: Music Videos from Soundies to Cellphones*, eds. Beebe and Jason Middleton (Durham, NC: Duke University Press, 2007).

Berg, Charles M. "Visualizing Music: The Archaeology of the Music Video," *OneTwoThreeFour: A Rock 'n' Roll Quarterly*, no. 5 (Spring 1987).

Biancorosso, Giorgio. "Global Music/Local Cinema: Two Wong Kar-Wai Pop Compilations," in *Hong Kong Culture: Word and Image*, ed. Kam Louie (Hong Kong: Hong Kong University Press, 2010).

Brooks, Peter. *The Melodramatic Imagination: Balzac, Henry James, Melodrama, and the Mode of Excess* (New Haven, CT: Yale University Press, 1976).

Brophy, Philip, ed. "Music for the Films of Joel and Ethan Coen: Carter Burwell in Conversation," in *Cinesonic: The World of Sound in Film* (Sydney, AU: Australian Film Television and Radio School, 1999).

Brown, Royal S. *Overtones and Undertones: Reading Film Music* (Los Angeles: University of California Press, 1994).

Browning, Mark. *Wes Anderson: Why His Movies Matter* (Oxford, UK: Praeger, 2011).

Brunette, Peter. *Wong Kar-Wai* (Chicago and New York: University of Illinois Press, 2005).

Burwell, Carter. "Composing for the Coen Brothers," *Soundscape: The School of Sound Lectures, 1998-2001*, eds. Larry Sider, Diane Freeman, and Jerry Sider (London: Wallflower, 2003).

Calico, Joy H. *Brecht at the Opera* (Berkeley and Los Angeles: University of California Press, 2008).

Chion, Michel. *David Lynch*, trans. Robert Julian (London: BFI, 1995).

Coates, Norma. "(R)Evolution Now?: Rock and the Political Potential of Gender," in *Sexing the Groove: Popular Music and Gender*, ed. Sheila Whitely (London: Routledge, 1997).

Collins, Jim. *Film Theory Goes to the Movies*, eds. Jim Collins, Hilary Radner, and Ava Preacher Collins (New York and London: Routledge, 1993).

Connelly, Marie Katheryn. *Martin Scorsese: An Analysis of His Feature Films, with a Filmography of His Entire Directorial Career* (Jefferson, NC: McFarland, 1993).

Conrich, Ian, and Estrella Tincknell, eds. *Film's Musical Moments* (Edinburgh, UK: Edinburgh University Press, 2006).

Cook, Nicholas. *Analysing Musical Multimedia* (Oxford, UK: Clarendon, 1998).

Cook, Pam. "Portrait of a Lady: Sofia Coppola," *Sight and Sound*, November 2006.

Cooke, Mervyn. *A History of Film Music* (Cambridge, UK: Cambridge University Press, 2008).

Corrigan, Timothy. "The Commerce of Auteurism: Coppola, Kluge, Ruiz," in *A Cinema without Walls: Movies and Culture after Vietnam* (New Brunswick, NJ: Rutgers University Press, 1991).

Coulthard, Lisa. "Torture Tunes: Tarantino, Popular Music, and New Hollywood Ultraviolence," *Music and the Moving Image*, vol. 2, no. 2 (Summer 2009).

Cubitt, Sean. "'Maybellene': Meaning and the Listening Subject," in *Reading Pop: Approaches to Textual Analysis in Popular Music*, ed. Richard Middleton (New York and Oxford, UK: Oxford University Press, 2000).

Culler, Jonathan. *Structuralist Poetics: Structuralism, Linguistics, and the Study of Literature* (Ithaca, NY: Cornell University Press, 1975).

Dancyger, Ken. "The MTV Influence on Editing I," in *The Technique of Film and Video Editing*, fourth edition (Amsterdam and Boston: Focal, 2007).

DeCurtis, Anthony. "What the Streets Mean," in *Martin Scorsese: Interviews*, ed. Peter Brunette (Jackson, MS: University of Mississippi Press, 1999).

De Man, *Aesthetic Ideology*, ed. A. Warminski (Minneapolis: University of Minnesota Press, 1996).

Denisoff, R. Serge, and William Romanowski. *Risky Business: Rock in Film* (New Brunswick, NJ: Transaction, 1991).

Denisoff, R. Serge. *Inside MTV* (New York: Transaction, 1988).

Deppman, Hsiu-Chuang. *Adapted for the Screen: The Cultural Politics of Modern Chinese Fiction and Film* (Honolulu: University of Hawai'i Press, 2010).

Devlin, William J., and Shai Biderman, eds. *The Philosophy of David Lynch* (Lexington, KY: University of Kentucky Press, 2011).

Donn, Allegra. "Sofia's World," *Times Magazine*, October 7, 2006.

Donnelly, K. J. "The Hidden Heritage of Film Music," in *Film Music: Critical Approaches*, ed. K. J. Donnelly (New York: Continuum, 2001).

Donnelly, Kevin. "The Classical Film Score Forever? *Batman, Batman Returns* and Post-classical Film Music," in *Contemporary Hollywood Cinema*, eds. Steve Neale and Murray Smith (New York: Routledge, 1998).

Dougan, Andy. *Martin Scorsese* (New York: Thunder's Mouth, 1998).

Drazin, Charles. *Charles Drazin on "Blue Velvet,"* Bloomsbury Movie Guide No. 3 (New York: Bloomsbury, 1998).

Dyer, Richard. *Heavenly Bodies: Film Stars and Society*, second edition (New York and London: Routledge, 2003).

Eco, Umberto. "Postmodernism, Irony, the Enjoyable," in *Modernism/Postmodernism*, ed. Peter Brooker (London: Longman, 1992).

Ehrenstein, David. *The Scorsese Picture* (New York: Carol, 1992).

Elsaesser, Thomas. "Tales of Sound and Fury: Observations on the Family Melodrama," in *Home Is Where the Heart Is: Studies in Melodrama and the Woman's Film*, ed. Christine Gledhill (London: BFI, 1987), 50.

Elsaesser, Thomas. "Vincente Minelli," in *Genre: The Musical*, ed. Rick Altman (Boston: Routledge & Kegan Paul, 1981).

Evans, David, ed. *Appropriation* (London: Whitechapel Gallery; Cambridge, MA: MIT Press, 2009).

Frayling, Christopher. *Spaghetti Westerns: Cowboys and Europeans from Karl May to Sergio Leone*, second edition (New York: I. B. Tauris, 2006).

Friedman, Lawrence S. "The Sound(s) of Music: From the Bands to The Band," in *The Cinema of Martin Scorsese* (New York: Continuum, 1997).

Frith, Simon, and Andrew Goodwin, eds. *Sound and Vision: The Music Video Reader* (New York: Routledge, 1993).

Frith, Simon, and Angela McRobbie. "Rock and Sexuality," in *On Record: Rock, Pop, and the Written Word*, eds. Frith and Andrew Goodwin (London: Routledge, 1990).

Gabbard, Krin. "Spike Lee meets Aaron Copland," in *The Spike Lee Reader*, ed. Paula J. Massood (Philadelphia: Temple University Press, 2008).

Garner, Ken. " 'Would You Like to Hear Some Music?' Music In-and-Out-of-Control in the Films of Quentin Tarantino," in *Film Music: Critical Approaches*, ed. K. J. Donnelly (New York: Continuum, 2001).

Garwood, Ian. "Pop Music as Film Music," in *Close-up 01*, eds. John Gibbs and Douglas Pye (London: Wallflower, 2006).

Gilchrist, Todd. "Interview: Sofia Coppola, the Marie Antoinette Director Talks about Making a Post-Modern Period Piece," *IGN.COM* (2006), http://movies.ign.com/articles/739/739308p1.html.

Giles, Dennis. "Show-Making," in *Genre: The Musical*, ed. Rick Altman (Boston: Routledge & Kegan Paul, 1981).

Goldmark, Daniel. "*O Brother, Where Art Thou?*: A Musical Appreciation," *Xavier Review* 23, no. 2 (Fall 2003).

Gooch, Joshua. "Making a Go of It: Paternity and Prohibition in the Films of Wes Anderson," *Cinema Journal*, vol. 47, no. 1 (Fall 2007).

Goodwin, Andrew. *Dancing in the Distraction Factory: Music Television and Popular Culture* (Minneapolis: University of Minnesota Press, 1992).

Gorbman, Claudia. "Auteur Music," in *Beyond the Soundtrack: Representing Music in Cinema*, eds. Daniel Goldmark, Lawrence Kramer, and Richard Leppert (Berkeley and Los Angeles: University of California Press, 2007).

Gorbman, Claudia. "Ears Wide Open: Kubrick's Music," in *Changing Tunes: The Use of Pre-Existing Music in Film* (Burlington, VT: Ashgate, 2006).

Gourley, Bob. "Brian Reitzell," *Chaos Control Digizine*, 2009, http://www.chaoscontrol.com/?article=brianreitzell.

Grant, Catherine. "www.auteur.com?" *Screen*, vol. 41, no. 1 (Spring 2000).

Gunning, Tom. "The Cinema of Attractions: Early Film, Its Spectator, and the Avant-Garde," in *Early Cinema: Space, Frame, Narrative*, eds. Thomas Elsaesser and Adam Barker (London: BFI, 1990).

Hainge, Greg. "Weird or Loopy? Specular Spaces, Feedback and Artifice in *Lost Highway*'s Aesthetics of Sensation," in *The Cinema of David Lynch: American Dreams, Nightmare Visions* (London: Wallflower, 2004).

Hoberman, J. "French Confection; Sofia Coppola pays opulent tribute to the innocent boredom of a teen queen," *Village Voice*, October 3, 2006, http://www.villagevoice.com/2006-10-03/film/french-confection/.

Holm, D. K. *Independent Cinema* (Harpenden, UK: Kamera, 2008).

Howard, Rachel. "Constant Sorrow: Traditional Music and Fandom," *Echo* 4, no. 2 (Fall 2002), www.echo.ucla.edu.

Hubbert, Julie. "Whatever Happened to Great Movie Music: Cinema Verité and Hollywood Film Music in the Early 1970s," *American Music* 21/2 (Summer 2003).

Hutcheon, Linda. *A Poetics of Postmodernism: History, Theory, Fiction* (New York: Routledge, 1988).

James, William. "Reflex Action and Theism" (1881), reprinted in James, *The Will to Believe and Other Essays in Popular Philosophy* (New York: Dover, 1956).

Jameson, Frederic. "Historicism in *The Shining*," in *Signatures of the Visible* (New York: Routledge, 1992).

Jenkins, Henry. *Convergence Culture: Where Old and New Media Collide* (New York and London: New York University Press, 2006).

Johnson, Jeff. *Pervert in the Pulpit: Morality in the Works of David Lynch* (Jefferson, NC, and London: McFarland, 2004).

Johnson, Victoria. "Polyphony and Cultural Expression: Interpreting Musical Traditions in *Do the Right Thing*," in *Spike Lee's 'Do the Right Thing,'* ed. Mark A. Reid (Cambridge and New York: Cambridge University Press, 1997).

Jones, Andrew F. *Yellow Music* (Durham, NC: Duke University Press, 2001).

Kandell, Steve. "Quentin Tarantino Talks *Inglourious Basterds* Soundtrack," *Spin* 2009.

Kaplan, E. Ann. *Rocking Around the Clock: Music Television, Postmodernism and Consumer Culture* (London: Methuen, 1987).

Kassabian, Anahid. *Hearing Film: Tracking Identifications in Contemporary Hollywood Film Music* (New York and London: Routledge, 2001).

Kelly, Mary Pat. *Martin Scorsese: The First Decade* (1980) and *Martin Scorsese: A Journey* (New York: Thunder's Mouth, 2004).

Keyser, Les. *Martin Scorsese* (New York: Twayne, 1992).

Kinder, Marsha. "Music Video and the Spectator: Television, Ideology and Dream," *Film Quarterly*, vol. 38, no. 1 (Autumn, 1984).

Klawans, Stuart. "The Queen is Dead," *Nation*, November 6, 2006, http://www.thenation.com/doc/20061106/klawans/single.

Kolker, Robert. *A Cinema of Loneliness* (Oxford, UK: Oxford University Press, 2000).

Leonard, Marion, and Robert Strachan. "Authenticity," in *The Continuum Encyclopedia of Popular Music of the World*, vol. 1, eds. John Shepherd, David Horn, Dave Laing, Paul Oliver, and Peter Wicke (New York: Continuum, 2003).

Levine, Josh. *The Coen Brothers* (Toronto: ECW, 2000).

Levy, Steven. "Shot by Shot," *The Coen Brothers Interviews*, ed. William Rodney Allen (Jackson, MS: University of Mississippi Press, 2006).

Longworth, Karina. "Tetro Review," in *SPOUTblog*, 2009, http://blog.spout.com/2009/06/08/tetro-review/.

Lopate, Phillip. "Introduction," in *The Art of the Personal Essay: An Anthology from the Classical Era to the Present* (New York: Anchor, 1995).

Lynch, David. *Lynch on Lynch*, ed. Chris Rodley (London: Farber and Farber, 1997).

Marcus, Greil. "Corrupting the Absolute," in *On Record: Rock, Pop, and the Written Word*, eds. Simon Frith and Andrew Goodwin (New York: Pantheon, 1990),

Marcus, Greil. "Introduction," in *Stranded: Rock and Roll for a Desert Island*, ed. Greil Marcus, second edition (New York: Da Capo, 2007).

Martin, Adrian. "Possessory Credit," *Framework*, vol. 45, no. 1 (Spring 2004).

Mason, Stewart. "Laurie Anderson: *Bright Red*," *All Music Guide*, fourth edition (San Francisco: Backbeat, 2001).

McCarthy, Todd. "Review of *The Hudsucker Proxy*," *Variety*, January 31, 1994. Reprinted in Paul A. Woods, ed. *Joel & Ethan Coen: Blood Siblings* (London: Plexus, 2000).

McCarthy, Todd. "Sofia's Choice Is a Modernist 'Marie,'" *Variety*, May 29, 2006.

McClary, Susan. *Feminine Endings: Music, Gender, and Sexuality* (Minneapolis: University of Minnesota Press, 1991).

McCourt, Malachy. *Danny Boy: The Legend of a Beloved Irish Ballad* (New York: New American Library, 2002).

McGowan, Todd. *The Impossible David Lynch* (New York: Columbia University Press, 2007).

McHale, Brian. *Postmodernist Fiction* (New York: Methuen, 1987).

McLean, Craig. "Low-Key Queen of Her Own High Court," *Sunday Independent* (Ireland), October 29, 2006, http://www.independent.ie/entertainment/film-cinema/lowkey-queen-of-her-own-high-court-136302.html.

McLean, Craig. "Pop," *Daily Telegraph*, October 28, 2006.

Mendelsohn, Daniel. "It's Only a Movie," in *How Beautiful It Is and How Easily It Can Be Broken* (New York: HarperCollins, 2008).

Meyer, Marianne. "The Rock Movideo," *Rolling Stone Review*, Ira Robbins, ed. (New York: Charles Scribners & Sons, 1985).

Miklitsch, Robert. "Audiophilia: Audiovisual Pleasure and Narrative Cinema in *Jackie Brown*," *Screen*, vol. 45, no. 4 (Winter 2004).

Miller, Mark Crispin. "Hollywood: the Ad," *Atlantic Monthly* 265/4 (April 1990).

Mitchell, Elvis. "Film Review; an American in Japan, Making a Connection," *New York Times*, September 12, 2003, http://www.nytimes.com/2003/09/12/movies/film-review-an-american-in-japan-making-a-connection.html?pagewanted=all&src=pm.

Mitchell, William J. *Picture Theory* (Chicago and London: University of Chicago Press, 1994).

Modleski, Tania. "Time and Desire in the Woman's Film," in *Home Is Where the Heart Is: Studies in Melodrama and the Woman's Film*, ed. Christine Gledhill (London: BFI, 1987).

Mottram, James. *The Coen Brothers: The Life of the Mind* (London: BT Batsford, 2000).

Muecke, D. C. *Irony and the Ironic* (London and New York: Methuen, 1982).

Mulvey, Laura. "A Phantasmagoria of the Female Body: The Work of Cindy Sherman," *New Left Review* 1/188, July/August 1991.

Mundy, John. *Popular Music on Screen: From Hollywood Musical to Music Video* (Manchester, UK, and New York: Manchester University Press, 1999).

Naremore, James. *More than Night* (Los Angeles: University of California Press, 1998).

Natoli, Joseph. "Ethan and Joel Coen," *Postmodernism: The Key Figures*, eds. Hans Bertens and Joseph Natoli (Malden, UK: Blackwell, 2002).

Neumeyer, David, and James Buhler. "Analytical and Interpretive Approaches to Film Music," in *Film Music: Critical Approaches*, ed. K. J. Donnelly (New York: Continuum, 2001).

Newman, Melinda. "Independent thinking key to smaller scores," *Hollywood Reporter*, November 1, 2007, http://www.hollywoodreporter.com/news/independent-thinking-key-smaller-scores-153961.

Newman, Michael Z. *Indie: An American Film Culture* (New York: Columbia University Press, 2011).

Newmark, Kevin. *Irony on Occasion: From Schlegel and Kierkegaard to Derrida and de Man* (New York: Fordham University Press, 2012).

Nochimson, Martha P. *The Passion of David Lynch* (Austin, TX: University of Texas Press, 1997).

Nyce, Ben. *Scorsese Up Close* (Lanham, MD: Scarecrow, 2004).

Odell, Colin, and Michelle Le Blanc. *David Lynch* (Harpenden, UK: Kamera, 2007).

Olsen, Mark. "Interview: Sofia Coppola Cool and the Gang," *Sight and Sound*, January, 15, 2004, http://vnweb.hwwilsonweb.com/hww/results/results_single_fulltext.jhtml;hw wilsonid=NRPLOLMFRVDIHQA3DIMCFF4ADUNGIIV0.

Olsen, Mark. "The Virgin Suicides," *Sight and Sound*, June 2000, http://www.bfi.org.uk/ sightandsound/review/573.

Palmer, R. Barton. *Joel and Ethan Coen* (Urbana, IL: University of Illinois Press, 2004).

Perez, Gilberto. *The Material Ghost: Films and Their Medium* (Baltimore, MD: Johns Hopkins University Press, 1998).

Perkins, Claire. "Remaking and the Film Trilogy: Whit Stillman's Authorial Triptych," *Velvet Light Trap*, no. 61 (Spring 2008).

Phillips, Patrick. "Genre, Star and Auteur: An Approach to Hollywood Cinema," in *An Introduction to Film Studies*, ed. Jill Nelmes (London and New York: Routledge, 1996).

Poirier, Agnes. "An Empty Hall of Mirrors: Sofia Coppola's Latest Film Is a Disgrace and Betrays the Disturbing Trend of Art as Marketing," *Guardian*, May 26, 2006, http://www.guardian.co.uk/commentisfree/2006/may/27/comment.filmnews.

Powrie, Phil, and Robynn Stilwell, eds. *Changing Tunes: The Use of Pre-existing Music in Film* (Aldershot, UK, and Burlington, VT: Ashgate, 2006).

Robson, Eddie. *Coen Brothers* (London: Virgin, 2003).

Rodman, Ronald. "The Popular Song as Leitmotif in 1990s Film," in *Changing Tunes: The Use of Pre-existing Music in Film*, eds. Phil Powrie and Robynn Stilwell (Aldershot, UK, and Burlington, VT: Ashgate, 2006).

Rogers, Anna. "Sofia Coppola," in *Senses of Cinema*, http://archive.sensesofcinema.com/contents/directors/07/sofia-coppola.html.

Romney, Jonathan, and Adrian Wootton, eds. *Celluloid Jukebox: Popular Music and the Movies Since the 1950s* (London: BFI, 1995).

Romney, Jonathan. "Family Album," *Sight and Sound*, vol. 12, no. 3 (2002).

Roth, Michael S. *The Ironist's Cage: Memory, Trauma, and the Construction of History* (New York: Columbia University Press, 1995).

Rowell, Erica. *The Brothers Grim: The Films of Ethan and Joel Coen* (Lanham, MD: Scarecrow, 2007).

Sangster, Jim. *Scorsese* (New York: Virgin).

Sarris, Andrew. "Notes on the Auteur Theory in 1962," reprinted in *Theories of Authorship: A Reader*, ed. John Caughie (London and New York: Routledge, 1981).

Scorsese, Martin. *Scorsese on Scorsese*, eds. David Thompson and Ian Christie (London: Faber & Faber, 1989).

Scott, Ellen. "Sounding Black: Cultural Identification, Sound, and the Films of Spike Lee," in *Fight the Power! The Spike Lee Reader*, eds. Janice D. Hamlet and Robin R. Means Coleman (New York: Peter Lang, 2009).

Seeger, Anthony. "Reflections on Anthologized Recordings: The Alan Lomax Collection on Rounder Records and the John A. and Ruby Lomax 1939 Southern States Recording Trip on the Library of Congress American Memory Website," *Echo* 4, no. 2 (Fall 2002), www.echo.ucla.edu.

Seeger, Pete. *Where Have All the Flowers Gone: A Singer's Stories, Songs, Seeds, Robberies* (Bethlehem, PA: Sing Out Corp., 1999).

Severn, Stephen. "Robbie Robertson's Big Break: A Reevaluation of Martin Scorsese's *The Last Waltz*," *Film Quarterly*, 56/2 (Winter, 2002–2003).

Sheen, Erica, and Annette Davison, eds. *The Cinema of David Lynch: American Dreams, Nightmare Visions*, Directors' Cuts Series (New York: Wallflower, 2004).

Smith, Gavin. "Martin Scorsese: Interviewed (1990)," in *Martin Scorsese: Interviews*, ed. Peter Brunette (Jackson, MS: University of Mississippi Press, 1999).

Smith, Jeff. "Popular Song and Comic Allusion in Contemporary Cinema," *Soundtrack Available: Essays on Film and Popular Music*, Arthur Knight and Pamela Robertson Wojcik, eds. (Durham, NC: Duke University Press, 2002).

Smith, Jeff. *The Sounds of Commerce: Marketing Popular Film Music* (New York: Columbia University Press, 1998).

Smith, Jeff. "Taking Music Supervisors Seriously," in *Cinesonic: Experiencing the Soundtrack*, ed. Philip Brophy (North Ryde NSW, AU: Southwest Press, 2001).

Straw, Will. "Music Video in its Contexts: Popular Music and Post-Modernism in the 1980s," *Popular Music*, vol. 7, no. 3 (October 1988).

Taubin, Amy. "Martin Scorsese's Cinema of Obsessions," in *Martin Scorsese: Interviews*, ed. Peter Brunette (Jackson, MS: University of Mississippi Press, 1999).

Taylor, Ella. "I Don't Like Being Told What to Do," *Guardian*, October 13, 2003, http://www.guardian.co.uk/world/2003/oct/13/gender.uk.

Teo, Stephen. "Wong Kar-wai's *In the Mood for Love*: Like a Ritual in Transfigured Time," in *Senses of Cinema*, 13 (April 10, 2001), http://www.sensesofcinema.com/2001/13/mood/.

Tichi, Cecilia. *High Lonesome: The American Culture of Country Music* (Chapel Hill, NC: University of North Carolina Press, 1994).

Tincknell, Estrella. "The Soundtrack Movie, Nostalgia and Consumption," in *Film's Musical Moments* (Edinburgh, UK: Edinburgh University Press, 2006).

Tobias, Scott. "Interview: Sofia Coppola, Virgin Territory," *Onion*, May 3, 2000, http://www.avclub.com/articles/sofia-coppola,13656/.

Vernallis, Carol. *Experiencing Music Video: Aesthetics and Cultural Context* (New York: Columbia University Press, 2004).

Viera, Maira. "The Institutionalization of the Music Video," *OneTwoThreeFour: A Rock 'n' Roll Quarterly*, no. 5 (Spring 1987).

Ward, Brian. *Just My Soul Responding: Rhythm and Blues, Black Consciousness, and Race Relations* (London: University College London Press, 1998).

Wilson, Eric G. *The Strange World of David Lynch: Transcendental Irony from Eraserhead to Mulholland Dr.* (New York: Continuum, 2007).

Winter, Jessie. "Sofia Coppola's Mystery Girls: Dreamlife of Angels," *Village Voice*, April 18, 2000, http://www.villagevoice.com/2000-04-18/film/sofia-coppola-s-mystery-girls.

Wright, Robb. "Score vs. Song: Art, Commerce, and the H Factor in Film and Television Music," in *Popular Music and Film*, ed. Ian Inglis (London and New York: Wallflower, 2003).

Wyatt, Justin. *High Concept: Movies and Marketing in Hollywood* (Austin, TX: University of Texas Press, 1994).

Yacowar, Maurice. *Sopranos on the Couch: Analyzing Television's Greatest Series* (New York: Continuum, 2003).

Yueh-yu Yeh, Emilie, and Lake Wang Hu. "Transcultural Sounds: Music, Identity, and the Cinema of Wong Kar-wai," *Asian Cinema*, 19/1, Spring/Summer 2008.

Žižek, Slavoj. *The Art of the Ridiculous Sublime: On David Lynch's* Lost Highway (Seattle, WA: University of Washington Press, 2002).

INDEX